COMPLETE PHOTO GUIDE

Matching the color palette of the Namibian desert below, this hot air balloon draws the eye up into the serenity of the frame. Negative space isolates the balloon, designating it as the photograph's focal point.

NATIONAL
GEOGRAPHIC

COMPLETE PHOTO GUIDE

I HOW TO TAKE BETTER PICTURES

HEATHER PERRY

NATIONAL GEOGRAPHIC
WASHINGTON, D.C.

Photographing into the sun can add a dynamic element, especially when beams backlight the petals of a flower.

PART III
TECHNOLOGY & THE ART

This portrait from Cape Town, South Africa, depicts a moment of camaraderie with more impact than a typical pose would.

A LIFE OF **LOOKING**

MARK THIESSEN

STAFF PHOTOGRAPHER, NATIONAL GEOGRAPHIC

Ever since I was a kid, I've wanted to be a photographer. In fact, when I was a teenager, I delivered the local newspaper, the *San Gabriel Valley Tribune,* and every afternoon before I set out on my bicycle, I'd flip through every page of the paper, noting all the photographs and which photographer shot what. These photographers were my heroes.

As a freshman in high school, I befriended one of those heroes—Raleigh Souther, a photographer who shot the photos at our high school's football games. I told him I wanted his job. He suggested I get a scanner that picks up police and fire radio traffic so I could chase down news. Photographing breaking news events was a great way to get a foot in the door, he told me. The only problem was, I was still too young to drive.

Early one summer morning, when I was 14, I heard on my scanner that a freight train had hit a car nearby. I talked my always adventurous mom into driving me to the wreck. Off we went in our Ford Pinto. Mom dropped me off at the scene, where I found the car resting against a brick wall. The hood had been ripped off and the engine was lying a few feet away. It turned out the car had stalled on the tracks. Luckily, the driver had jumped out at the last minute and was unscathed as the train blasted through his vehicle.

I shot the scene with my newly purchased wide-angle lens, and then my mom drove me to the newspaper office. I was ushered into the photo department, where I delivered my roll of black-and-white film to one of the photo editors, another one of my heroes. He said they had just sent a photographer to shoot the wreck so they might not need it, but I should leave the film anyway, just in case.

Truth be told, it didn't matter to me if they published my photos. I was in awe—I had met

Mark Thiessen's work as a National Geographic photographer has taken him around the world and into situations both fascinating and dangerous. A certified wildland firefighter, he has photographed fires and firefighters for 25 years.

one of my heroes and had made it into the inner sanctum of the newspaper's photo department. A moment I remember to this day.

That afternoon, as usual, a delivery truck dropped off a stack of papers for me to fold and deliver on my paper route. And there on the front page was my first published photo, with my name, in the form of a photo credit, printed right below it. I couldn't believe it. My photo, on the front page, where I'd seen my heroes' photos countless times before. As I rode my bicycle through the neighborhood, I porched every one of those papers. I was so proud.

And I was hooked.

Since then, I have shot hundreds of thousands of pictures—first as a newspaper photographer and then in my current role as a staff photographer for National Geographic. Even after three decades with National Geographic, I'm still growing as a photographer. There is always more to learn.

Every time I look at another photographer's pictures, I put myself in his or her shoes and think about the creative decisions I can see that they made. What direction is the light coming from? How is the image composed? What were the moments like leading up to the picture? The result of these decisions, and more, are frozen in time in the photograph. I became a better photographer by paying attention to the thought process that a good photographer goes through when approaching a shot.

GETTING THE SHOT

Let me take you through my thought process that led up to one of my more dramatic fire photographs (pages 12–13). But first, let me back up and tell you what got me into this situation in the first place.

My first job out of college was working as a

photographer for the *Idaho Statesman,* a newspaper in Boise, Idaho. I covered a lot of fires that summer. Then, a few years later, when I was working for National Geographic, I was looking for a personal project, something I could go back to every year. A friend suggested I do my project on wildland firefighters. He said he could get me the training that would both keep me safe and give me access to this very insular world.

Wildland firefighters are the men and women deployed to do the dangerous job of extinguishing wildfires. They have a subculture all their own, one I knew I would fit right into. To get the access I needed to tell their story, I attended a week of fire school to earn a "red card" and become a certified wildland firefighter. Not only did this certification give me access to the frontlines of these forest fires, it showed my subjects that I was one of them and that I would have their backs just like they would have mine.

Firefighters talk about getting bit by the "fire bug," and it's true—it's what keeps me going back again and again. When I'm photographing fires, I get to see one of nature's fiercest forces up close and personal, and the power and energy is just amazing.

Back to the photograph. A few days earlier, fire authorities had predicted Santa Ana winds—the strong winds that blow from the mountains to the coast in southern California—and they had issued a red flag warning. I knew surely there would be wildfires, so I hopped on a plane from Washington, D.C.

So now, I'm in Santa Clarita, California. It's after dark, and I'm standing in front of a house at the top of a hill that is fully engulfed in fire. The flames are being fed by hot, dry winds, which are approaching 50 miles an hour. The front porch is pockmarked with burn holes from the blizzard of embers blowing sideways through the air, and an American flag is flying there.

I NEED A PERSON

As tragic as this scene is, this is what I flew all the way across the country for. I am looking for pictures that tell the human impact of wildfires for a story that will appear in *National Geographic* magazine. It's surreal to be standing there in front of this burning house, with no one else around, because all the residents have been evacuated.

So, I start shooting this remarkable scene in front of me from different angles, making sure to include the flag. But I'm disappointed. These pictures are useless unless I can show how wildfire affects people; a burning house alone isn't enough. I need a person.

Then, out of nowhere, I see a guy coming out of the darkness, walking toward the house. He's wearing a dust mask. He can't believe this house is burning. I can't believe he is here. He says to me that he knows the owner of the house and, in fact, he was here earlier in the day for a child's birthday party. He keeps walking toward the house, and I think to myself, "Here is my person!"

My mind begins working out how best to capture this moment. I anticipate that to leave, this guy will have to use the driveway, which is dark. I turn on the camera's flash; otherwise he will be a black silhouette against the bright light of the fire. I take a few test shots to make sure the light level of the flash is balanced with the light level of the burning house. I add a subtle warming gel (filter) on the flash so that the image won't have that chalky white flashed look.

I take pictures of him as he is walking around, with the burning house in the background. All the time, I'm keeping him between the house and the downhill driveway. I know I will have only one chance to capture him walking toward me, and I don't want to blow it. He scrambles around, frustrated by the helplessness of the situation, but I can tell he wants to do something—his friend's house is burning to the ground.

He sees the American flag, full of holes and flapping hard in the wind against the front porch roof. He grabs a ladder that is leaning against the house, climbs up, and saves the flag. Then he grabs golf clubs and a painting leaning against a retaining wall—anything he can find to save for his friend. I shoot all of this.

I can tell he is now ready to leave. With the painting under his arm, golf clubs over his shoulder, and the singed American flag in hand, he begins to walk down the driveway. I'm right there in front of him, shooting away. I have an entire sequence of this guy as he surveyed the house in a panic—probably 250 shots altogether—but in only one did everything come together just right.

Every successful photo like this contains lessons learned. After a photo shoot, as I edit my photos, I always review my thought process and the decisions I made. Every once in a long while, I'll shoot a picture that I can't believe I took. This is one of those photos. Not only is it dramatic, it also tells the story I traveled to California to tell: the human impact of wildfires.

Photographing wildfires can be full of boring stretches, either waiting for a fire to happen or waiting at a fire for something worth shooting to happen. And then other times, it can be crazy. Sometimes when I'm out photographing fires, it just gets too dangerous and

A show of bravery: in the friend who rescued his neighbor's belongings, including a U.S. flag, from blazing destruction—and in the photographer who captured this moment

it's time to leave—but that's when the pictures are just getting good. You never know what's going to happen next. You have to be flexible, resilient, and patient. But the most important thing is you have to be out there.

A NEW PERSPECTIVE

One way to improve your photography is by studying your own favorite photographs. Look critically at your best pictures. What was the mental path that led you there? Were you tempted to veer down a different path, but your intuition told you otherwise? Do you see a common theme among your favorite photographs? Looking back now, what made your choice of lens and angle work? Did you find that choosing a darker exposure than what your camera meter said made for a moodier image? Does a picture you shot by mistake look surprisingly interesting? Are there ways your images could be improved? Would you take them differently now?

We all have our own ways of seeing; that's why it's important, for the sake of becoming a better photographer, for you to explore exactly how you see. Take the time to understand your natural tendencies—your preferred subject matter, style, aesthetic, and composition—and you will begin to approach your photography with greater intent.

If you want to grow as a photographer, you also need to push beyond your comfort zone. Explore with reckless abandon. Try shooting subjects that you aren't comfortable shooting. Experiment with a different composition, shoot all verticals, or maybe try shooting closer, then closer still, and finally, very close to your subject, which can lead to a composition you hadn't expected. You will improve as a photographer when you challenge yourself

and try different techniques from the ones you already practice.

For a 2018 *National Geographic* story on human performance, I took a chance with experimentation, and it paid off. I was sent to Lawrence, Kansas, to photograph swimming phenom Michael Andrew at his house, where he has an enclosed two-lane training pool. My research showed it was lit with drab fluorescent lights from above. Ugh. I decided at the last minute to throw in a pair of underwater strobes, modified so that when I took a picture, the strobes would fire.

I had Michael place them at the bottom of the pool, pointing across the lane he was swimming in. Then we turned off the overhead lights. He and his coach—his father—began going through their workout routine.

I shot a test picture. Wow! The light was amazing. It took the strobes a few seconds to recycle after each picture, so I could get only one shot each time Michael swam by.

It's an example of how experimenting, and pushing beyond the boundaries of your everyday photography practice, can get you an even better picture. I photographed him both from the front and side of the pool and got some great shots. Ultimately, this one (opposite) made it into the magazine. I could have used strobes above the pool or the available fluorescent lights, but neither choice would have produced results as interesting as the underwater strobes did.

THE PHOTOGRAPHIC JOURNEY

It's been 40 years since my first photo was published, and as you can see, I keep learning with every assignment, every photograph I make. I'm always looking for ways to

Photographic creativity involves awareness of composition, color, and lighting. Turning off the overhead fluorescents and triggering underwater strobes made this picture work.

make more interesting pictures. That's the beauty of photography. It's a never-ending process that takes practice and dedication. It's easy to get overwhelmed with all your different camera settings. In this book, we'll help you learn to pay attention to the ones that matter. The more you practice, the better you will get.

Photography can make our lives so much richer as we capture images of the people and places we encounter. It can be the vehicle to explore other cultures as we travel and the way we hold and share our memories through the years. Photography has the power to change the world, whether drawing attention to a local polluted beach or portraying a volunteer who works tirelessly to educate underprivileged children. It has the potential to reach deeply into people's characters, by catching the glint in a little boy's eyes or the beauty of an old woman's wrinkled smile.

What you hold in your hands is a collection of photographic knowledge designed to take you beyond the basics and make you a better photographer, no matter your current abilities and talents. Here are tips and tricks of National Geographic photographers, expertly explained, with terms defined and examples provided.

It has been a pleasure to contribute to this book, and we hope you find it useful and enlightening.

And, most important, we hope it shows you how taking better pictures can be a lot of fun.

ABOUT THIS BOOK

National Geographic's *Complete Photo Guide* is designed to provide the tools and information you'll need to elevate your photography practice, regardless of where you begin.

National Geographic magazine published the first photograph in its pages in 1890, and since then, National Geographic books and magazines have continued their tradition of photographic excellence—printing groundbreaking, jaw-dropping images from around the world, made by some of the very best photographers. Here, in these pages, not only will you see some of those extraordinary photographs, but you will also learn to create your own masterpieces, fine-tune your skills, share your unique perspectives, and make photographs that will hold meaning for you and others for a long time to come.

The lessons and images throughout have three main goals: to educate, inspire, and motivate you to go out into the world with your camera in hand, put what you've learned to use, and have a great time doing so.

LESSONS
Learn precisely what makes a great photo, how cameras and other equipment work, and how to improve your skills.

CROSS-REFERENCES
Want to know more about a certain subject? You'll be directed to where related topics are discussed in depth in the text.

ZOOM IN SIDEBAR
Here you'll be given either a concise distillation of the lesson or a suggestion for how to apply what you've learned.

WHY I LOVE THIS PHOTO

In each chapter, hear a National Geographic photography expert point out the key features of an exemplary image.

ASSIGNMENTS

At the end of every chapter, find creative exercises that challenge you to practice what you've learned.

TIME LINES

In Part II, explore how the art, science, and societal impact of photography has evolved throughout the years.

PART I
SEEING
YOUR WORLD

CHAPTER ONE

THE ART
OF SEEING

Professional photographers often say they "make," rather than "take," pictures—a distinction that implies the creative collaboration between machine and operator, rather than a simple confluence of light and space. In any carefully considered photograph, four tangible elements are vital: subject, composition, light, and exposure. When those technical basics have become second nature, photographers are well on their way to mastery.

But what of the *intangible* elements—those that make a simple photograph something more? When you approach photography with more than just eyes—with gut, heart, and perhaps most important, patience—you begin to

really *see*. This is when photographers begin to grow in the medium and develop voice. This in turn yields an ability to create a photograph that becomes successful—even powerful. When you use more than just your eyes to see, you can make a photograph that tells a story; that becomes art.

The great artist Georgia O'Keeffe once said, "To see takes time." In this first chapter, you will be challenged to think beyond the nuts and bolts of how to take photographs and begin to examine the elements needed to make *great* photographs. You are invited to take the time to consider your approach to photography before picking up the camera, and in doing so, you will learn to see in a new, complete way.

A climber on lower Ruth Glacier in Denali National Park, Alaska, is silhouetted against a bright sky in the top portion of this photograph. Below, the glacier extends beyond where the imagination can reach.

YOUR SMARTPHONE AS YOUR FIRST TOOL

Always on hand, smartphone cameras have become a valuable part of the photographic process, from mapping ideas to capturing excellent photos.

▶ FOR MORE ON SMART-PHONE PHO-TOGRAPHY, SEE PAGES 224-5

▶ FOR MORE ON SMART-PHONE EDIT-ING, SEE PAGES 378-9

You might think that professional photographers would shun the use of a smartphone as a camera, but in fact, most don't. Technology continues to get better every year, and most phone cameras are capable of capturing fantastic images and are showing up more frequently in professional photographers' kits.

More important, these compact devices, which most people have on hand all the time, can be your first and best tools for learning to see in a new way. The familiarity and comfort most people feel with their phones allows you to frame the world around you casually, yet thoughtfully. Freed up from camera buttons and dials, you are better able to

At a panoramic overlook in West Virginia, Swikar has just proposed to his girlfriend, Bethany, and commemorates the moment with a selfie. When done thoughtfully, this popular smartphone technique can result in a meaningful photograph.

A visitor to the Taj Mahal gets a higher than normal view with a selfie stick, one of an endless array of smartphone accessories that make phone cameras capable of new perspectives.

focus on scene and mood, sometimes even from right within the action. With the low profile of something so commonplace as a phone, you can be more at ease and open to capturing the meaningful essence of everyday. A phone can also be a visual notebook for developing ideas over time. And when used openly and respectfully, a phone allows you to make photographs of willing subjects while being much less intimidating to them. When taking risks as a photographer, the stakes seem much lower with equipment that's always in your pocket. And so, your phone becomes an excellent tool for cultivating photographic vision and voice.

The concepts in this book will apply to both DSLRs (digital single-lens reflex cameras) and smartphones—with regard to photographic technique and how to best employ available technology to your efforts. But for now, consider your phone as an always present tool with which you can begin to knock down hurdles between you and your vision as a photographer.

FOCAL POINT

A strong focal point offers a quick clue about the story of a photograph, giving the eye a place to start and end its journey throughout the frame.

▶ FOR MORE
ON POSITIVE
& NEGATIVE
SPACE, SEE
PAGES 60–61

▶ FOR MORE
ON STREET
PHOTOGRA-
PHY, SEE
PAGES 124–5

Every successful photograph has a culminating point of interest, and that point should be clear to the viewer. The focal point of an image might be the subject of a larger story, or it might be an element important to and supportive of a story. It might even be as abstract as the general mood you'd like to evoke in the viewer.

Before committing to a focal point, consider what you are trying to say with the image. Think about how the place-ment and nature of your subject, in concert with its context, might support that story.

CAPTURING FEELING

Are you trying to evoke a sense of chaos in a bustling city street? Then perhaps you could photograph a subject that appears still amid a sea of movement. The eye will then flow toward that focal point and rest there. Are you trying to convey the vast emptiness of a mid-

In an ancient water well in Jaipur, India, two women in brightly colored saris anchor the eye before and after the steps' geometric pattern directs viewers through a scene of muted tones.

A ladybug rests on a prickly pear cactus bloom. The creature, tiny but bright, grabs and holds viewers' attention in the otherwise softly focused field of yellow and green.

western prairie? Consider a focal point that will stand alone—an old barn or a fence post—on one side of a frame otherwise filled with nothing but grass and sky.

DIRECTING THE VIEWER'S GAZE

A focal point pulls the viewer into the image as the starting point of its story and gives the eye a place to return after exploring the rest of the frame. In general, an image that lacks a strong focal point—even when full of other successful elements—will cause the eye to wander aimlessly across the image, and likely won't hold the viewer's attention for long. Once you develop a sense of what you want to say and where you want to focus the viewer's attention, call on technology and your photographic skills to create an image that supports that story. Composition, exposure, color, and light are the tools photographers use to direct the viewer's attention to the focal point of an image, and in turn, the heart of the story within the frame.

ZOOM IN

▶ Consider an element in the scene you want to draw attention to. This is your focal point, and your task is to guide the viewer's eye to that spot.

POINT OF VIEW

Point of view helps shape the story of a photograph, through placement and perspective from both within the scene and behind the camera.

Made from the heart of the action—this photo conveys the energy of the marching band in a parade in the Philippines, as well as the fascination of kids watching as the band passes by.

▶ FOR MORE ON ARCHITECTURE, SEE PAGES 166-7

▶ FOR MORE ON CELEBRATIONS, SEE PAGES 118-19

Every story has a point of view, and so should every photograph, whether a stand-alone image or part of a larger set contributing to a whole. The *geography* of point of view is quite simple: You can photograph something from above, below, from the side, or straight on, with a variety of subtle angle shifts between. Photographing a building from below, looking up, may allow the viewer to see the entire structure, while photographing a group of people from above, looking down, may reveal each face in a way that a picture at eye level might not. Getting down on the same level as a small child or pet may yield a portrait that gives us the most accurate view of their face.

PSYCHOLOGY OF POINT OF VIEW

But the *psychology* of point of view is

── ZOOM IN ──

▶ What do you want to say about the subjects of your photograph—about their strength, size, or place in the world? Where can you position them and the camera to convey that to the viewer?

worth considering before you decide where to place yourself and the subject in the scene. If a subject is placed high in the frame, it might convey lightness, celebration, or elevation. If placed low in the frame, it might project small-ness, weight, or even burden. Likewise, when you position yourself in the scene and change your point of view of the subject, you translate part of that perspective, further informing what viewers might feel themselves.

If you lie on the ground and point the camera up at a tree, allowing it to tower over the viewer, you might convey that the tree has more age, strength, and maybe even wisdom than you. If you photograph from high above a small child or animal, you might convey your own power or prominence over a diminutive subject. When point of view is combined with actions or expressions of the subject, feelings of dependence, trust, or admiration may be implied. And then there is the impact of look-ing a subject straight in the eye, which sug-gests equality. This perspective may be particularly impactful with children or animals with whom we rarely have the opportunity to see eye to eye. Consider also the impact of making a photograph from within the action itself—in the midst of a parade, or among danc-ers at a celebration. Capturing a photograph from within a crowd infuses the image with energy and sensory cues that are missed when looking at the action from afar.

COMMUNICATING PERSPECTIVE

Remember that by creating an image, you effec-tively become the eyes of the viewer, studying

The view from high on El Capitan illustrates the height and sheer nature of its cliff face. Looking down on climber Alex Honnold—without a rope—evokes anxiety and awe.

a scene unfolding before you. If focal point directs viewers to the subject of the photo-graph, point of view is your tool to influence how they *feel* about it.

Point of view allows you to tell more than one story—or one side of a story—at a time. When you make a choice about position in a photo-graph, the resulting image not only conveys the perspective of the subject, but also your own.

Mauli Dhan climbs down a hand-woven bamboo rope ladder to harvest hallucinogenic honey from a cliff face in the jungles of eastern Nepal.

COLOR

Use the eye-catching colors in a scene or find a vivid element to add to an ordinary tableau in order to make a photograph with impact.

▶ FOR MORE ON COLOR OF LIGHT, SEE PAGES 74-5

▶ FOR MORE ON BALANCE & TENSION, SEE PAGES 44-5

Of all the elements you'll consider in a scene when making an image, color may possibly have the most powerful pull. As visual artists, photographers often find themselves drawn to large areas of color, regardless of what shape or form they take. Sometimes color in and of itself seems enough of a subject to make one raise a camera. The combination of the color of the light and colors of the objects within a frame work together to form a palette, which has an important influence on mood and tone. Saturation—the range of intensity of color, from vibrant to muted—is also important. Almost universally, vivid colors invigorate, while neutral tones soothe. Think of the bright lights of carnival rides versus the soft pastels of a sunrise at sea.

PSYCHOLOGY OF COLOR

It is not only the palette and saturation of colors that guide interpretation of an image, but also the way in which available colors are used. For example, an uninterrupted visual constant can evoke a feeling of calm. Use of a single color in varying shades, repeating or overlapping throughout the frame—say, the earthy greens of prairie grasses or the warm browns of sand dunes—creates rhythm and harmony. Alternatively, a small, vibrant object in an otherwise neutral field carries a lot of visual weight—a *pow!*—and will pull the eye more easily than something much larger in a muted tone. The robust red of the matador's cape, or the bright yellow of an inflatable raft on a lake—these punctuative elements are transformative in a frame, and should work with composition and light to craft the image's overall impact.

Color is personal. Most people find themselves attracted to objects or images featuring their favorite color. Photographing scenes with hues you find most stirring is one way to begin identifying a look for your photographs and your style as a photographer. Look for colors that catch your eye most, and work with composition and light to make the viewer feel the same. As always, the story you want to tell and the way in which you want to move your audience are at the heart of choices you make when photographing colors in the world around you.

ZOOM IN

▶ Examine a scene that features your favorite colors. How do they influence the way you feel? How can you make a photograph that will create the same response in the viewer?

A blue sky and emerald sea set the tropical tone of this scene off Mexico's Isla Holbox. A red hammock in the vigorous breeze captures the imagination, adds energy, and elevates this photograph from average to extraordinary.

PATTERN & TEXTURE

Patterns and textures are more than just superfluous detail—they are a direct route to making the viewer feel something beyond what is seen.

Sometimes a break in pattern can highlight a particular object, or be an orienting element in an otherwise abstract frame, as is the case with this striped tail, which stands out against the otherwise polka-dotted bodies of these cheetahs.

▶ FOR MORE ON DIRECTION OF LIGHT, SEE PAGES 78–9

▶ FOR MORE ON CONTROLLING DEPTH OF FIELD, SEE PAGES 238–9

The human brain naturally seeks patterns to make order out of chaos, to find something to latch onto and follow through a scene. Likewise, texture—even when seen and not physically experienced—can further describe and give context to a subject. When photographed skillfully, texture may even evoke a sense of physical touch in a viewer.

Even when framed tightly and excluding anything else, a pattern can create an experience in a photograph that goes beyond just sight. For example, the pattern in a circuit board may add energy to an image, while the soft ripples in the seafloor may create a sense of calm in their predictability. The stripes of a shop's awning or gaps in a picket fence can be hypnotic—an effect that may transcend the clear identity of the subject itself.

PHOTOGRAPHY WITH FEELING

Texture can add depth to a photograph by creating a multisensory experience for viewers. We know how soft a baby's first hairs are, or how gritty sand feels on bare feet, and so when the eye finds these textures well represented in a photograph, the viewer may *feel* something deeper. And when examined closely, you'll often see that within texture, a pattern emerges.

Creative use of direction of light, depth of field, and color (or lack thereof in some cases) are all effective means to make texture stand out, and possibly even become the focal point of a photograph. A solid understanding of photography basics helps a photographer bring pattern and texture to their full impact and potential in an image.

Consider the pattern and texture in the ordinary scenes around you. Notice how a photograph of a forest tells a different story than a photograph of the shadows its trees cast on the snowy ground. One tells a story of habitat and safety in numbers, the other a story of light and where it comes from, perhaps the time of day, and an indication of what comes next. It may even make the viewer feel cold, or like it's time to go home.

Being conscious of pattern and texture forces a photographer to pay attention to details that ultimately add to the story within the scene. Tapping into these elements to capitalize on their intrinsic impact in the human brain gives you a sophisticated tool to evoke understanding and emotion from an audience.

Intriguingly disorienting, these multi-angled mirrors on a building's facade in Tokyo reflect hundreds of shoppers. With a jumbled pattern that denies the viewer of rhythm, the image evokes the scene's chaotic energy.

BREAKING THE RULES

Understanding the human response to imagery helps a photographer recognize elements that make for powerful photographs—as well as the instinct to push against them.

▶ FOR MORE ON IDENTIFY-ING STORY, SEE PAGES 24–5

▶ FOR MORE ON DEFINING COMPOSI-TION, SEE PAGES 42–3

A famous quote says something to the effect of, "Learn the rules so you can break them effectively." It's hard to pin down with any certainty who said it first, but without question it is good and relevant advice for photographers.

Learning more about the rules—both applying and breaking them—will help on your quest to make great pictures using your own photographic voice.

The difference between "taking" and "making" a photograph is not simply about mastery of techniques and technology. It's about having the ability to perceive and gather information about what's happening beyond what the eye can see. Sometimes this means that the image you create in pursuit of a powerful story or feeling is one that is not technically perfect. That's okay. It's important that you rely on your heart, your gut, and all your senses—not just your learned skills. If your instincts guide your camera a certain way, go with it.

This image offers just enough of a horse to identify the tools of shoeing. The earthy palette grounds us in the stable, the tail evokes the feel of the animal being tended to, and the pop of blue draws the eye to the rider's connection to the scene.

ZOOM IN

▶ Pay attention to what is compelling in a scene, but don't get bogged down trying to make an image perfect. Immerse, feel, and take chances. Every frame is an opportunity to learn or say more.

The soft palette of dresses and backdrop contrasts with the beautiful richness of skin tones, while the twins' artful and spontaneous position—gently leaning while staying connected to each other—evokes a carefree intimacy.

HEEDING YOUR INSTINCTS

Once you are fully present with a subject, or in a scene, inhabiting an open mental space, you can call on what you know about the mechanics and process of photography. If your skills are second nature, they will kick into gear, helping you realize your vision and make a photograph that tells a deeper, more complete story. Often, this process requires a commitment, and always, it requires practice and patience.

Being able to recognize a strong or pleasing image requires *seeing* beyond what your eyes can show you. That perception begins before you pick up the camera. To strengthen the metaphorical muscles needed to do this, it is important to first learn the basic rules of composition as centuries of artists and designers have assembled them by studying the human response to visual material.

And although it is incredibly valuable to know and practice the basic guidelines to composition and design, it is important, too, to heed what your instincts tell you about impact. In some instances, the best photographs are created when the rules go out the window. If it works, it works.

ASSIGNMENT

A peaceful spot in the Cape Sebastian forest in Oregon feels special,
even sacred, when early light streams through the morning fog.

TAKE A NEW LOOK AT A FAMILIAR PLACE

Choose a familiar place to visit. And, rather than bringing your most technical camera, bring only a smartphone or sketchbook.

SIT AND OBSERVE your surroundings. Notice how you feel. Is this spot noisy and energetic? Or is it serene and calm? Do you feel warm or cold? As you take in the entire scene, pay attention to all your senses. This may sound counterintuitive in a photography book, but close your eyes. Your other senses will become stronger when not overpowered by sight.

IDENTIFY A STORY in this place—it could be the story of an animal, of another person you are observing, or of how time spent here changes you. Make notes, sketches, or smartphone photos of elements that support the story. Be sure to note colors, patterns, textures, and other details. Choose a focal point for a single image and consider point of view. Do you want your audience to relate to a particular subject, or is this story best told from your own perspective?

REFLECT ON YOUR EXPERIENCE throughout the rest of the day, what it was like to look at that familiar place with more than just your eyes. Consider a photograph you could make that would best describe the place to a viewer. What elements would it need to include, and where should you be to create a frame that tells us what you want to say? Return the next day with your camera, and using any technical knowledge you already have, try to make a photograph that is different from any you may have made here before.

CHAPTER TWO

COMPOSITION

Look up the definition of *composition* and you'll find some inspiring phrases. Composition is . . .

" . . . a product of mixing or combining various elements . . . "
" . . . an intellectual creation . . ."
" . . . arrangement into specific proportion or relation and especially into artistic form . . ."

Especially into artistic form. This is central to the *making* of a photograph—the difference between a mere snapshot and a thoughtful image that moves the viewer to feel. And so, artful composition becomes important whether a photograph is a singular work or a contribution to a larger story, whether purely an artistic endeavor or a tool for explaining the world in which we live. Photographers know that the more appealing an image's aesthetic is to an audience, the more successful it becomes, no matter its function.

It's interesting to note that although photography is a means to accurately reproduce what is seen, a photographer still has the opportunity to curate what elements go into each frame, and how they are arranged, even if only by rearranging the camera position within the scene. To achieve a composition that elicits a desired reaction, there is an abundance of knowledge to study and consider.

The so-called rules of composition are merely guidelines—pointers for evoking a response in the viewer. And sometimes, for reasons that may or may not be easy to articulate, an image will resonate even when breaking those rules. The better photographers know the rules, the more effectively they might break them. This chapter will explore the concepts that come from centuries of design theory, and will help you hone your power to communicate as a photographer.

Photographed from above, a simple hat becomes the dominant subject in this unusual portrait, casting the woman beneath as an evocative mystery. Composition plays a key role here, with all but her lips obfuscated.

DEFINING COMPOSITION

Composition guides viewers to the payoff of an image with a careful curation of elements within a frame.

These two rowboats, with their elegant forms and vivid color, make compelling, crisp subject matter as framed by the placid waters and soft reflections in Katanuma Lake in Narugo, Japan.

▶ FOR MORE ON FRAMING, SEE PAGES 52–3

▶ FOR MORE ON ANTICIPATING COMPOSITION, SEE PAGES 64–5

The rules of composition may help define something many developing photographers instinctively know. When you take in a scene, perceiving it with all your senses, and give yourself time to consider what appeals to your own aesthetic, you'll likely make compositional choices reflecting that appeal. This is called having a photographic eye. And, although many people are gifted with a natural eye (some more than others), this ability certainly can be developed and improved upon with study and practice. Enter the rules of composition: universally accepted guidelines about the way humans respond to elements of design that artists and designers alike have passed down through the ages.

At its most basic definition, composition describes the placement of relative objects and elements in a photograph. This includes not only the positioning of objects, but also decid-

Photographed from above, this image is full of texture. The tiny truck carrying bunches of oil palm fruits adds context, interest, and a sense of scale to the lush green pattern of the palm fronds.

ing whether or not to include them at all. *National Geographic* magazine photographer Joel Sartore put it best when he said, "If it's in your frame, it's either working for you or against you." In short, if it doesn't contribute to the concept of your photograph, it shouldn't be there. This can create a visual problem for a photographer. In some instances, you may actually be able to arrange elements, as in portrait or still life photography. But, with something more journalistic like street photography, you'll rely heavily on anticipation—the predictive waiting for moving elements to reach a compelling position in the frame. This means thinking

ahead about the next three seconds or the next three minutes, with your camera out and ready to go. In circumstances where you are powerless to move anything, as in landscape photography, moving yourself is your best tool for solving visual problems.

Composition is a powerful means of directing the audience to the most important elements of a photograph. Attention to details like framing, position, angle of view, and more helps determine what exactly to include, and where. The photographer's job is to guide the viewer to the payoff of the picture. The map of that journey is yours to make.

ZOOM IN

▶ In a scene with stationary subjects, explore how repositioning the camera changes the composition of the frame. Which position gives the final image the most impact, and why?

BALANCE & TENSION

Balance and tension in a photograph impact the viewer's equilibrium, fostering pleasing comfort or eliciting a longer, more thought-provoking look.

▶ FOR MORE
ON COLOR,
SEE PAGES
32-3

▶ FOR MORE
ON FRAMING,
SEE PAGES
52-3

When objects are framed by the bounds of a photograph, their positions within that frame relative to one another automatically create either balance or tension in an image. The result has an impact on viewers, so those choices should be made consciously, aiming for the intended goal of the image.

Just as in the real world, balance in a photograph is a function of weight. Although gravity governs weight and balance in the physical world, the weight of an element in a two-dimensional image is purely visual—determined often by color, size, or shape. Like balancing a seesaw, visual balance is achieved when weight is distributed evenly across the frame. The most obvious path to balance is symmetry—two like objects placed evenly on either side of an axis. But balance can also be achieved asymmetrically—when one object with a lot of visual weight is

The three young girls playing on a farm in Kentucky are arranged in a meaningful balance in this frame. The girl in the center, arms outstretched, is flanked by a companion on each side.

Angle of view and subject placement conspire to create an intriguing tension in this image from Paris, with the weighty, round top of a carousel threatening to engulf the scene, and the elevation of the Eiffel Tower rocketing the eye up and out of the frame.

opposite two or more objects of lesser weight. Artists typically seek to create balance in an image, because the result is a feeling of stability and comfort to the viewer.

CREATING TENSION

Tension is created when objects in the image are asymmetrically placed and out of balance. Such an arrangement disrupts the equilibrium within an image and creates conflict or work for the viewer. This may or may not be a bad thing. If tension is the result of thoughtless compositional choices, it may cause the audience to misunderstand or lose interest in the image. Placing a subject precariously against the edge of the frame, for example, with little or no breathing room around it, leaves the viewer's eye with nowhere to go but out of the bounds

of the picture. If constructed creatively, however, tension may intrigue, compelling viewers to stay longer and look deeper. Placing a subject one-third into the frame, with a little negative space around it but nothing directly balancing it, holds a viewer's attention, perhaps leading them to consider where the subject has come from or is headed. This technique makes use of the rule of thirds.

Balance and tension are powerful in creating a feeling with a photograph. If the goal is to create an image that is simply pleasing to the eye and makes viewers comfortable, you'll seek a balanced composition. If the image is meant to feel unstable and create deeper interest or intrigue, compositional tension will achieve that. As always, the story you are trying to tell should dictate your compositional choices.

THE RULE OF THIRDS

Placing the subject in one-third of your image commands viewers' attention, then directs them to seek more information in the rest of the frame.

Taken in Big Piney, Wyoming, the main subject of this image commands the viewer's attention with shape, proximity, and placement in the right third of the frame. Beyond her, a dynamic cast of characters provide context about the scene.

▶ FOR MORE ON BREAK-ING THE RULES, SEE PAGES 36–7

▶ FOR MORE ON ATHLETIC EVENTS, SEE PAGES 144–5

One tried-and-true path to creating interest and energy in an image is by implementing the rule of thirds. Imagine a grid of nine (three-by-three) equal squares over your scene. Some cameras have functions that put a grid overlay right into the viewfinder.

Centuries of studying visual perception and design have revealed that placing a subject along one of these grid lines—or even at their points of intersection—will result in an image with more dynamic tension and interest than if the subject were placed right in the middle of the frame.

In addition to sheer aesthetics, the rule of thirds provides room to add more context to an image. Imagine a photograph of a mountain biker in profile headed down a steep trail. With the subject placed on the left line of the grid and the hill spilling down and away from her, the viewer has room to consider her trajectory and where she's headed as it's revealed in the rest of the frame. When the subject occupies one-third of the image, the viewer is called to begin there, take it in, then continue to the secondary information in the other two-thirds of the field. In that space may be a counterpoint to the subject, something that more fully defines the story, or there may be nothing at all, which is called negative space—the weight and potential of which will be discussed later in this chapter.

RULE BREAKING

As with all rules, there are times when breaking this one will result in a more compelling image. If a subject is particularly striking—for example, a set of stunning eyes looking right at the camera, from beneath the hood of a jacket, against the backdrop of a snowstorm—it's possible that putting the subject dead center will make an arresting image.

Take the time to experiment with positioning your subject both along the grid and in the center. See which orientation speaks to you most as you consider what is distinct about your subject, the story you're trying to tell, or the feeling you are trying to evoke in an audience.

GETTING INTO POSITION

Making effective use of the rule of thirds may mean moving around and changing your own perspective to line up the most important elements in the frame along the grid. This requires thought *before* triggering the shutter—a good practice whether or not you end up applying this compositional rule.

In this photograph of a Kenyan warrior in Samburu National Reserve, the pool of water essentially doubles the image, with subjects and reflections covering all four points of intersection of the grid illustration.

HORIZON LINE

The horizon is an orienting element in an image, a foundation of information. Its placement in a photograph taps into the viewer's intrinsic response to stature and what lies ahead.

▶ FOR MORE ON POINT OF VIEW, SEE PAGES 28–9

▶ FOR MORE ON ADJUSTING FRAME, SEE PAGES 362–3

The horizon is where this world meets atmosphere. It's the line where land or sea meets the sky, as well as the zone where the subject of an image visually meets the background of the scene. This important interface should be carefully considered in a photograph—both in its placement within the frame, and with regard to the subject's position relative to it.

Think about an image that features nothing but land and sky, and how the position of the horizon determines what is expressed. If the horizon is in the bottom of the frame, the sky becomes the subject—it may be vast and open, full of foreboding clouds, or even illuminated by a rainbow. It may speak to potential, lightness, or great, impending forces. The size of the sky may make a viewer feel small, or it may leave room for possibility.

A horizon toward the top of the image gives weight and prominence to

In this photograph, made on the streets of Havana, Cuba, the horizon separates a city scene from its reflection in a puddle, doubling the color, shapes, and impact of design in the frame.

━━━━━━━ ZOOM IN ━━━━━━━

▶ Photograph a subject from above and below, noting how its position changes relative to the horizon. How does a change in orientation impact the story of the image?

what lies below it. The earth becomes long, stretching out ahead, the viewer's attention directed down toward it. It may give a sense of a long journey to come, or the size and grandeur of the world. A horizon right in the middle of an image may evoke a feeling of calm and equanimity, and the junction itself may become the subject.

POINT OF VIEW

Consider point of view, and how the camera's position changes the subject's position with regard to the horizon line. This decision in turn affects the perceived prominence of the subject.

If you get low and look up at an elephant, its head and shoulders rise above the horizon, giving the animal stature in a photograph. If you stand above a small child in a field, the child will appear fully below the horizon line, seeming small and not so powerful, perhaps needing care.

In general, it's important to keep the horizon line—whatever or wherever it may be—level in the scene, and parallel with the top and bottom of the frame. This allows it to contribute to the image without throwing viewers off balance. If used effectively and with intention, an uneven horizon line can evoke a sense of mayhem or chaos, action or adventure, but a horizon that is just a little off reads as a mistake, detracting from the power of an image.

THE HORIZON'S IMPACT

Humans intrinsically relate to the concept of horizon. Its relative position orients a body in

The relatively low position of the camera allows this moai on Easter Island to reach above the horizon and into the sky. In addition to creating a clean, blue backdrop, this orientation gives the figure stature and prominence.

physical spaces, and simplifies interpretation and navigation of even complex landscapes. Conceptually, horizon symbolizes what is to come. And so, this ubiquitous intersection has the significant ability to convey meaning in very little space—sometimes in no more than a simple line.

LEADING LINES

Leading lines bring the viewer on a visual tour through the frame from starting point to payoff, guiding the eye from element to element, building the story of a scene.

Two students walk along the tracks as they return home from school in Nanu Oya, Sri Lanka. The tracks lead into an uncertain point in the distance, enhancing the visual description of their journey.

▶ FOR MORE ON LEADING LINES IN GARDENS, SEE PAGES 94–5

▶ FOR MORE ON LEADING LINES IN ARCHITEC-TURE, SEE PAGES 166–7

Leading lines are elements in a composition that carry the viewer's attention to a point of interest. Not always straight, lines can connect elements in the frame, tying them together in a relationship otherwise overlooked. A leading line is most effective when it starts from a corner of the frame, often at the bottom, and directs the audience into and through the rest of the scene—a winding road to a castle, a city street to a boy with a ball—something that can guide the viewer through the story of the image and on to its payoff.

Sometimes the payoff is infinity. When leading lines start in the bottom corners of a frame and continue toward each other, up and into the picture to a vanishing point—the point at which their distinction is no longer visible—the result is a message of potential,

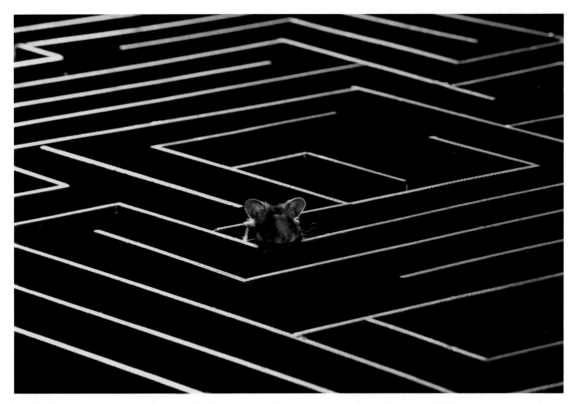

This golden hamster adds context and a dynamic, visual stopping point along the path of a laboratory maze. In this case, the lines guide the eye through the frame without a clear end, emphasizing the animal's challenge.

longevity, or an infinite distance to be traveled. In this way, the perspective of lines can create a three-dimensional quality in a two-dimensional image, and the viewer is drawn more deeply into the frame. More subtly, lines can be visual cues for an emotional response: Horizontal lines convey serenity, vertical lines emphasize power, and diagonal lines may invoke action.

ENVIRONMENTAL LINES

Most photographs contain lines: Some are obvious, like a path or a river; others are more subtle, like a shaft of light or the folds in a scarf. Cityscapes are full of these linear elements—from roads and sidewalks to telephone poles and building facades—lots of opportunities to draw the eye to the focal point of an image. Most often, lines are found rather than created in a scene. The photographer's challenge is to record, interpret, and harness their power, with placement of an important element at the point to which the lines lead. Most often, this is best done by moving the camera and making strong, creative choices when framing a scene.

ZOOM IN

▶ Identify a leading line in a natural space nearby and place a subject along its path. How can you reposition yourself to maximize the effect and influence where the viewer's eye will go?

FRAMING

Beyond using the bounds of an image to define a scene, framing can be accomplished when one element in a photograph is bordered by the structure of another.

▶ FOR MORE ON TECHNOLOGY OF FOCUS, SEE PAGES 234-5

▶ FOR MORE ON ADJUSTING FRAME, SEE PAGES 362-3

The concept of framing is universal in everyday life. The outside world is viewed through windows, TV programs are shown on a rectangular screen, and artwork is typically appreciated within the confines of a frame. In the same way, a framing element within a photograph—usually an object in the foreground such as the leafy branches of a tree or the mouth of a cave—can emphasize the focal point, by creating a sort of border or boundary around it, adding both depth and context.

FOCUS & FRAMING

At their most effective, framing ele-

The driver within the illuminated, purple interior of a taxi in Rajasthan, India, is neatly framed by the window and contrastingly dull exterior of the vehicle. A potential passenger's hand on the door adds an additional layer of information.

A lone elephant is framed by a gap in the trees in Kenya's Samburu National Reserve, and the entire scene is further framed by the double rainbow in the sky above the scrubby hillside.

ments in a photograph are part of the story or environment and have some aesthetic contribution or suggestion of circumstance. Viewing men in orange jumpsuits through the openings of a chain-link fence may imply confinement, for example, while photographing a window in an adjacent building through the window of the room you are in uses repetitive shapes to convey predictability and order.

A frame can be identifiable but completely out of focus and still add an important layer of information. Consider the reflection of a woman's face within the in-focus frame of a mirror, or a bird on a distant branch seen through a gap in blurred leaves right in front of the camera—both of these scenarios include elements that frame the focal point and add context, regardless of their degree of focus.

Framing can also refer quite literally to what is included in the image. By moving the camera one way or another, you can edit your view of the scene. For example, wildflowers may fill the bottom of an image, obscuring a trash can on a trail, or a doorway may block a parked car when the intended focus of the photo is a group of kids playing in the street. When you creatively combine the edges of the image as seen by the camera with framing elements within, you have the power to constructively eliminate clutter and emphasize the subject, commanding the viewer's full attention to the focal point of the photograph.

WHY I LOVE THIS PHOTO

ike any work of art, a photograph succeeds or fails primarily on strength of composition; an understanding of light, focus, color, and texture; and the more subtle but important rule of thirds and sense of scale. This picture, taken in Bhutan by Lynsey Addario, is a wonderful example of a photographer's utilization of these guiding principles. The monks move from darkness into light, walking a serpentine path that naturally leads viewers' eyes through the frame from top to bottom, from right to left and back again. Their soft, red flowing robes create an organic and sharp color contrast against the hard and linear edges of the white stone that surrounds them. The composition is also very democratic: By choosing a deep depth of field, Addario gave all the monks equal priority in terms of focus, thus conveying equal importance to viewers.

—CHARLES BORST
Photo Editor

LAYERING

Skillful use of layers gives a photographer more than one plane with which to tell a complete story within a frame.

The three distinct layers of this photograph of a waterfront fish market on Lake Tanganyika, Tanzania, provide a complex description of the scene, featuring fishermen, shore support, and catch, all within one frame.

▶ FOR MORE ON HIERAR-CHY, SEE PAGES 58–9

▶ FOR MORE ON CON-TROLLING DEPTH OF FIELD, SEE PAGES 238–9

Layering is an advanced compositional technique that photographers use to add depth and dimension to the story or theme of a photograph. Adding one, two, or more layers to a two-dimensional image allows multiple aspects of a story to be told, with relevant information in the foreground, middle ground, and background. In this way, newspaper and magazine photographers often make good use of the whole frame to show context,

telling more of the whole story in an image or two.

A simple example of effective layering in an image would be a chewed-up teddy bear in the foreground, the feet of a grown-up who found it in the middle ground, and the humbled, guilty-looking dog in the background. Within a single frame, it's clear that there has been a household crime, that the perp has been identified, and that he knows a reckoning is coming.

——— ZOOM IN ———

▶ Squat behind a catcher at home plate. Frame to include the batter and pitcher beyond him. Capturing the actions of all three in different layers may tell a more complete story than a view of the game in profile.

This photograph uses light and texture to define layers and add dimension to a summer scene as storm clouds advance over the Dugout Ranch within Bears Ears National Monument in Utah.

CREATING EFFECTIVE, DISTINCT LAYERS

Even with alternating planes of focus—some may be sharp, others may be soft and offer a mere suggestion of important elements—layers help photographers tell a more complex and complete story in one photograph. The trick, of course, is making sure each layer is well composed and contributes to the whole, without adding anything distracting or counter to the goal of the image. It's also effective if the most important elements in each layer have some particular definition—either through color, focus, or separation. A little negative space between them or other means of distinction helps ensure that each element is impactful. This takes careful consideration, attention to detail, and practice.

At its most successful (and challenging), layering can do more than create cohesion between elements; it can also direct viewers through each element in order of its importance. This takes layering to the next level of complexity in its use of hierarchy—the implied importance of elements in the photograph based on their arrangement.

HIERARCHY

Hierarchy is the ranking of subjects in the scene through visual cues of composition. The result is a subliminal road map for the viewer to navigate the image.

▶ FOR MORE
ON PATTERN
& TEXTURE,
SEE PAGES
34–5

▶ FOR MORE
ON DEFINING
COMPOSI-
TION, SEE
PAGES 42–3

Hierarchy, and specifically visual hierarchy, refers to the arrangement of elements in a frame that suggests a ranking of their importance, as well as the order in which viewers are guided to view them. Many of the compositional and visual techniques discussed so far, including color, patterns, texture, leading lines, and framing, can be used to plot the viewer's path through the image. Other characteristics that can make certain elements stand out are contrast, shape, size, deviation from alignment, and space surrounding the subject.

A DOMINANT ELEMENT

An object that stands out from the rest of the elements in a photograph will attract the eye first, and perhaps hold a viewer's interest longer. Imagine a carton of eggs, with one of the dozen

In this portrait of two girls through the window of a home in remote Peru, the eye first goes to the smaller girl whose face jumps out in contrast to everything else. The line of the sheer curtain leads next to the other girl, who is gently leaning toward the edge of the frame.

Bright and dominant in the photograph, the cliffs in this split frame grab the eye first. The change in color and texture at the water's surface lead to the downward motion of the fur seals playing just beneath.

badly broken. A number of compositional elements will lead the viewer's eye to the broken egg first, including deviation of the pattern of rows containing two whole eggs, texture, contrast in content, and pop of color if the bright yellow yolk is visible. And so, while taking in the context of normal eggs in the periphery, the viewer's attention will jump to the broken one first as the one that stands out as different. After examining the rest of the eggs, the eye will likely return to the broken one.

Essentially, successful hierarchy helps the audience navigate a photograph. And when carefully crafted, this road map for traveling through the frame can add structure and visual organization that supports the story within the image, adding emphasis along the way.

SPOTTING EXISTING HIERARCHY

It's worth noting that intentional, plotted use of visual hierarchy in a photograph, especially one that involves multiple subjects in motion, presents quite a challenge to any photographer. It's rare to have total control over all the elements in a scene and their relative positions within the frame. With many of these guidelines, and with hierarchy in particular, the best approach is to learn to recognize compositional opportunities as they arise naturally in scenes as you are photographing.

Whenever possible, make thoughtful decisions about what's most important to the story of your photograph, and reposition yourself and the camera to emphasize these elements in your frame.

POSITIVE & NEGATIVE SPACE

Areas of an image are classified by their contents—whether subject or void, positive or negative—and these work together to advance the story of the frame.

▶ FOR MORE
ON BALANCE
& TENSION,
SEE PAGES
44–5

▶ FOR MORE
ON ANTICI-
PATING
COMPOSI-
TION, SEE
PAGES 64–5

A photograph is essentially a rectangular canvas on which you compose an image. It's important to remember that everything within the frame—not just the elements you intend to emphasize—makes up the final picture. "Positive space" describes the areas of the image occupied by subject matter. The empty space around those objects is considered "negative space," and although these areas may seem secondary, they still carry weight, emphasize the subject, and help advance the story. In general, leaving a little negative space between elements will make for a stronger composition, allowing for the shape of each object to be discernable, particularly for silhouettes.

Looking for separation between elements requires patience, timing, and a good deal of anticipation when subjects are in motion. Imagine waiting for the moment when there is separation between buffalo roaming on the prairie, allowing viewers to see exactly three big creatures, rather than an unquantifiable, indistinguishable herd. Often, simply moving around and changing the perspective of the camera can create negative space between objects.

Large empty spaces created by sky, fields, a wall without windows, or other simple elements also contribute to an image and ultimately the way it impacts viewers. Negative space can be used as an element unto itself to creatively balance or visually support a subject, or to evoke an emotion about the scene. For example, empty space in front of a hiker may imply the nature and length of his journey in the mind of the viewer. Negative space may say something about the vastness of a place, or perhaps trigger a feeling of desolation or loneliness. Large swaths of space can also suggest calm, possibility, and potential.

To that end, think of negative space as one more creative tool to further reinforce your message. This is true both in the way you use it to frame and emphasize your subject, as well as the placement of large empty areas or blocks of solid color within the image to add more context or leave room for imagination. Play with balance, tension, and other compositional precepts and consider space as another object within your photograph.

ZOOM IN

▶ Photograph two friends standing two feet apart. Move around them and note when their figures overlap and when they are separated by space. How does the negative space influence the impact of the image?

Vast, black negative space indicates the size and epic nature of Kacna Jama cave in Slovenia, while the white space created by a beam of light accentuates the explorer's feat and indicates the way back out.

SENSE OF SCALE

Coupling known objects and unknown elements within one picture provides viewers with a frame of reference, capitalizing on existing knowledge to make a photograph more meaningful.

▶ FOR MORE ON LANDSCAPES, SEE PAGES 152–3

▶ FOR MORE ON ENVIRONMENTAL PORTRAITS, SEE PAGES 114–15

You've seen it, that common photograph of someone "holding up" the Leaning Tower of Pisa. The particular placement of the person in the foreground and the tower in the background tricks the eye into seeing something we know is false (if posed accurately side by side, of course the structure would be much bigger than any person). It's a compositional illusion that takes comedic advantage of sense of scale, or in this case, a distorted sense of scale.

A FRAME OF REFERENCE

Scale adds to a photograph by triggering the viewer's understanding of the size of a common object—a pencil or person, for example—and juxtaposing it with a subject, the size of which might not otherwise be obvious. Imagine a photograph with a penny placed beside an insect, or a microchip on the tip of a human finger. Existing knowledge about the size of the penny and a human finger offers a frame of refer-

Tourists view the city of Paris, tiny in the distance, from behind a giant clock face in the tower of the Musée d'Orsay. The surreal perspective of unusual proportions makes this image unique and intriguing.

Photographed from below, this cat appears large and looming in comparison to other elements in the frame. Had it been photographed from above, it would appear much smaller and less significant.

ence for subjects previously unexperienced (the insect and microchip).

PROVIDING CONTEXT

Looking at a landscape photograph, the viewer's brain automatically makes a series of calculations based on what they know—they've likely seen many photographs of the Grand Canyon, so when they see another, they can easily interpret the size of it. This becomes a little more challenging with unfamiliar places or certain natural features like waves. By including a person enjoying the surf, a photographer can emphasize the massive shore break she is trying to capture.

In the case of the Leaning Tower of Pisa gag, note that placement of the objects in concert with perspective of the camera can manipulate perception—by having the person close to the camera beside the tower in the distance, the human looks large enough to hold up the tower, and illusion distorts reality.

Adding an object for sense of scale may provide useful reference, but consider a way to offer a size comparison that also meets your aesthetic preference for the image. For example, including a bike messenger riding past a concrete wall covered in vivid graffiti offers a sense of the size of the wall and the breadth of the graffiti, while also adding a contextual yet artful element to a photograph about a city street. The successful inclusion of any object in a frame may require consideration of more than one compositional rule and will contribute to the image in more than one way. In other words, when adding an element for sense of scale, be sure to consider other ways it might contribute to the overall impact of the photograph.

ANTICIPATING COMPOSITION

Anticipation is the predictive selection of a decisive moment with a second-nature sense for the most compelling composition of elements in the scene.

With immersive observation, a photographer can anticipate the action that defines a dynamic moment—in this case, all four boys in the air and throwing water from buckets at the same time.

▶ FOR MORE ON DEFINING COMPOSITION, SEE PAGES 42–3

▶ FOR MORE ON CANDIDS, SEE PAGES 122–3

Whether consciously or not, viewers are always using information from prior experiences to interpret what they see in a photograph. By examining this idea in yourself and understanding it in others, you can make subtle but effective choices when you consider composition. The more familiar you are with the elements that make a photograph really work, the more efficiently you can make choices about composition. You will not only begin to choose the best moments to photograph, but you will also begin to anticipate them.

SELECTING THE MOMENT

The phrase "anticipating composition" means predicting and selecting one important moment from the ebb and flow of life. Perhaps an even better word for what a photographer does is *selecting*, rather than *creating*, an image. With observation and presence, you will

—— ZOOM IN ——

▶ Examine the two photographs on this spread and try to imagine the scenes seconds after each capture was made. Would the impact be the same if the buckets were empty or the skier had already landed?

By framing in advance and being prepared for the pace of action in the scene, the photographer was able to anticipate and respond to the moment this skier took flight, even at high speed.

begin to recognize patterns of movement, behavior, and other dynamic elements that shape a scene. A classic example is the presentation of a birthday cake. You might be prepared to capture your child blowing out the candles. But what about the moment he first sees the cake, his eyes wide in anticipation? With practice, you will be able to see the moment before it happens, and harness the impact of multiple elements of composition together in a single frame. Photojournalist Henri Cartier-Bresson called this the "decisive moment," the capture of an image of life at its most revealing.

Of course, you do need to plan ahead to be ready for what unfolds before the camera. Batteries should be fresh, memory cards should have plenty of space available, and exposure settings should be adjusted to the current conditions. But presence of mind and a broader perception will make the difference between a grabbed snapshot and something more artful, more meaningful. To capture a remarkable moment in time, it's important that the rules of composition be second nature so you can anticipate and quickly recognize opportunities to apply them, or make an informed decision to discard them.

ASSIGNMENT

This photograph of a girls' soccer training program in Jharkhand, India, makes wonderful use of perspective, framing, and layering.

A BALL, A ROPE
& A FEW FRIENDS

Collect a few inanimate objects—perhaps a beach ball, a rope, or other simple, flexible items. Ask a few friends to join you and be ready to embrace their sense of play.

HEAD TO A WIDE-OPEN LANDSCAPE—a grassy field, a sandy beach, or even an empty parking lot. Ask your friends to toss the ball back and forth and move around.

EXPERIMENT WITH COMPOSITION as they do. Try placing the ball on the ground close to the camera and see how far into the background your friend needs to stand to be the same size. Have your friends use the rope to connect themselves to one another, or create a leading line between themselves and the ball. Move yourself and the camera, looking for separation of elements and large areas of negative space.

EXPLORE THE RULES OF COMPOSITION, and try as many of them as you can, using these basic elements and moving subjects. Stand on a chair and look down at the action, or lie on the ground and photograph objects flying overhead as you play with perspective. Use the rules, break the rules, and let the scene swirl around you. Try to anticipate what will happen next as you select moments in time to capture. Go home and review the results—see what appeals to your aesthetic and what doesn't. Intentional experimentation with composition (and being willing to make some photos you don't like) is one of the best ways to begin to understand your voice as a photographer.

CHAPTER THREE

LIGHT

The word *photography* stems from the Greek words for "light" and "drawing," and indeed, without light, there would be nothing to see or make photographs with. Eyes and cameras are only able to register objects once light has touched them. Light is both a critical constant in photography as well as a tool for great creativity.

Photographers think constantly about light—the amount, quality, and nature of light available, and how it paints objects, allowing them to be seen and photographed. And so, a deep understanding of light—its behavior and how best to harness it—is essential to becoming a skilled photographer.

Light reveals the world in an ever changing display of shadows and subtleties, highlights and penetrating glare. Although much can be said about the light a photographer can create, this chapter will look deeply into available light—how to anticipate and interpret it, how to reflect and shape it, and most important, how to work within it. To make the most of available light, it's important to master the fundamentals of photography as well as any technology specific to the camera being used. But above all else, it is important to recognize that, ultimately, light is the illuminating force for everything you do as a photographer.

National Geographic photographer James Stanfield says, "It's not the light, but where you are in it." Just as with composition, the photographer's challenge is to accept things that cannot be controlled, and to find a place from where the story can be told in the most effective way.

The better you understand light, the more skillfully you will be able to tap into all that it has to offer. If presence and composition are your foundation for seeing, consider light as the gift that allows your compositions to shine.

One of the most magnificent natural displays of light, an aurora is caused by collisions of gaseous particles in Earth's atmosphere with charged particles released by the sun. Here, the aurora borealis swirls over a fjord in Tromsø, Norway.

AWARENESS OF LIGHT

Beyond simply illuminating a scene, the source and path of light give it distinct properties that can make a photograph powerful, more descriptive, and unique.

▶ FOR MORE
ON COLOR
OF LIGHT,
SEE PAGES
74-5

▶ FOR MORE
ON RANGE
OF LIGHT/
HISTOGRAM,
SEE PAGES
250-51

Light is a critically important ally in conjuring emotion with a photograph. As such, an understanding of light's nuances is essential to successful photography. To have an awareness of light, you must also have an awareness of shadow. Paying attention to the patterns of light and shadow on your subjects will help you add depth and mood to your photographs, as will an understanding of the character of the light available to you.

CHARACTER

Light's properties—source, strength, and direction—can create completely unique effects in a photograph. The soft pink pastels of a sunrise may wrap your subjects in a gauzy air that invokes a sleepy or contemplative start to their day. If you're forced to shoot in direct midday light, its harsh, bold, and unapologetic properties might just be the best expression of the energy and busyness of the

With a sky illuminated by the reflected light of the moon, the silhouetted figures of migrant Somalis searching for cell service on the Djibouti seashore are made visible. The light from their phones adds points of interest that carry the eye through the scene.

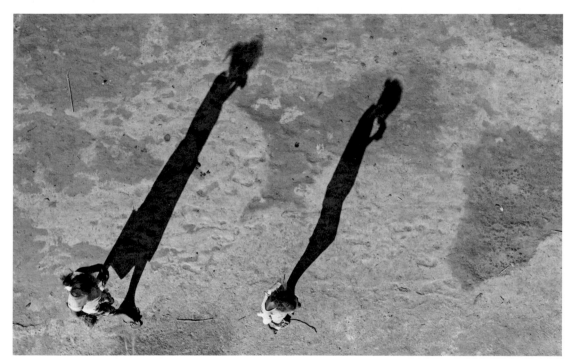

With the sun low in the sky, long shadows of these children contrast with the red glare of a dry landscape in Bekily, Madagascar. From this perspective, the illuminated ground becomes a canvas for their distinct shadow shapes.

scene. The ferocious oranges of a dramatic sunset can give a romantic glow to the focus of the frame. The way light touches each thing in an image is so potent that it's sometimes hard to discern if it reflects, or in fact creates, the mood of the scene.

FLOW

Begin to notice light's flow, the way it enters, moves through, and leaves the frame. The goal is to use the camera to harness and convey the flow of light in the same way our eyes see it. Beginning photographers may adhere to the idea that light should always come from behind the camera to illuminate the subject evenly. More experienced photographers know that when light comes toward a subject from the side, it may create something more dramatic and sophisticated; it may enhance texture and add context about time and place. And very brave photographers may opt to shoot directly into the sun—transforming a subject into a stunning, haloed silhouette.

When you are truly aware of light, you are able to recognize what is available, and can surf the wave of how this force, so dominant in a photograph, shapes the mood and story of the scene before you. The even better news is that once you start observing light in this way, you cannot ever stop.

ZOOM IN

▶ Look at a favorite photograph made by someone else. Try to determine the source of light, and how it illuminates the subject and influences the tone of the entire image.

QUALITY OF LIGHT

Depending on the nature of its source, the quality of light—whether hard or soft—sets the tone for the image and should enhance composition.

Hard afternoon light creates crisp shadows and brings out the vibrant colors of treasured bedsheets—the only items many Sudanese women refugees carried when they fled to Uganda.

▶ FOR MORE
ON FOG &
HAZE, SEE
PAGES 82-3

▶ FOR MORE
ON BRIGHT
LIGHT, SEE
PAGES 84-5

The quality of light is always changing. During different seasons, in various types of weather, and even at different times of day, light has unique attributes. The tonal range of light includes its gamut of shadows, highlights, and mid-tones—the ratios and blending of which shift as the quality of light changes. The aim for photographers is to make the most of what is available so that it aligns with—and enhances—the content of an image for maximum emotional effect.

HARD LIGHT

Hard light comes from a single, defined point source—the sun, a spotlight, an unmodified flash, or a bare bulb, for example. High in contrast, this sort of light reveals an unvarnished realism in a photograph. Brilliant sunlight, particularly at midday, produces sharp-edged shadows and highlights with clear lines of definition between the two. Sunlit areas show bright colors, while shaded areas turn nearly black. And although the combination of these extremes may enhance a strong composition, it's important to keep in mind that details may be lost in both deep shade and bright highlights, as a camera's digital sensor may not have the capacity to discern information in these extremes.

In the mid-tones of an image, however, colors may be accurate and intense, unless the light is so harsh that it washes them out with glare. If glare is unavoidable, use it to help advance the story of the image. With an appropriate subject and composition, a bright, bleaching glare may convey extreme heat, as in a photograph of a cactus in a scrubby desert, or discomfort, like a picture of a hitchhiker sitting on a hot, empty road, or even joy, as in a photograph of kids flying a kite at the beach.

SOFT LIGHT

In photographs with soft light, the source isn't as clearly defined—the light seems to come from everywhere and wrap around the subject. Soft light doesn't have the same extremes as hard light in either highlights or shadows, and a subject will cast only a faint shadow, if any. A lack of glare means that both subtle tones and rich hues will be well reproduced in the final photograph. Images with very soft light are rarely dramatic, but they still evoke mood when made well.

Soft lighting can convey gentleness, calm, mystery, or solemnity—think of a woman staring out to sea from the bow of a boat on a foggy day, or a father's hands holding a baby, beside a window with sheer curtains. Portraits made in soft, gentle light may be very flattering, and leave room for the subject's expression to be the major focus. When working with what's available, photographers often embrace the tone created by light in the scene, capturing its effect as it washes over and influences a subject. The result is a photograph that truly reflects the mood of the moment.

The soft light that gently illuminates a great egret hunting for fish in a calm lake in Maine complements the bird's graceful shape and the subtle contours of the water's ripples, conveying a feeling of serenity and quiet.

COLOR OF LIGHT

Light has color depending on its source and its path to the subject. Photographers may embrace the mood that color creates, or choose to neutralize it.

▶ FOR MORE ON THE SENSOR, SEE PAGES 216–17

▶ FOR MORE ON WHITE BALANCE, SEE PAGES 258–9

The human brain perceives color based on the wavelength of light that enters the eye. When light hits a yellow lemon, it reflects back to us the wavelengths we perceive as yellow and absorbs all of the others. An object that appears white has reflected all the light's wavelengths, whereas an object that appears black has absorbed all the wavelengths and reflected none. Those different wavelengths and colors are referred to with terms like *warm* and *cool*.

TEMPERATURE

Color temperatures, which are measured in the unit of kelvin, refer to the color of a light source, which ranges from red to blue. Light sources with a lower temperature (3500K or less), have a warm, red to yellow appearance, and will color the subjects they light accordingly. In the same way, light sources with a mid-range temperature (3500K to 5000K) have a white or neutral appearance, and sources with a higher temperature (5000K and up) will have a cool, bluish appearance.

So, although the red end of the scale is actually cooler than the blue end of the scale, photographers typically use the term *warm* to describe the rosy glows of pink to orange light, and *cool* to refer to blue light.

EMOTION & MOOD

But what *effect* does the light's color have on a photograph? The camera precisely documents the color of light as it impacts the subject. The orange glow from the light of sunset, low in the sky, may bathe a subject with a look of warmth, calm, or romance. The cool tones of light bouncing off a field of snow may evoke a feeling of cold, desolation, or mystery.

Photographers must choose to embrace the colors the camera sees—and the moods they evoke—or correct the image to a neutral temperature. This can be done with in-camera white balance adjustments when taking the photo or in the editing process. As with many aspects of photography, working with the color of light means merging a technical understanding with a creative choice. Recognize the color of the light available to you and call on your understanding of science and technology to make the most of it.

ZOOM IN

▶ Look at the light out your bedroom window at dawn, noon, and dusk. What is the color that comes to mind with each? What mood does each color evoke in you?

As this young woman is illuminated by light passing through a stained-glass window, the predominant yellow light on her face and hand creates a warm appearance overall, in spite of the blue, cooler light seen elsewhere in the frame.

AMBIENT LIGHT

Ambient light is the light available in any scene. Learn to make the most of it by recognizing its qualities and learning how to modify it to your needs.

The delicate leaves of a plant in Myanmar are lit by the soft ambient light of an overcast day. With exposure control, the photographer has kept the background nearly black, allowing the hypnotic illuminated pattern to artistically dominate the frame.

▶ FOR MORE ON SEASONS, SEE PAGES 154-5

▶ FOR MORE ON OTHER ACCESSO-RIES, SEE PAGES 282-3

Light may be a photographer's most critical tool. Given the dynamic nature of *ambient* light—the light available at any given moment without any added—a photographer must know how to identify, understand, and anticipate the most advantageous light conditions for a particular type of photograph.

DYNAMIC LIGHT

Every season, weather condition, and time of day offers unique types and qualities of outdoor light, but there are some general observations to consider. In the morning hours, before the sun is high in the sky, the light is typically clean and white and makes for good landscape and cityscape photography. Midday is typically not an optimal time for making photographs. When the sun is directly overhead, the shadows are short but deep, carving sharp contrast into everything they touch. It's an especially challenging time for portraits, when a subject's face will be riddled with unforgiving highlights and distracting shadows. The low sun of late afternoon offers light that is typically warm and diffuse, casting long shadows. Many photographers favor the special light in the hour just after sunrise and just before sunset—the golden hours.

WORKING WITH WHAT IS

Skilled photographers can work effectively with whatever light is available. Even when the source of light is beyond their control, they have ways to modify it, to shape and soften it, and even to change its direction.

A diffuser is any object that allows the passage of some light and spreads it more evenly as it passes through. Any translucent medium can diffuse light, from a sheer curtain to a nylon parasol, and diffusing is a great way to soften light from a direct, harsh source. A portable dif-

fuser is an inexpensive accessory, and is usually a round or oval disk of stretched, white nylon that collapses into a small pouch for transport. It's a great add to any camera kit, though it may require an extra set of hands to use effectively.

A reflector changes the impact of harsh light by bouncing it into areas of dark shadows. Bouncing light requires a solid, reflective surface, like a bright piece of poster board. Bounced light will carry the color of the surface reflecting it, so most professional reflectors are white, silver, or even gold, which adds a little warmth. When used skillfully and in combination with a flag—a dark surface that will block light—a reflector can change the direction of light altogether. A setup like this, although requiring many hands or stands, can be a great solution when available light is not ideal.

The low, ambient light of late day illuminates the hand of a Labuan Bajo man working on a canoe in Indonesia. The man's face is in shadow, further highlighting the work, rather than the worker.

DIRECTION OF LIGHT

Direction impacts not only the quality of light, but also the way it paints a subject in both highlights and shadows, influencing mood and message.

▶ FOR MORE ON AMBIENT LIGHT, SEE PAGES 76–7

▶ FOR MORE ON LAND-SCAPES, SEE PAGES 152–3

Ambient light is often in a fixed position and not easily moved. So, as you consider the direction of light and how it will impact your subject and photograph, it's important to understand that, barring the use of modifiers, a change in light direction will most likely require moving either the subject or the camera relative to the light source.

DIRECTION & IMPACT

Before making any big moves, first consider the impact of light coming at the subject from different directions. In general, light from above can be unflattering, casting shadows beneath brows, noses, and lips for portraits, and is relatively harsh and uninteresting for landscapes. Though sun coming from behind the camera might be a popular

Light from above is reflected back on the women, who are preparing a meal in an Afghan home. Made soft and diffuse by the steam and from light bouncing off a reflective surface, the three-quarter angle of illumination creates a natural, almost painterly effect.

ZOOM IN

▶ Look at these two photos and determine the direction of the light on the subjects. What is the effect on tone? How would that change if the light came from another direction?

---

choice among beginning photographers, when light shines on a subject from directly in front, it can appear flat and undefined, as it lacks variety in highlights and shadows. A more interesting approach is light from one side, illuminating the subject while creating natural shadows with everything it touches. This oblique lighting, from a window for example, can make a portrait captivating. If the subject is at a 90-degree angle to the light source, half her face will be lit and the other half obscured by shadow—possibly to dramatic or even mysterious effect. The most common angle of light for a portrait is the flattering three-quarter view, when light illuminates the subject from the front and slightly to one side. The result is shadow on a portion of the face, usually with a triangle of light beneath the far eye. This natural look is known as Rembrandt lighting, for its resemblance to the look captured by the great master of portrait painting.

THE GOLDEN HOUR

The golden hour is when the sun is low and its light makes its longest journey through the atmosphere, creating a softer, warmer glow. This typically occurs in the hour just after sunrise and just before sunset, when the sun is at its lowest visible point in the sky. The results are long shadows, rich colors, and soft light. Many landscape photographers choose this time to make images with greater depth, mood, and impact. To optimize your chances of catching golden hour and the fleeting magic light it produces, search for websites and apps that offer local information on the exact time of sunrise and sunset, as well as atmospheric conditions.

The light is reaching the face of this great horned owl from about 90 degrees to its side, illuminating half of its face, while obscuring the rest in shadow, to a dramatically mysterious effect.

PREPARED FOR GOOD LIGHT

When on location, plan ahead and be ready to make photographs in the early and late parts of the day. Photographers prepare by scouting locations in advance, and having their gear ready to go with charged batteries and fresh memory cards. A solid understanding of the way light plays in a photograph, combined with use of data, technology, and anticipation, will help you make the most of available light, no matter where it comes from.

During Ganga Dussehra, a Hindu festival in Haridwar, India, oil lamps float down the Ganges River.

WHY I LOVE THIS PHOTO

Twilight is the perfect low-light situation for a skilled photographer like John Stanmeyer to capture the energy, beauty, and pulsating verve of India's annual Ganga Dussehra festival along the banks of the Ganges River. Notice how the streaks on the river dance and lure you into the frame. They entice your eyes to float down the river to the right, where the bright street lamps guide you from one side to the other until you return back to the foreground to find the bright spots in the candlelit crowd. Lighting in a photograph can be a powerful tool. The gorgeous blue hue in this image, in combination with the blurred crowd, adds to its success. They create an energetic mood that envelops me with the importance and excitement of the moment.

—STACY GOLD
Senior Director, National Geographic
Image Collection

FOG & HAZE

Suspension of matter in the air defines and diffuses light in creative ways, but may also require some adjustments for proper exposure.

The intense dust kicked up at a rodeo festival in Coahuila, Mexico, becomes a giant diffuser, softening even harsh midday light. Light bouncing off matter suspended in the air washes out the image—an effect that works well in this context.

▶ FOR MORE ON EXPOSURE, SEE PAGES 230-31

▶ FOR MORE ON EXPOSURE COMPENSATION, SEE PAGES 254-5

On misty mornings, the moisture that envelops trees in the woods, or rises in soft pillows from the surface of still waters can add a feeling of freshness, eeriness, or mysticism to a scene. Rays of illumination become defined as they penetrate fog and haze, giving shape to light and wrapping everything they touch in a soft, even glow.

THE NATURE OF FOG & HAZE

Like clouds, fog is the suspension of millions of water droplets in the atmosphere close to Earth's surface. Haze is the suspension of other particulate matter from sources like smoke or dust in the air. Both act like natural diffusers of light, softening it and reducing contrast. But the particles—whether water or other matter—create surface area for light to reflect, broadening the light source, which can potentially confuse your camera's metering system.

In this sophisticated image of fog enshrouding the Golden Gate Bridge in San Francisco, the lights of the city softly, but also brightly, illuminate portions of the fog blanket, giving the entire image a varied and artistic effect.

COMPENSATING FOR FOG & HAZE

Both fog and haze have varying densities. The suspension of particles can be white or gray, thick or thin, making a balanced exposure a challenge. When a camera is set to an automatic mode, the settings it uses are based on its meter reading. But, in the case of fog and haze, it's possible the camera might actually *underexpose* the image in a sort of overreaction to the excess light bouncing off suspended matter in the air.

To expose the scene correctly, a photographer may need to override the camera's settings and intentionally *overexpose* the image. This can be done by choosing the aperture and shutter speed manually, or by using a fully or partially automatic mode in combination with the exposure compensation function available in most cameras. With either option, choosing to overexpose by a half stop or more will push the exposure to create an image closer to what your eyes see.

ACCENTUATE THE SUBJECT

Fog or haze can swallow up considerable contrast, resulting in a flat photograph that lacks punch. Exposure tweaks and composition are your best allies here. To work with a loss of sharp detail, focus on shapes and silhouettes. Mist in the air acts as a clean backdrop when you set your exposure for the fog and lets a shapely subject fall to nearly black. Leaving negative space between shapes will likely create the strongest composition. For more color and contrast, move close to some of the elements in the frame, reducing the amount of fog between the camera and that part of the scene.

Although the goal is to understand both the conditions and your equipment well enough to zero in on the best settings for the circumstances, experiment and adjust after reviewing each capture to make the most of the conditions before the air clears.

BRIGHT LIGHT

When bright light is unavoidable, assess the options and make creative exposure choices to direct viewers to the focal point of the image.

▶ FOR MORE ON AMBIENT LIGHT, SEE PAGES 76-7

▶ FOR MORE ON EXPOSURE COMPENSATION, SEE PAGES 254-5

Certain photographs can work in midday sun, especially if the story will benefit from high contrast, or a feeling of starkness or severity. But working when the sun is bright and high means challenges to overcome and choices to make.

White sandy beaches and snowy fields are like mirrors in high, bright sun. The abundant light, which seems to come from everywhere at once, may confuse a light meter, and a camera in automatic mode may respond with settings that actually underexpose the scene. To compensate, manually choose settings that let in a little more light, whether by opening the aperture further or by slowing down the shutter speed. Alternatively, set the camera to automatic, but also engage the exposure compensation function, which will consistently let in more light.

When deep, contrasting shadows are

To block and diffuse the sun shining right into the camera while photographing Mount Everest and Lhotse on the horizon, the photographer made creative use of Tibetan prayer flags, adding context, color, and a distinctive framing element to the photograph.

problematic, one way to modify the light is to bounce some back onto the subject. A reflector helps do this by filling dark areas with bounced light. If you cannot modify the light, consider setting the camera to expose the focal point properly. This is most easily done in manual mode, or by using the exposure compensation function. If the subject occupies a small percentage of the frame, though, it may have a significant impact on the rest of the image—either by overexposing it and "blowing it out," or darkening it to almost black.

LENS FLARE

Lens flare is a quirk of very bright light created when stray light bounces back and forth between layers of glass in the lens before reaching the camera's sensor. Zoom lenses, with their numerous glass panes, may be more prone to them.

Flares appear in the final image in one of two ways: either as a series of bright circular artifacts, or as a haze across the frame. Either can be used as a creative element that contributes to the story of the image, accentuating a feeling of heat, happiness, or even the serenity of a sunny day. But successful incorporation of flare may take some trial and error to avoid it obscuring an important element or subject.

Making a successful photograph in bright light often requires choosing which element to draw the viewer's attention to, and how. Sometimes that's done through composition, and sometimes it's done with exposure and creative use of the abundant light in the scene.

Exposing for a bright sky allows for creative use of silhouettes, with subjects in the foreground that are underexposed. This free diver and the cypress trees beyond form dramatic, dark shapes in a surreal photograph made from underwater in Ginnie Springs, Florida.

LOW LIGHT

Although camera performance in low light is improving, a solid understanding of exposure and technology will make the difference between a good low-light image and one that is unusable.

A high ISO allowed the photographer to maximize depth of field and freeze gentle ripples on the water's surface as a swan drifted across this lake in Norway just before dawn.

▶ FOR MORE ON ISO SENSITIVITY, SEE PAGES 246–7

▶ FOR MORE ON HIGH DYNAMIC RANGE, SEE PAGES 318–19

Many of life's most subtle yet meaningful moments happen in low-light conditions. As the day wraps up and action winds down, a hint of fatigue often paints a scene with a sense of calm. Campers around a fire, kids walking home after a day of play, friends gathering as a wedding celebration starts to wane—moments like these are when people often drop their guard, revealing a softer, more authentic version of themselves.

LOW-LIGHT CONSIDERATIONS

These gentle, end-of-day moments come with unique photographic challenges. Wide apertures, long shutter speeds, and high ISO settings make low-light exposures viable, but each of these factors has its potential pitfalls. The shallow depth of field from a wide aperture may mean too much of the scene is out of focus, and a long shutter speed may cause blur from either camera shake or subject movement. Selecting a high ISO (the setting that determines how sensitive the sensor is to light) leaves room for safer aperture and shutter speed choices, but comes with a price—noise. Noise is the graininess, or digital "dust," that appears in an image as a result of maximizing sensor sensitivity.

Each year seems to bring improvements in digital camera technology. Sensors have become more accurate and sensitive, creating sharper low-light images with higher dynamic range (numerous degrees of brightness across the frame) and reduced noise even at high ISO settings.

And although it's never been easier, a photographer cannot rely on technology alone to make successful low-light pictures. Large areas of shadow can throw off the meter reading for a focal point in the frame, so try center-weighted or spot metering to ensure the subject is exposed correctly. Images made with higher ISO settings will yield more noise with even minor edits made later on a computer, making it even more important to be accurate on capture. The camera's autofocus function might struggle to find edges on which to focus in low light. One work-around is to shine a flashlight on the subject during autofocus, then shut it off for capture, or turn autofocus off altogether and focus manually.

KNOWLEDGE & TECHNOLOGY

Knowing your equipment—its strengths and limitations—is essential to successfully making an image in low light. In general, cameras that produce large, RAW-format files work best at capturing and preserving details in the low-light zones that challenge a sensor's capacity. That

This image is exposed for the rosy glow of the backdrop behind this ballerina who is mostly in shadow, giving her and the image a dramatic, elegant feel.

said, smartphone cameras continue to improve, as does their ability to make quality photographs in low-light situations.

As with bright light, striking the right balance in the exposure of a dimly lit scene requires paying close attention to the camera's settings. Practice and a deep understanding of light and exposure will help you decide when to rely on the camera's automatic modes, or when manually selecting your settings is the best bet for making an image that tells the moody, low-light story you envision.

—— ZOOM IN ——

▶ Don't be afraid to use darkness in your photograph. Rather than trying to fully expose your subject, work with the mood set by the low light in the scene—exposing for small portions that have caught the light.

THE NATURE OF ARTIFICIAL LIGHT

Ambient light can come from artificial sources that determine its character, quality, and strength. Mixing these light sources with the powerful sun makes for complex conditions.

▶ FOR MORE ON WHITE BALANCE, SEE PAGES 258-9

▶ FOR MORE ON FILL FLASH, SEE PAGES 296-7

Although sunlight is always the same—it is the circumstances through which it passes and the objects on which it falls that give it a rich variety of masks and personalities—artificial light varies in character depending on the mechanism by which it is created. There is the warm orange glow emitted from a campfire or an oil lamp, the yellow cast of a standard tungsten bulb, and the sharp bluish green tone of a gymnasium illuminated by fluorescent tubes. Each of these types of light has a different temperature, and a specific color that it brings to the subject. Because the camera sees the color of light as it is, the result is somewhat surprising in photographs made with vari-

While lighting a large petroglyph with an artificial light source, the photographer also used a long shutter speed to expose for the ambient light of the night sky over Comb Ridge in Utah.

The vibrant, solar-powered artificial light of Singapore's Supertrees is bright enough for visitors to make photographs using only the ambient light of the scene.

ous artificial light sources. The photographer's options are to correct the color or use it to emphasize the story of the image. When artificial light from multiple sources is at play in a scene, the effect of the mix can be complex.

THE QUALITY & STRENGTH OF ARTIFICIAL LIGHT

As with sunlight, the quality of artificial light depends on how the light comes to a subject. A lampshade softens light in the same way a cloud or diffuser does, whereas light coming directly from a bare bulb is brighter and more harsh.

When working with ambient light from both the sun and manufactured sources, it becomes clear just how strong and powerful our sun really is. There are almost no artificial light sources as bright as daylight, and the camera's

light meter proves it. In artificial light, apertures are wider, shutter speeds are slower, and ISO settings are higher than when photographing in daylight.

THE COMBINATION OF LIGHT

When natural and artificial light sources are combined in a photograph, color, quality, direction, and power of light become more complex for the camera and the photographer. Perhaps this is why fill-flash photography—using a photographic flash to balance or fill shadows created by the great light of the sun—is one of the more advanced techniques in photography, and one of the most intimidating to try. But really, light is light. And as your observations and understanding of it deepen, the more powerful and creative a photographic tool it becomes.

ASSIGNMENT

In this iconic photograph of the Kremlin visible through lace curtains in a window in Moscow, the pears ripening on the sill are bathed in both highlights and shadows as created by the setting sun.

A PEPPER & THE LIGHT

Choose a curvy object that will hold its shape and can stand on its own. A bell pepper would work perfectly. Place the pepper in the middle of a white sheet on a table, either using the sun as the light source outdoors, or next to a window or bright lamp indoors.

QUALITY OF LIGHT First, photograph the pepper in hard, unmodified light—either at high noon on a clear, sunny day, or beside a bare lightbulb. Next, find something translucent—sheer fabric or waxed paper will do—and ask a friend to hold it between the light source and the pepper, to diffuse the light. Make any necessary exposure adjustments and photograph the pepper again. Note how the diffuser changes the quality of light, and how, in turn, that changes the final image. Note the shadows, highlights, contrast, shape, and mood.

DIRECTION OF LIGHT Ask a friend to hold a flashlight or a bare lightbulb to one side of the pepper. Make a photograph. Now move the light source the way the sun would move throughout the day, in an arc, from left to right, above the pepper and back down. Photograph the pepper at several points along the way. Repeat the exercise with the light source directly in front of the pepper, moving in an arc over the top of it until the light is coming directly from behind the pepper. Notice how the patterns of shadows and highlights change, both on the white sheet and on the pepper itself. How do the quality and direction of light impact the tone of each image?

CHAPTER FOUR

PHOTOGRAPHING
THE FAMILIAR

To some extent, making compelling imagery in exotic places is a little bit of a layup, as strangeness and intrigue are built into the content, which is new to most viewers. But what about the familiar subjects from an ordinary day? A photographer's goal is to create an image that makes viewers feel something, and whether that is empathy, concern, or joy, a successful photograph moves them and makes them look longer. This is true even—and maybe especially—when the subject matter is less once in a lifetime and more everyday life.

Making a photograph that is intriguing or relatable requires a photographer's contemplation, patience, presence, and anticipation. It requires seeing the ordinary in an artful way. Being able to mine extensive knowledge of a familiar place or person adds depth and intimacy to the photographic effort. And when combined with strong composition, awareness of light, and mastery of camera skills, the result is an image with deeper meaning and soul—one that tells a more complete story that new visitors might not readily see, or one they might better recognize through the lens of personal relevance.

A successful approach to photographing the familiar is to seek balance between drawing from existing knowledge about a subject, and seeing it in a new and compelling way. Making extraordinary photographs of ordinary moments requires a lot from a photographer, including deep reflection of both self and subject. The reward is a photograph that tells an authentic story, and has the power to reach farther into the viewer's own life history and experiences to make them feel deeply at home.

The unique setting and perspective of the photographer make this photograph of children at play on a sand dune in Moab, Utah, at once artful, intriguing, and relatable.

GARDENS

Learning to see a common garden through the lens of composition and light can set your photographs of plants apart.

Blocks of green surprise the eye in this view of Chicago's City Hall and its rooftop garden. Photographing from above the scene with a wide-angle lens puts this garden into its delightful urban context.

▶ FOR MORE ON PATTERN & TEXTURE, SEE PAGES 34–5

▶ FOR MORE LENS OPTIONS, SEE PAGES 232–3

Colorful and still, gardens are often good starting points for new photographers, but the results can be hackneyed and stale. To make pictures that will surprise an audience, strive to see the garden in a new way. Great havens of color, texture, and patterns, gardens hold stories about science, beauty, and the art of design.

A garden is a visual feast at a variety of angles. A wide angle can illustrate how the garden fits into the human story of a place—whether as the periphery of a suburban backyard, or as a rooftop oasis in the midst of a city. A narrower field of view focuses on textures and patterns, like mixed shades of green, foliage variety, or branches tracing lines of interest through swaths of colorful leaves. And then wonders of the tiniest kind can be examined with a macro lens—insects feasting on nectar and drops of dew bejeweling blades of grass.

A GARDEN'S DESIGN

Cultivated gardens are thoughtfully designed and maintained, making photographic composition a collaboration between photographer and gardener. Change perspectives to highlight design beyond what can be seen at eye level. Photograph from above (where possible) to emphasize leading lines of curving beds and blocks of color. Photograph from low to the ground to make colorful blossoms statuesque, set against a backdrop of sky. Frame one plant through the foliage of another to illustrate the gardener's organization and layering. Consider early green shoots, plants that have wilted, and the brown evidence of decay—vegetation often shows the first signs of the seasons' transitions.

As always, wait for good light and use the right tools. Dawn is an extraordinary time, with dew-covered plants and the promise of blooms on the verge of unfurling. Colors pop against the long shadows of a low sun, and insects and birds are busy. Consider backlit leaves and water droplets glowing with the sun shining through them. A slow shutter speed softens the flow of a water feature, and adds movement to a photograph when combined with wind. A tripod will help keep the image crisp when using a slow shutter speed or a macro lens, and a reflector can bounce extra light on subjects in dappled shade.

Take the time to immerse yourself in a garden and let it speak to you. Listen with all senses to learn its secrets, and to interpret the stories it embodies. More than just documenting, compelling garden photography makes the most of a designed gathering of natural elements that transport viewers into a world where plants are prime.

Dappled sun falls on freshly picked carrots. Photographing through the foliage at a low angle frames the subject with carrots yet to be harvested, and including the farmer's hand adds the element of her work.

STATIC SCENES

From inanimate objects, artful photographs can be made. When texture, history, light, and shadow combine, you may see something new in a familiar, static scene.

▶ FOR MORE
ON LOW
LIGHT, SEE
PAGES 86–7

▶ FOR MORE
ON DETAILS,
SEE PAGES
168–9

Simple works of art are everywhere in the form of common, inanimate objects. The story of a static scene will reveal itself the longer you look. It might be the shape of a vase and the shadow it casts on a wall, or the history of an old tool hung on a hook decades ago. A slight change of perspective or careful framing may bring out an arresting juxtaposition of shape, color, or texture in a scene you look at nearly every day.

If a static scene is outside or near a window, how the light hits it changes throughout the day. Low light will create long shadows that may give an object a sculptural look, adding an abstract quality or even drama to a still life composition. Sometimes a shadow is more intriguing than its object.

Zoom in on a portion of a common object for an abstract distillation of its essence. Imagine the weathered handle of an old barn door, or the worn,

From a simple cup of Turkish tea comes a variety of patterns and shadows. The light illuminates the tea within the elegant glass, and makes a distinct shadow on the table as it passes through.

——————— ZOOM IN ———————

▶ Look longer at an everyday object. Place a laundry basket on a table by a window. Zoom in on it to distill the gaps in its sides and the shadows it creates.

By eliminating the sides of the display case that holds them, the photographer has turned these leather shoes in a Moroccan market into a work of art, a mosaic of color and pattern.

scuffed toe of a dancer's shoe. A tight view of the intersection of multiple objects—a pile of laundry or a stack of books—might transform the ordinary into an artful arrangement of textures and colors. Before pushing the button, photographers often frame a subject with their hands, to envision what the elements will look like in the photograph, out of the context of their surroundings.

DRAMATIC DETAILS

Atmospheric conditions can animate and add context to inanimate objects. Window light might illuminate dust on an antique dresser, enhancing its old, storied character. Rain on a glass door may distort the look of rubber boots inside a mudroom. A breeze might cause a gauzy curtain to billow, stirring a calm corner of a room.

When a static scene meets light and other ephemeral elements, the ordinary and still can be transformed into something artful and alive. Most often, a compelling still life photograph requires no special equipment—just an openness to the possibility that ordinary things can be both recognizable and inspiringly beautiful.

FOOD

A fan favorite, food can be tricky to photograph in an appetizing way. By following a few guidelines, you can inspire viewers to ask for seconds.

▶ FOR MORE ON QUALITY OF LIGHT, SEE PAGES 72-3

▶ FOR MORE ON A SENSE OF STORY, SEE PAGES 130-31

Food is a universal desire, and yet it is challenging to photograph in an appealing way. Whether a smartphone shot of lunch, or a professional DSLR photograph for advertising, keeping food imagery clean and simple is key.

Like meals, photographs of food are best with quality ingredients—greens without wilt, fruits without bruises or splits. Prepared items look best fresh out of the oven or just off the grill.

Natural light makes food look best. Whenever possible, photograph food near a window where soft, indirect light can add a natural and appealing glow to both ingredients and plated meals. Try photographing from directly above a platter or cutting board for a clean backdrop that gives the food full focus, or from table level for a bowl of stew to accentuate rising curls of steam.

ATTENTION TO DETAILS

Food on a table should be part of an appealing arrangement with organized utensils, full glasses, and a clean place setting without soiled, extraneous clutter. Car keys and cell phones, wrinkled paper napkins, and more can ruin a photograph of a carefully prepared meal at a restaurant, unless intentionally incorporated. Everything in the frame should add to the story of the meal.

But the story of food is much larger than the ingredients or the meal itself. Shopping yields colors and textures aplenty. Food preparation is often dynamic, with kitchen tools covered in seeds and sauces, puffs of steam wafting from pots and pans, and grills or ovens glowing with flame and heat. Chopping, mixing, and plating offer opportunities to add action and energy.

Photographing diners enjoying a meal is tricky, as people rarely look good with food in their mouths, but the end of a meal is a relatable moment, with dirty plates and empty glasses—a reflection on time enjoyed together.

Food preparation and pleasure convey larger themes of family and culture, and photographs of these subjects evoke vivid memories of flavor and feasting. Making carefully considered photos of the tastiest part of a meal can trigger a multisensory experience that will make the viewer's mouth water.

ZOOM IN

▶ Make a PB&J and place it on a plate. Make pictures from above and from table height and then with a bite out of it. What can you do to make it look as good as it tastes?

Creative use of arrangement and depth of field make these blueberries from Maine pop out of the photograph. Containers full beyond their bounds add to the impact with a sense of plenty.

PEOPLE YOU KNOW

Build on your connection to the people you know to make photographs that are distinctly, uniquely them.

▶ FOR MORE ON ANTICI-PATING COMPOSI-TION, SEE PAGES 64-5

▶ FOR MORE ON POR-TRAITS, SEE PAGES 112-13

Everyone has a story. Chances are, if you are photographing someone familiar, you know their story. Whether you are making a formal portrait or something more candid, the most successful photographs of people come from a photographer's effort to understand the subject. Consider who you're photographing—their story, life history, struggles, and hopes—and approach your work together from that place. Anticipation is key, and familiarity means having a sense of what a subject might do next. Will they make a distinctive gesture? Will they react to a certain sight or sound? Be ready to capture an expression that reveals feeling or emotion. These are the personal attributes that make someone both unique and familiar. Building on existing relationships gives photographers shortcuts to seeing and portraying their subjects authentically.

For a formal portrait, set a scene familiar to both you and your subject, or just be yourself with them in a staged setting to help them feel at ease and

This portrait of a woman at home in Costa Rica feels very natural and genuine. Surrounded by her things, she is clearly comfortable in her space and with the photographer. Soft light from the window beside her enhances the feeling of contentment.

─── ZOOM IN ───

▶ Think about someone you love and the gesture or habit that most defines their character. How can you capture that in one photograph?

Knowing that your friend is an artist, a reader, or a daredevil means you can be ready to capture the moments that tell their story best. Here, the photographer was ready when this young man did a backflip into his favorite swimming hole.

comfortable. If you know they love to dance, ask them to describe the feel of a tango. For a more candid approach, rely on your familiarity to fold yourself into the scene itself. Participation offers photographers an opportunity to get in close and vary perspectives without disrupting the action or making people feel self-conscious.

GET ACTIVE

Focus on an activity or moment that most represents the person—perhaps he has a passion for running and is cooling down after a sprint, or she loves to travel and is spinning a globe looking for her next destination. Have the camera ready

for spontaneous photographs of people doing what they do, being most themselves.

Be creative and critical with composition and light. Don't confuse loving the person in front of the camera with loving a photograph of them, when it could be better. Be objective and work the scene, being careful not to disrupt the action, until you find the best angle and light to photograph the story most effectively.

Overall, your intuition, sensitivity, and familiarity with someone will foster a setting that allows for an authentic photograph—an honest picture that says something deep, true, and meaningful about the person in the frame.

FAMILY PICTURES

You know your family well enough to predict authentic, meaningful moments. The challenge is to be objective and have a critical eye when photographing the ones you love most.

Although this family portrait is posed, the subjects' seeming discomfort and the shadows in the scene give it a dramatic edge.

▶ FOR MORE ON DEFINING COMPOSITION, SEE PAGES 42-3

▶ FOR MORE ON CANDIDS, SEE PAGES 122-3

Everyone wants family photos—evidence that you were all together, in one place at one time—but the average person with a camera will struggle to get anything other than the requisite lineup in Grandma's living room. As subject matter, though, family members combine two ideal elements—familiarity and access. Consider what makes a family, and in particular, what makes your family unique. Think about the familial relationships and connections. Natural, relaxing moments—preparing meals, reading, and playing—make for authentic images that define a family at home. To get many people in one frame and capture how they interact with one other, take advantage of activities like a football game, talking around the table, or even greetings and departures. To elevate these photos to something special, pay extra attention to light and composition.

Look with an artful eye beyond the happy, easy moments. Rarely are instances of struggle, discontent, and the mess of real family life photographed, but they can be powerfully relatable when they are. Photographing family during difficult moments requires masterful consideration of point of view and perspective, as well as courage and compassion.

When someone asks you to make photographs of his or her family, take time to get to know them so that you embrace the goals of the request and understand how best to represent them. A family's instinct in a photo session may be to huddle up in a pose. Make a few frames this way, then throw in a prop or one of their favorite items. Ask them to describe it to one another, and observe, camera at the ready. Anticipate laughs or special moments, and be

poised for when the arc of their energy reaches its peak. When the momentum naturally wanes, have them move on to something or someplace else.

Compelling candid photographs of people in motion are the result of anticipation, practice, and often many exposures in an intentional, focused effort. Batteries should be fresh and memory cards should have plenty of room, and settings should be dialed in for the available light in the scene. Especially when photographing your own family, be clear in your role in the gathering. Are you there as a photographer or as a family member? The family photographer's concern is to be at once a loving member and its documentarian—the challenge to do both concurrently and well is full of both struggle and reward.

Great perspective, good use of the rule of thirds, and appropriate separation of key elements make this photograph of a man exploring nature with his granddaughters more than just a simple snapshot.

BABIES

Babies are animated and delightful, full of softness and big-eyed wonder. Until they can crawl, you've likely got a very willing subject.

▶ FOR MORE ON AMBIENT LIGHT, SEE PAGES 76-7

▶ FOR MORE ON POINT OF VIEW, SEE PAGES 28-9

New to this world, babies represent everything fresh and cute. Observing the face of a baby is a charming tutorial in expression. Wave after wave of emotion and physical sensation passes through them—lips, eyes, and brows all engaged in a variety of ways—and it appears as if they are discovering their face muscles for the first time. They are constantly in motion, but don't actually move very far or fast (until they do), which makes babies manageable subjects. The goal is to capture the heart of the viewer as if they were there, hearing the coos and smelling that sweet baby scent.

Point of view is most often the key compositional consideration when photographing babies. Photograph them at their level—on the floor or bed—to fill the frame with their wide eyes and drooling lips. Isolate parts of a baby that are unique to this stage of life, like tiny fingers and toes, chubby thighs and shoulders, that soft tuft of hair. A wide aperture and shallow depth of field are often effective here, with the featured body part sharp, and everything else falling to softness. Alternatively, looking straight down as a baby sleeps or looks up at you from a clean, clear surface—a white rug or an heirloom quilt—can add poignant context and a sense of scale to the photograph.

BABY SOFT

Similar to what babies prefer in life, the best light for baby photography is typically soft and natural. Windows with sheer blinds or drapes make great soft boxes, casting a gentle glow that wraps around the subject, and may illuminate those fine hairs atop the head.

Think more deeply about the experience of caring for a baby as you set out to photograph one. It's not all soft gurgles and gentle slumbers. There are tears. There are messes. Photos of faces full of food, small spoons strewn about, and bleary-eyed parents speak to the larger story of babyhood.

Having a baby around means having a seemingly always-willing subject, and you may feel compelled to capture every minute and milestone. But remember to be present and let them see your face too, without a camera constantly in front of it.

ZOOM IN

▶ Alert, sleepy, hungry, confused, delighted, and full of awe are expressions you may witness on the face of a baby, sometimes all within minutes. How many can you capture on one baby's face?

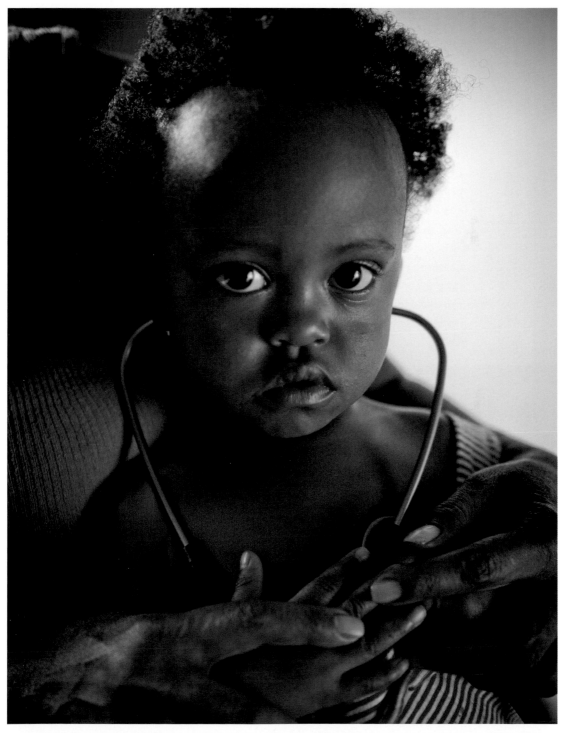

A woman uses a stethoscope to listen to the lungs of a baby girl with asthma. Photographing hard moments with a little one juxtaposes the purity of infancy with the challenges of life.

CHILDREN

Familiar kids are an endless source of photographic inspiration. Be efficient and discreet to capture their most authentic moments, and know when to put the camera down.

▶ FOR MORE
ON FRAM-
ING, SEE
PAGES 52–3

▶ FOR MORE
ON ANTICI-
PATING
COMPOSI-
TION, SEE
PAGES 64–5

If you have children of your own, the arc of their childhood is a story you know better than anyone else. You know what brings your kids joy, and the ways they show happiness and satisfaction. To capture expressions worth hanging onto, anticipate these moments and have a camera ready. But consider also that fatigue, anger, sadness, and boredom can make for compelling photographs if done with creativity and care. The caveat here is balance: You are in the best position to determine when you have the space and time to make a photograph, or when your children need your attention right now, and not the attention of a photographer, documenting the moment.

BE DISCREET

Photographing your kids in both harmonious interactions as well as in conflict with siblings or friends makes for compelling imagery and illustrates the

Shallow depth of field makes this photograph of a girl lost in laughter really pop. Find a spot that has composition you like and wait for special moments with the kids you know best.

harder side of childhood. Focus on personality and emotions, framing and composition. Move discreetly to edit what's captured, without disrupting the interaction. Kids in play move fast. Stay on your toes. Make sure your camera functions and compositional technique are second nature to freeze the best moments of action.

When photographing children other than your own, always be sure to ask their parents' permission first and let them know what your intentions are for the images. If you photograph the same kids frequently, they will learn to either accept or ignore your efforts, meaning fewer posed moments and more authentic pictures. But be sure to pay attention to the energy of the room—if your presence is becoming antagonis-tic, back away. When kids are done with the photographic process, you should be, too.

Balancing parenthood and photography is a trick indeed. Professional photographers try to master this dance with their families, though it often results in their loved ones' love-hate relationship with the camera. It can be difficult to navigate the uncharted waters of sharing professional photos of your children online. As children age and can make their own decisions about their internet presence, it's good practice to revisit their feelings about the photographs you've made and shared that involve them. Giving kids a say in their participation in your photographic efforts will likely ensure better access to them with a camera for years to come.

Kids and bubbles almost never disappoint. This photograph, made in Yoyogi Park in Tokyo, is full of pleasing shapes, colors, and young faces lost in play. Other parents with cameras add to the context of the scene.

PETS & OTHER FAMILIAR ANIMALS

Capitalize on the behaviors you know and love from your pets to make portraits that say something meaningful about the furriest members of the family.

Having pets adopt human characteristics can make them oddly more relatable and always gets a smile, like this dog wearing shades at the Columbian Flower Festival in New York City.

▶ FOR MORE ON POINT OF VIEW, SEE PAGES 28-9

▶ FOR MORE ON DETAILS, SEE PAGES 168-9

As with photographing people you love, concentrate on the attributes that most define a pet's irreplaceable place in the home. Whether they are always waiting by the door for a walk, or perpetually curled up at the foot of a bed, focus on the things that make any pet a unique, contributing member of the family.

Make the most of responses you can expect, like a head tilt when hearing a whistle, a funny rear wiggle when preparing to pounce on a toy, or swimming to the top of the bowl when the lid comes off the fish food jar. Anticipate, compose, and capture. Be mindful of when a pet has had enough, and be sure to come equipped with plenty of treats.

Whether your pet is horse or ferret, dog or cat, experiment with angles and point of view to make a photograph different from the plethora of other pet

── **ZOOM IN** ──

▶ Working with a pet is good practice for making strong exposure and compositional choices quickly and without fuss. Play with framing and slow shutter speed to capture fast movements in an abstract way for pet portraits that stand out.

Pets often do unexpected things, turning mundane moments into meaningful images. Having your camera ready ups your chances of capturing a compelling photo. Case in point: this recently adopted cat punching through his temporary pet carrier.

pictures out there. Get on a pet's level for a full-frame authentic portrait. Let the dog lick the lens (you can clean it later). Try getting below them with the sky as background, giving the pet more stature. Or photograph from above them as they look up at you, demonstrating loyalty and obedience.

Note the way light brings out colors in your pet's coat or eyes, or how shadow accentuates musculature and whiskers. Catch the shapes a dog makes while catching a Frisbee, or the cat makes stretching out in the sun. Focus on the details you know so well from years of affectionate pats—big paws, a speckled nose, or mismatched ears.

Perhaps the most poignant thing about pets is their connection to their people. Imagine a boy's stockinged feet resting atop a warm pup beneath the kitchen table, or the way the cat drapes himself around the shoulders of a family elder. Maybe the family parakeet likes to take sunflower seeds right from your daughter's mouth. These moments tell the story of pets' place in the home and heart of a family. If done right, a photograph of a pet will make viewers feel the love, too.

WHY I LOVE THIS PHOTO

Sometimes a picture isn't just a picture; sometimes, it's a time machine. At least, that's what I see when I look at (or maybe it's through) George Mobley's candid 1968 street scene of a snowy May Day in Finland. Here is a different era: vintage fashions, picturesque traditions, and a color palette that could only come from a film stock—Kodachrome—that has since been discontinued. A gust of cold, wet snow wreaks havoc on the fragile umbrellas and bouquets of balloons layered across the desaturated landscape, providing the few pops of color for the eye to follow off into the distance alongside the strolling revelers. In this park, on that afternoon, Mobley captured a single, frozen, perfect snow globe of a moment in his own time.

—MELISSA FARRIS
Creative Director, National Geographic Books

A spring stroll through the park turned snowy in this image taken in May 1968 in Kaivopuisto Park in Finland.

PORTRAITS

Creating an authentic portrait of someone you know requires a combination of both interpersonal and photographic skills. Make the most of an existing connection for success.

▶ FOR MORE ON PHOTO- GRAPHING PEOPLE YOU KNOW, SEE PAGES 100–101

▶ FOR MORE ON PHOTO- GRAPHING PEOPLE YOU DON'T KNOW, SEE PAGES 140–41

A portrait, at its best, is much more than a mere photograph of a person's face. A good portrait goes beyond a person's physical appearance to capture their personality. Creating an environment of trust is essential to achieving rapport, so starting with someone you know should offer a shortcut to a familiar ease.

Even so, the first handful of images may be stiff and emotionless. Don't worry, that's to be expected. People often feel awkward if they are not used to being in front of a camera and may express doubt that they "photograph well." Perseverance and attention to a subject's comfort helps both the photographer and subject throughout a session.

Clear the room of anyone who's not being photographed if your subject is shy. Consider asking if they have an angle they prefer. Playing music may create a lighter, less inhibited mood, and might inspire creative movement. Conversation and interaction lead to natural moments. These can be gently directed to harmonize with light and composition. Get in close. Look and listen. Encourage the subject to talk about something meaningful, guiding them to inhabit that mental space. Be prepared to capture these moments with your camera at the ready—the settings should be second nature and dialed in to prevent any unnecessary pauses.

GO WITH THE FLOW

Most formal portrait sessions have a few cycles of opportunity for authentic photographs. Pay attention to the arc of the experience, noting the ebb and flow of energy, and reading the subject for signs of anxiety or fatigue. Be sure to take breaks and note when a change of scene or styling might help give both photographer and subject a chance to reset. Vary poses and capitalize on natural movements.

Making a portrait is an intimate experience. It requires trust and respect that allows for the reveal of something personal and defining. Most important, if your subjects enjoy the experience, they will more likely love the photographs, seeing themselves in the flattering way you see them.

— ZOOM IN —

▶ Begin a session with a friend by recalling a mutual favorite memory, or by having her flip through some photos from a special time you've shared. Don't raise the camera until you're both feeling a connection.

Rapport between photographer and subject allows for playful experimentation with props that may yield something both authentic and unique. This tourist on an Antarctic expedition poses with a feather she found, resulting in a creative but natural-looking portrait.

ENVIRONMENTAL PORTRAITS

Environmental portraits tell more of the subject's story through setting and background, with literal or creative details included in the frame.

By making this environmental portrait of a ballerina in Brooklyn Bridge Park at night, the photographer sets a scene not unlike that of a theatrical stage, with evening ambience and dramatic lights.

▶ FOR MORE ON LAYER-ING, SEE PAGES 56–7

▶ FOR MORE ON IMAGE SELECTION, SEE PAGES 360–61

An environmental portrait is one that includes more context about the subject in the frame, showing them in their element. Examples might be an avid gardener photographed among blooms, a lawyer photographed in a courtroom, or a librarian surrounded by books. And although environmental portraits supply more detail about the nature and skills of the subject of the photograph, they don't always have to be literal. Imagine a pilot photographed in midair above a trampoline, with headset and sunglasses to convey flight, or a race car driver photographed in front of a fan, hair and scarf blowing in the breeze to suggest speed. An environmental portrait is an opportunity for creative expression by and about the subject.

This is also an opportunity to tell someone's story in a single frame. Spending time in a workshop with a passionate woodworker will give you an

ZOOM IN

▶ Study the exposure and composition choices in the two environmental portraits on these pages. Which rules have been applied, and how do they add to the subjects' story?

idea of how and why they do what they do, working with precision, immersed in the smell of sawdust, and the infinite possibilities implied by their tools. Imagine a photograph of a firefighter who has just returned to the station, sitting in a pile of sooty boots and gear, sweaty and exhausted from the work. Unselfconscious photographs of someone in a moment of effort, either in play or work, will tell a more complete story of who they truly are.

Pay attention to light and composition, looking for backgrounds filled only with elements that define a scene, and light that suits the mood of the moment. Note layers of detail that advance the story—discarded high-heeled shoes at the end of a wedding, a paint-covered smock hanging in an artist's studio—and edit the frame to include these clues. Look for leading lines that connect the subject to other elements, forming a cohesive narrative within one photograph.

Make many frames as the person settles into and interacts with the environment, anticipating a defining moment, and perhaps directing attention toward the camera once in a while. The more photographs you make, the more options you'll have later in the selection process of an environmental portrait full of context and character.

Mirrors add perspective and layering to this detailed portrait of a girl and her friend at a body piercing studio in Austin, Texas.

CELEBRATIONS

Gatherings of familiar people are opportunities to put anticipation, composition, and exposure to work for imagery that looks as good as being there feels.

Revelers at a Holi celebration in Queens, New York, give over to color and merriment. This photograph uses composition and framing in the moment to convey the energy of the scene.

▶ FOR MORE ON ISO SENSITIVITY, SEE PAGES 246-7

▶ FOR MORE ON WIDE-ANGLE & FISH-EYE LENSES, SEE PAGES 276-7

Gatherings and parties bring many people into one familiar space. Celebrations are usually times when people are feeling good and will most likely be willing (or expecting) to be photographed. Consider the tone of the occasion, and use composition and light to express the mood in your photographs. For example, if the gathering is an exciting time of joy, photographs might reflect movement and action, with subjects filling frames full of light. For more

somber or formal occasions, the mood might be best expressed by reflections of stillness and ample negative space, with more emphasis on dramatic shadows or dim corners lit by candlelight.

Think in advance about the space and people who will gather there. Consider the rooms or corners with the best light or cleanest backgrounds so that the interaction of friends and loved ones is the focus of any photograph. Select camera settings in advance to be ready

This photograph of a boy celebrating his bar mitzvah shows smart decisions in the use of negative space and framing. By including a background of mostly white, the black hats and coats pop and form interesting shapes, further framing expressions of satisfaction and joy.

for available light in the space. Avoid using a flash as it's distracting and will most often produce bad results in crowded rooms or intimate spaces. Instead, opt for a high ISO and a wide-angle lens with big aperture to maximize light. Keep shutter speeds high enough to hand-hold the camera for flexibility and improvisation. Make lots of photographs to ensure a few really special frames.

ANTICIPATE SPECIAL MOMENTS

Stay alert to what's happening in the space. Anticipate sweet, candid moments between people, and reactions to special gifts or surprises. Look for old friends reuniting, or a couple kissing at the stroke of midnight. Arrive early and stay late to go beyond the obvious moments of the occasion. Consider the preparation of food and

decorations, and hosts anxiously awaiting arrivals. Seek ordinary moments that yield unexpected photographs, like someone cleaning up a spill, or stealing a taste of dessert, or maybe a dog hiding under the table. Wrap up the story by capturing the afterglow, with countertops full of leftovers, dirty dishes in the sink, piles of wrapping paper, and exhausted hosts collapsed in chairs. Make best use of composition and light to create moving photographs of the mundane.

As a photographer and guest, strive for balance between making merry and making pictures. Familiarity with fellow revelers allows a photographer to take full advantage of the best of the gathering. And remember: Reserve some time to put down the camera and be in the moment with the people you enjoy.

CANDIDS

Though candid photographs honor spontaneous moments, a lot of preparation is required on the part of the photographer. Sink into the scene and be ready.

The photographer moved into the perfect spot to capture these three Morehouse graduates in their revelry after receiving their diplomas in Atlanta, Georgia.

▶ FOR MORE ON ANTICIPATING COMPOSITION, SEE PAGES 64–5

▶ FOR MORE ON ACTION, SEE PAGES 302–303

Most photography genres require some skill at making strong candid imagery—photographs of fresh, unguarded moments that employ great composition and light, without choreography. Whether of familiar people or of strangers, in intimate situations or on crowded streets, successful candids almost always reveal something more telling than formal portraits can.

New photographers will often stand at a distance and use a long lens to grab shots of action without being seen. But for something more evocative and impactful, grab a wide-angle lens, be brave, and move in to where the story is unfolding. Fully immerse yourself in the experience, with all senses alert to what is happening. Whether the subjects are kids playing a game of kickball in the street, or old men fishing on a pier, become part of the action and photograph from within the mood. Great candid photography requires that a photographer wear two hats—that of participant, riding the ebb and

---

ZOOM IN

▶ Consider how fleeting the expressions captured in photographs on these pages may have been. Immerse yourself in an active scene. Observe and tap into the rhythm of the action. See if you can *feel* the moments coming before they happen.

In a playful moment, a young man in a field of poppies photographs his girlfriend in a sweater of the same color. The photographer was prepared for just the right moment, having already lined up a compelling composition.

flow of the energy and action of the scene, and that of observer, with second-nature control of the camera and creative choices.

To take photographic advantage of a defining, natural moment, fluency in the language of composition and exposure is a must. The camera should be ready—set for the available light and proper exposure for the focus of the frame. Carefully positioning the camera relative to the subjects could mean the difference between a standard snapshot and something extraordinary. Anticipation is everything in good candid photography—predicting the exact moment when there will be separation between moving subjects, when one may leap into a field of otherwise nega-

tive space, or when the elements will all come together in a way that makes the image special.

Familiarity with the subject matter is a distinct advantage, both in connecting to the scene and anticipating the most powerful moments. Take time to observe for a while to get a feel for the flow. The most powerful candid photographs are of ephemeral moments captured because the photographer's focus, skill, and energy are in perfect alignment with one of life's significant moments. They are at once surprising and relatable. This may sound challenging and somewhat nebulous, but observation, courage, and practice will lead you into the pocket of successful candid photography.

STREET PHOTOGRAPHY

Walk the streets you know best with a camera, anticipation, and an openness to the photographs arising all around you, waiting to be made.

▶ FOR MORE
ON APER-
TURE &
DEPTH OF
FIELD, SEE
PAGES 236-7

▶ FOR MORE
ON WIDE-
ANGLE &
FISH-EYE
LENSES, SEE
PAGES 276-7

Street photography is an intriguing combination of the familiar and strange. You may know the neighborhood, or what to expect in general from the hustle and bustle of a city street, but the subjects passing by are likely total strangers. Their decisions and movements may be predictable, or they may surprise you. Either way, successful street photography is the product of camera preparedness combined with careful observation and anticipation of compelling, often fleeting moments.

There are a few ways to approach making photographs of life as it happens out in the busiest parts of the world. One is to wander, taking note of the flow of life and activity all around you. When something catches your eye, look closer and think about ways to capture the feeling that made you stop. Alternatively, pick a spot with a great

With great framing, and preparedness for just the right moment, the photographer has caught this break dancer in a compelling position. The rest of the frame is filled with other onlookers attempting the same, adding to the liveliness of this street scene in Chicago.

In Queens, New York, the photographer has positioned the camera low in the scene, for a silhouetted view of this skateboarder against a backdrop of sky. Anticipation allowed for the capture of the exact moment of separation between skater and board.

setting that well represents the location—a subway platform at rush hour, or an outdoor café on a cobblestone street—compose the frame in your viewfinder and wait for life to pass before the lens. Pay close attention to moment, composition, and the way light touches the scene.

ORIENT IN ACTION

Festivals, parades, and other congregations are places where people expect to see someone with a camera. Other contexts might require discretion or even a permit. If appropriate, introduce yourself and ask permission. If the number of people or circumstances makes an introduction impossible, step back from the scene and be unobtrusive with the camera. Some street photographers actually shoot from the hip, with the camera balanced and steadied against their bodies, fingers poised on the shutter button. Many camera models have tilting LCD screens that allow you to look down and compose, but others require an acute understanding of the lens's angle of view to be able to interpret what the camera is seeing. Wide-angle lenses and small apertures (light and shutter speed permitting) work best to ensure a broad capture zone and sharp focus in most of the scene.

In general, it's best to be up front with anyone who notices you and your camera and is wondering what you're up to. Be kind and open, explaining your photographic efforts with confidence, and consider showing them a few frames on the playback screen of your camera. More often than not, people will be intrigued and delighted with the creative way you've seen the street on which they walk every day.

ASSIGNMENT

This man is hard at work filling his water truck on federal land in Utah. Imagine riding along with him on the job, and being there, camera ready, as he heads home for the day. Imagine telling his story in pictures.

CURIOUS ABOUT GEORGE

Pick someone with whom you have a trusting, comfortable relationship—let's call him "George." Discuss your plans to create a photographic personality profile of him. Plan the photo sessions in advance, and over the course of a week, be a fly on George's walls.

TELL GEORGE'S STORY IN PICTURES Tag along on George's morning commute and capture him working. Visit his home one evening, photographing him walking in the door, at the dinner table, relaxing, or playing with family and pets. With permission, photograph nighttime routines like brushing his teeth and climbing into bed. Focus on George's relationships with family members, capturing personal interactions and authentic moments. Look for static scenes featuring his most used objects—books on a bedside table, a ball he throws for the dog—the details that make George's story unique to him. Make the most of available light, working each scene as unobtrusively as possible without compromising artful composition. Strive to make extraordinary photographs of George's most ordinary moments.

TWO PORTRAITS OF GEORGE Plan to make two portraits: the first, a more formal portrait at the start of the week, and the second, an environmental portrait at the end. For the latter, feature George in one of his spaces, surrounded by elements that tell a more complete story of who he is. Note how your week working with George informs the second portrait—his openness, your connection, and the creative choices these inspire. Compare the two portraits, noting how focusing on one subject and fully inhabiting his world makes a difference in your photographs.

TRAVEL &
ADVENTURE

Travel enriches the human experience by expanding our perspectives beyond a zone of familiar comforts. Whether visiting an unknown corner of your home state or a completely foreign country on the other side of the globe, travel has the effect of inspiring curiosity and appreciation for things considered mundane at home. The way people dress, how they eat, the work they do, the places they dwell, and the look of the landscape all become intriguing in a new place. The aspects of a stranger's "normal" become compelling subject matter for travelers and their cameras.

Adding the element of photography into travel can be equal parts rewarding and complicated. It is essential to plan and prepare for picture making far from home, even when parts of the journey itself may be spontaneous and uncharted. Research the culture in advance to understand customs and appropriate photog-

rapher conduct in various circumstances. And although it might seem obvious, it's important that photographers are equipped with clothing and camera gear suited to the weather and types of adventures ahead.

Well in advance of departure, decide whether photography is the primary mission of the trip, or the secondary mission, a medium through which you document and share the experience. This distinction is important, and all parties will be best served if the focus of the journey is clear.

Regardless, photography should remain a way of enhancing an experience abroad, and should be a respectful means of communication—never predatory, gawking, or without dignity and consideration. Photography has the power to be both a foundation on which to build new relationships and a means to enrich existing ones.

The artful way light moves through Antelope Canyon in Utah inspires the senses and the photographer.

A SENSE OF STORY

Stories are everywhere for the making, but it takes courage and preparation to truly immerse in a new place. Sometimes the story is about the journey itself.

This photograph of a giant panda cub being weighed at a research center in China tells its story through the delightful juxtaposition of a wild animal in an office setting.

▶ FOR MORE ON PHOTO-GRAPHING PEOPLE YOU DON'T KNOW, SEE PAGES 140–41

▶ FOR MORE ON CHOOSING YOUR EQUIPMENT, SEE PAGE 263

As with photographing familiar subjects, knowledge, immersion, and anticipation are key in travel and adventure photography. Whether you are at a cultural event in a foreign city, on a rough-water rafting expedition on a wild river, or sharing a home-cooked meal at a new friend's home, doing research about the place and people you intend to visit will help you embrace time in a new location and thoroughly photograph the story of the experience.

Telling the story of a new place involves investigating its resources, landscape, wildlife, and history. But immersive travel experiences also give photographers opportunities to explore the stories of people who live there—how the landscape shapes the ways they work, eat, move, and dwell. Make an effort to inhabit their world for a while, eating, sleeping, working, and seeing as they do. Make photographs from this point of view—whether from high in the alpine-hilltop home of a cheese maker in Switzerland, or riding along with a New York City cab driver down on the Lower East Side of Manhattan—step fully into this new world, and provide answers to questions viewers might have about a story completely different from their own.

Photographing the story of people, as a culture or individually, may feel more intimidating than making pictures of landscapes in a new place. It requires courage and diplomacy to put yourself into someone else's space, introduce yourself, connect, and ask to experience and document their story. But be brave. This sort of personal adventure may reveal that their lives, even with different details, are more relatable than you realized. As always, light, composition, and camera expertise are your best allies in sharing the experience through pictures.

Like photographic endeavors at home, travel photography is filled with highs and lows, ebbs and flows of energy and excitement. There are periods where everything seems new and inspiring, the light is fantastic, and the photographs are there for the making. And there are times that feel like a struggle—the hours or days when equipment isn't working, the weather isn't cooperating, and fatigue and frustration cloud your creative impulses. Know that not only are these days normal and temporary, they too are an important part of a travel story.

When the story of a new place seems to evade you, turn the photographic process on the journey itself—the peaks and valleys, and what it really means to step out into the world with a camera.

Negative space, sense of scale, and framing make an impact in this photo of a climber rappelling down from the remains of a collapsed cave in Guangxi, China.

SEEK THE AUTHENTIC

The best route to a genuine, truthful photograph about a place is to get to know its people. Make a friend and let photography follow.

▶ FOR MORE
ON PHOTO-
GRAPHING
PEOPLE YOU
DON'T KNOW,
SEE PAGES
140-41

▶ FOR MORE
ON CULTURE,
SEE PAGES
164-5

Locations once remote are now accessible, which means more "canned," or heavily produced, experiences and diluted or inauthentic access to distinct cultures. As travel has become easier, finding (and photographing) truly authentic experiences has become more challenging.

One tried-and-true way to seek authentic cultural experiences is to get to know people in the area in which you are traveling. Find a safe place off the well-worn path—a café in a district without any tourist attractions, for example—and sit down for a while. Make yourself open and available for connection—it may be as simple as smiling and waving to people passing by or asking to join another patron sitting alone. Engagement encourages rapport. Make a friend. Be courteous and respectful with questions and listen intently to answers. People are often open to sharing their point of view with a traveler

While walking through neighborhoods in Tokyo, this photographer came upon a local celebration outside an apartment building—an encounter (and photograph) that would never have occurred if he'd stayed in a more touristy area.

── ZOOM IN ──

▶ If you're having trouble starting a conversation with a stranger, consider asking someone to use your camera to make a photograph of you. From there, you can ask to take their picture or ask for other spots you should visit.

who shows genuine interest in their story. It may result in a terrific recommendation for where to visit or eat next, or even an invitation to dinner at their home.

So, where does the camera come in? In many instances, a camera can be a point of connection. You can share what you've been photographing through the playback function and ask a local to advise you on where the next stop on your journey should be. But also consider leaving the camera alone at the start of a conversation. If you build a relationship through genuine interest and shared connection, it will likely result in better photographic opportunities in the long run, and in a better experience overall.

If connecting with strangers in a new place seems a little too far out of your comfort zone, look into hiring a local, private guide. Do some research in advance about reputable guide organizations and read reviews about reliability and safety. If possible, connect with a guide online before your arrival, and make them aware of your goal to experience and photograph things beyond ordinary tourist stops.

If you're traveling to a foreign country, add learning a few key phrases in the local language to your pre-trip research. It shows genuine interest in and respect for the culture. Be sure to learn a few photographic terms, too. Have a language translation app on your smartphone to aid in any conversations with locals about their stories as well as the possibility of making some photographs. Just as photographers seek the extraordinary in everyday moments at home, so should they seek the relatable with foreign scenes and subjects. Discovering the everyday somewhere

By focusing on just hands joined in prayer, this photographer was able to make a lovely and abstract image of an altar boy at Sanctuary of La Bénite Fontaine in Haute-Savoie, France.

else is key to an authentic experience. Check out local grocery stores, attend a religious service, visit a park where parents take their children and walk dogs, or wake early to find a spot to witness the daily commute in the center of town. Use composition and light, and be present in the moment to make compelling photographs that say something truthful about a place. Don't let the exotic do all the work—find and photograph the things that unite us all.

A Tuvan Uriankhai cowboy holds on tight to his rearing horse near Kyzyl in Siberia, Russia.

ADVENTURE

Participate and make photographs from the heart of the action for images that bring viewers along for the ride.

▶ FOR MORE
ON BRIGHT
LIGHT, SEE
PAGES 84–5

▶ FOR MORE
ON ACTION,
SEE PAGES
302–303

Great adventure photographs make a viewer's heartbeat quicken with the same adrenaline rush as if they were there. Bright, fast, splashy, muddy, high, and thrilling adventure photographs work best when photographers experience the action firsthand. This requires balancing active, wholehearted participation with keen observation of unfolding events. Anticipation is key, as is the ability to hold on tight.

Because of the nature of most adventures, camera equipment should be light and flexible, and if possible—rugged. Many models of adventure cameras on the market today are all these things, and typically have super-wide angles of view to take in sweeping scenery that is the backdrop for most adventures, keeping almost all of it in focus. The trade-off is that photographers need to be close to subject matter to give it prominence in the frame. Most adventure cameras come with a variety of accessories to fasten them to anything from bikes to surf-

With the photographer's kayak in the frame, this image was clearly made right from the heart of the action, transporting the viewer into the expedition among Antarctic icebergs and mountains.

This photographer made clever use of his own climbing ropes to frame his fellow mountaineer. Adding layers of the snowy environment and bright sun further illustrates his perspective and brings the viewer into the action.

boards to helmets, to capture the scene from the participant's point of view. This makes composition mostly a matter of making sure a photographer is at the most advantageous angle to the action, and the camera is pointed into the heart of the scene.

High shutter speeds and small apertures are typically important, to freeze fast action and keep elements in all layers of the frame sharp. Because most adventures happen in bright, outside conditions, these types of settings are best, and most adventure cameras include them as automatic options.

Techniques that include time-lapse or stop-motion capture of multiple stills in rapid succession are useful for creating high-impact presentations of intense action. Most models of adventure cameras have these functions built in, and can transfer media wirelessly to a smartphone for immediate sharing across social media platforms. As adventure photography technology advances every year, it's never been easier to bring a camera into the heart of the action. If you can experience it, you can photograph it. And now you can photograph the experience in a way that brings viewers closer to the thrill than ever before.

ZOOM IN

▶ Shutter speed is one key to photographing an adventure, either by freezing action or letting it blur through the frame. Which will describe the scene best?

THE CHALLENGE

Bring home more than memories of your journey with photographs that make viewers feel the way you did on location—the joy, the struggle, and everything in between.

▶ FOR MORE ON PACKING TO MAKE PICTURES, SEE PAGES 132-3

▶ FOR MORE ON SEEKING THE AUTHEN- TIC, SEE PAGES 134-5

Photography calls for an embrace of the technical principles of image-making, and then exercising them with *vision*—your most creative way of seeing. To fold this effort into travel and adventure—circumstances where comfort and personal resources are pushed and often depleted—is a challenge that tests a photographer's energy, commitment, skills, and resolve.

Take care of the logistics of your travel and safety first as you plan for any journey or adventure. Then, tailor your kit to the circumstances ahead and the type of photographs you'd like to make. Remember that portability is key, and really, you can make a good photograph with anything that will capture a still frame. Special equipment can enhance the creative effort abroad, but the difference between a snapshot from a trip and a compelling photograph from a journey is in the photographer's approach and vision.

You've done your research and are prepared to document the who, what,

A National Geographic photographer gets deep into his work—and the Manu River—in Manu National Park in Peru.

National Geographic photographer Ami Vitale wore a costume to gain proximity to giant pandas for an unprecedented photo story made at the Conservation and Research Center at Wolong, China.

when, where, and how of the people and places you intend to visit. But for added depth of meaning, imagine photographs that will also address the *why* of your journey. Dig deeper, self-reflect, and add another layer to the story—why you travel, why you've chosen this place, why the people you have encountered have captured your attention and curiosity.

Some travelers say that if you can find these answers within yourself, you will have made the most of your time away from home. Going further, if you can answer the *why* in pictures that help a viewer feel the way you did on location, you will have brought home much more than memories. Don't shy away from photographing the tougher moments. Being authentic in telling your own experience is as important as telling accurate stories of people you encounter along the way.

Travel combines elements of wonder, exploration, self-reflection, and expanding your view to a world beyond your own. A photograph offers a way to examine and preserve the unique and the relatable in unfamiliar places. Bringing back photographs that genuinely move a viewer to feel the warmth of an Ethiopian sunset, or the textures in a colorful Chilean sweater, or the joy of kids splashing in a hydrant release on a New York City street is a means of sharing authentic stories beyond language and across borders. There is no better feeling as a photographer than when your energy and inspiration for making photographs leads to powerful connections made in new places. New connections will do more than add strength to your photographs—they will ultimately enhance your experience.

CHAPTER SIX

SENSE OF
PLACE

Every place, whether a country or one family's home, has a set of characteristics that give it a distinct visual signature. Landscape—in urban and natural settings alike—sets the stage on which a culture forms. In turn, an area's climate and natural resources influence the way humans live in concert with a geographical area, shaping how they interact with nature and each other, how they build and dwell, work and eat, contemplate and celebrate. These attributes are inextricably woven together in a quilt of essence and tone that often make a place instantly identifiable in a successful, thoughtful photograph.

Really understanding a place requires both research and time spent fully immersed on the ground. If you're planning to travel, learn as much as you can before you go. Look at imagery from the locale to begin to appreciate its scene. Dominant colors, style of architecture, and manner of dress are just a few standout factors that make a place unique. Once you arrive, settle in and take the time to absorb distinct features that touch all the senses, including language, smells, textures, and flavors.

If describing your hometown, dig more deeply into its past to comprehend what historical forces brought people there and inspired the architecture and structures you experience every day. Wander familiar streets with a visitor's eye, noticing unique trees and plants, and try to make connections between the landscape and culture to form a renewed understanding of home, and how you fit into it.

As always, immersion and investment in a location will allow for photographs with more information, soul, and meaning. To capture the story, use both broad and tightly focused angles of view, making photographs that provide context and mood through the depiction of sweeping vistas, defined details, and abstract emotions. Weave these types of images together to form a comprehensive fabric that distinguishes a place.

Salvation Mountain is a folk art masterwork created by a local resident of Imperial County in the California desert. The colorful hillside art is intended to be both religious tribute and gift to all who come to visit.

SEASONS

Changes in season bring changes in many aesthetic attributes of a place, often while remaining in character with what makes the place distinctive.

▶ FOR MORE
ON PATTERN
& TEXTURE,
SEE PAGES
34-5

▶ FOR MORE
ON QUALITY
OF LIGHT,
SEE PAGES
72-3

Most places in the world undergo some sort of transition with the changing of seasons. There are obvious shifts in a setting—a change in foliage color in autumn, a ground cover of snow in winter—followed by changes in wardrobe and activities for its inhabitants. But photographers seek to illustrate seasonal shifts on a more subtle level as part of a complete story of a place. The goal is to add depth of context with the ways seasons inform what is distinct and constant to a place's character.

In any location, the tilt of Earth's rotational axis will alter its position relative to the sun, causing changes in temperature and hours of daylight throughout the year, but also in the quality of the light. As the sun shines from higher or lower in the sky, the distance it must travel through the atmosphere changes, impacting its quality and color temperature. Summer light is typically high and harsh through much of the day, whereas winter light is often softer and more diffuse as it trav-

Cold, sunny mornings immediately following a fresh snowfall are great for illustrating the impact of winter on the landscape, as snow clings to everything—like the branches of this aspen tree in Basalt, Colorado—before the warmth of day melts it away.

Village kids frolic in the sea to beat the heat in Freetown, Sierra Leone. Following one girl with the camera allowed the photographer to select a compelling moment of movement and energy.

els lower in the sky, casting long shadows from everything it touches. The light in both spring and autumn seems to bring combinations of these qualities, evoking a sense of transition.

Seasons often bring with them a shift in the color palette of a place, with bright greens, blues, and yellows in summer, followed by brown-tinged yellows, oranges, and reds in autumn. Winter paints a landscape with cool blues and grays, yielding to the watery pastels of green and pink in spring.

A SEASON'S TEXTURE

Seasons also add a variety of textures to a place. Summer feels lush with supple leaves and grasses, which eventually dry up into the crunchy feel of autumn. These organic crumbs are covered by winter's smooth sheets of ice and snow,

which melt in spring to reveal fragile shoots, fresh and prickly.

Investigate the light, colors, and textures as they transform with the seasons. Notice how these changes are reflected in culture, dress, activity, and lifestyle. Even in a city's public transport system, the seasons are apparent. In winter, in a subway, the concrete floors may be wet and muddy with slush from boots. And the cold winds blowing through tunnels cause people to hunch up with hands in their pockets. In summer, commuters swelter and sweat, and try to keep their distance from fellow passengers as they shed layers of clothes after work. These gestures and responses to environment provide photographers with illustrations of seasonal impact without losing sight of the character that makes a place unique.

VEGETATION

Always alive and responsive to landscape, seasons, and weather, vegetation provides texture, color, and context to the photographic foundation of a place.

▶ FOR MORE
ON FOG &
HAZE, SEE
PAGES 82-3

▶ FOR MORE
ON BLUR
EFFECT,
SEE PAGES
304-305

Vegetation is perfectly suited to a given landscape, designed to make the most of available light and water to maximize biological processes. In turn, the shape, texture, color, and growth patterns of vegetation add to the look and uniqueness of a place. Northern climes are characterized by dense forests of evergreens. Deserts are distinguished by low scrubby plants and cacti, perfectly designed to store water. Rainforests have many layers of undergrowth beneath high canopies, maximizing growing area in a condensed space.

Photographing the vegetal life of a place is a good starting point to explore its natural history, as plants animate a landscape with color and movement. Look for unusual views and details that provide more of the story. Get low to photograph plants with sky as backdrop, or get high for a view of growth patterns. Look for the ways topography influences vegetation, or areas where plant and animal populations mix and rely on one another. Distill down to textures and patterns with close examination of tree bark and ground cover, root patterns and communities of critters taking up residency in decay. Increase shutter speed to freeze seed parachutes dispersing in a breeze. Slow it down for soft waves of movement in tall grasses, or an abstract blur of color in a field of wildflowers.

Whether in bloom, wilted, or well past peak season, plant life is always available, giving photographers flexibility in choosing time of day with optimal light or other circumstances. Adjust settings for the bright light of open desert or plains, or the low light of dense woods. Late afternoon sun might give a prairie a golden glow, and sunset might be a perfect time to capture the silhouette of a baobab tree on an African savanna. In a dense stand of conifers or tropical rainforest, early morning might bring beautiful beams of light that filter through branches, illuminating mist or fog. Take note, too, of the way people appreciate botanical spaces.

Observation of this biological base layer will help you settle into the tone and color palette of a place, while providing a foundation of information about the life it attracts.

ZOOM IN

▶ Look for a row of vegetation and photograph it as you might capture a city skyline. Try a silhouette with separation between elements, and get low to isolate them above the horizon for dramatic effect.

In this photograph from the Muir Woods National Monument in California, the wet climate turns forest trees into landscape for more vegetation, as ferns grow into a lush ground cover, and moss textures all surfaces.

ANIMALS IN THE WILD

Knowledge and patience are your best allies in photographing animals in the wild—understanding their environment and behavior, then settling in and waiting for a special moment.

A long lens and patient observation of this flower in Mindo Cloud Forest in Ecuador yielded a vibrant photograph of life in the wild. The photographer anticipated the swift movements of these hummingbirds to capture a compelling composition.

▶ FOR MORE ON LENS OPTIONS, SEE PAGES 232-3

▶ FOR MORE ON TRIPODS, SEE PAGES 280-81

An area's wild animal population is part of what makes it distinct. From songbirds and backyard squirrels to giraffes and elephants, the cast of characters seen flying, foraging, migrating, and making the most of a locale's available resources is at once thrilling and orienting.

Wildlife photography generally takes years of patience and practice to do well. But research, planning, and antici-

pation can go a long way. Before you even step outside, thoroughly investigate what species you can expect to see. Learn about their behaviors, patterns of movement, and how you might best position yourself for an encounter. If working in your own backyard, consider creating a blind, or camouflaged shelter, where you can wait, obscured from view. Many adventure cameras have settings that will allow you to set up in an animal's path and, with a smartphone, see what the camera sees and remotely make a photograph. As most of these types of cameras have super-wide-angle lenses, be patient and let an animal get close enough to fill the frame. An unusual perspective of an inquisitive creature is well worth the wait. Many professional wildlife photographers use "camera traps," which are complex systems using motion detection or the break of a laser beam to trigger the shutter release. Some of these incorporate multiple flashes and have resulted in stunning, ground-breaking photographs of animal behaviors otherwise rarely witnessed.

For animals at a distance—whales breaching at sea or lions on the savanna—bring the longest lens you can. Many of these may require a tripod or additional support, which means setting up and working a scene without moving too often. Consider joining an organized wildlife tour, which can increase the odds of getting to where the animals are, and be prepared to jockey for position with other photographers hoping for the same photo. Vet safari companies thoroughly to find one using best practices for locating wild species in nature, rather than staging experiences with captive animals. Set your photographs apart by making skilled use of light and negative space. Anticipate movements and wait for clean backgrounds, separation, and contrast that make the subject stand out.

Wherever you are, settle in and try to become part of the scene. Think like the animal you seek, and notice how perfectly an undisturbed landscape meets its needs. Make a photograph that tells the story of this divine design.

From an accompanying boat, this photographer was able to capture other photographers in the midst of a spectacular encounter with a gray whale in the wild.

CULTURE

Cultural differences well represented in a photograph instantly orient viewers in location and circumstance, by defining something identifiably distinct, or highlighting something new and unfamiliar.

These artful dresses do double duty in this photograph from the Galápagos Islands, with vivid depictions of iconic regional wildlife on the skirts of women performing a traditional dance.

▶ FOR MORE ON CELEBRATIONS, SEE PAGES 118–19

▶ FOR MORE ON DETAILS, SEE PAGES 168–9

All the naturally occurring aspects of a place—its landscape, weather, vegetation, resources, and wildlife—pour themselves into the ethos of its people. These are the resources with which communities establish how they organize themselves into a society, and how they live their lives, day to day. The combination of regional factors and their influence on the character of its people constitutes the culture of a place.

Culture influences everything, from music to dress to body language. Thorough research in advance of visiting a place is a must to be fully prepared to live and work in its culture—essential for both a positive travel experience and for making authentic, meaningful photographs. Different cultures have different shared perceptions about behaviors that are appropriate or respectful. Doing your homework in this area in advance is a must to ensure you don't

— ZOOM IN —

▶ Pick one attribute of culture in a new place, whether a distinct fashion item or type of meal. Do a quick photographic study, making four or five photographs illustrating a vignette of this subject.

unintentionally offend. The true understanding of culture may only come after spending time within it, and photographers strive to have an immersive appreciation come through in their photographs.

Culture lives in physical spaces where people gather, like urban parks or crowded marketplaces, religious centers, schools, and homes. As you enter any of these areas, take a good look before picking up the camera. Notice the way a space reflects its people and vice versa. Identify culture in how a space is appointed and how people interact with it and one another.

CELEBRATIONS OF CULTURE

Holidays and festivals are occasions where culture is celebrated and passionately on display. Most people will be expecting to see photographers in these circumstances, so get in close and fill the frame with color and visual representations of noise and merrymaking. For a more organic and everyday example of traditions and customs, try to visit a family celebrating a significant event, or even just sharing a meal. And don't shy away from serious or somber occasions like religious rites and processions for the dead. An authentic photograph documenting how people grieve can be a powerful and moving representation of culture. In all cases, approach with transparency and respect, and seek any necessary permissions.

The things people do in their quietest moments add layers and depth to what is apparent in a culture. Get to know someone and get quiet with them. Look intently at how they eat, pray, prepare for the day or for bed, and how they show

This photograph features a Muslim-American man living in Houston, Texas, who performs as Elvis Presley. He has been a fan of the singer since he was a young boy in Pakistan.

affection and love. Make photographs that are as quiet and contemplative as the moments themselves. Use natural light and register small details. Seek an accurate illustration of how real people in another place demonstrate their distinct culture through their approach to the universal aspects of life. As in so many types of photography, a successful cultural photograph is at once definingly unique and also relatable, and should move the viewer to feel curiosity, compassion, empathy, admiration, and more.

DETAILS

Important contributing elements to a larger story, the small and often inanimate details of a location add layers of context and dynamic interest to a photographic depiction of a place.

▶ FOR MORE ON FRAMING, SEE PAGES 52-3

▶ FOR MORE ON CONTROLLING SHUTTER SPEED, SEE PAGES 242-3

If wide, sweeping angles of view illustrate the atmosphere of a place, the depth and soul of it are revealed in the details. Whether subtle and quiet or distinctive and loud, examine closely the living and inanimate particulars that create the texture of a place in its landscape, weather, natural wonders, architecture, and culture, and add layers to its composition.

Environmental elements like the way water has eroded a rock, or a deer footprint in snow, are artful distillations of larger natural processes. Old hands wrapped around a teacup or on the keys of a piano speak to the inhabitants of a dwelling, their mood, preferences, and customs.

Primeval initials carved into the stone wall of an ancient castle now in ruins or hip-hop monikers spray-painted in giant, colorful block letters on the wall of a subway station add layers to the view of a place, with context about its

A signature part of a Maasai warrior's outfit is beadwork and a fighting stick. The lines of the blue-and-white robe lead the eye to the focal point of interest—the beaded bracelets, which further carry attention to the top of the stick.

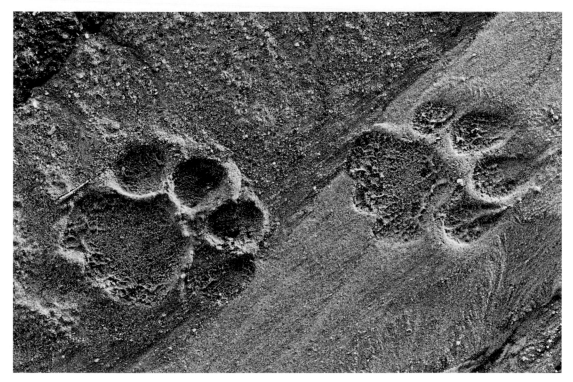

Lion tracks in the sand reveal evidence of what goes on in Tsavo National Park in Kenya, even when the animals themselves are not present. Details like this add texture and information about a location.

people, their history, and the universal, timeless desire for self-expression.

In your photographic pursuit of the details of a place, remember that low light from an oblique angle enhances texture, and a shallow depth of field makes a small, sharply focused element stand out from a busy background. Balance of even tiny components evokes calm and serenity, while tension adds interest that, when used well, captivates viewers and makes them look longer. Curate a view of inanimate objects with skillful framing that includes infor-mation but eliminates distractions. Consider adding portions of people interacting with objects—a hint about how and when items are used and by whom, or play with creative use of shutter speed to illustrate the flow of life around static elements.

Remember, too, that the accumulation and stacking of details makes the bigger picture. Trees make the forest, bricks make the buildings, and in the photographic depiction of the story of a place, great images of parts add depth to an overarching picture of the whole.

ZOOM IN

▶ Look at the two pictures shown here. Both draw attention to small, compelling, and informative elements that provide deeper understanding of culture and environment. These may have been missed without careful attention to tiny details.

| # ASSIGNMENT

Winter covers the landscape of a fishing village on a tiny island in west Greenland, where buildings are painted in different colors to indicate different functions—helpful for navigating the town in a land blanketed by snow.

A PLACE IN PICTURES

Whether at home or abroad, find a location you know well or would like to know better. Examine the visual signature of the location and create a sense of place in photographs.

SAME PLACE, DIFFERENT DAY Pick one spot that gives you a wide view of the landscape, architecture, or a bustling, populated center. Note the exact spot where you'll stand each time, and be sure to use the same lens. Pick days that are particularly distinctive to each season to make photographs there. Try to incorporate people or wildlife in the frame, to add scale and context with dress and activity. Put the photographs together in a set and examine how seasons and other aspects of time transform a place.

SIX TO 10 FRAMES Pick one building in the location you've chosen. Make six to 10 photographs. Incorporate landscape, architectural elements, how people use the space, and small details to provide a full picture of the building, its history, cultural significance, composition, and use. Vary cameras or lenses, perspectives, and points of view.

THE STORY IN ONE PHOTOGRAPH Pick a dynamic spot within your chosen location. Sit quietly and observe, immersing yourself in all the aspects that make it distinct. Think carefully about how you can capture the story of this place in one frame. Compose layers carefully and anticipate any movements that will add context. Make many photographs, then edit and select the one that does the job best.

PART II
CENTURIES OF SEEING

PHOTOGRAPHY
THROUGH TIME

Photography mirrors life. Whether the authentic documentary view of a journalistic image, or the enhanced, possibly augmented reflection of a fine art photograph, each image tells the story of a small slice of life as experienced and interpreted by the person who makes it.

The earliest primitive images, drawings etched on the side of caves—likely done from memory rather than sight—attest to human's ever present proclivity for self-expression. We want to document and share what we *see*—our experiences, our points of view—as an account of our world and our lives. What other explanation can there be for the consistent drive throughout history to record life, reflect our stories, and share them with others? Whether for science or social justice, as an artful exploration of beauty or the bad news from our darkest moments, we long to expand our understanding of the world through photographs, and rely on pictures as messaging. Perhaps even more fascinating is that we also seem to know instinctively that the more aesthetically compelling an image is, the more successful it becomes, no matter its intended function.

Photography freezes time. And yet, the rapid advancement of the technology we use to make photographs is happening at a pace that exceeds our full comprehension or measure of its impact. We now have the ability to preserve what might have been forgotten, to broadcast what is extraordinary, but also to project the mundane as something significant.

The phenomenon of photography doesn't fade. We keep making and looking at photographs with an appetite that has yet to be sated. Perhaps what we seek most in our persistent pursuit of a photograph is proof. Proof of what was, proof of what is. Proof that we are here, living, seeing, and surfing the wave of life before it's gone.

Black-and-white with hand-tinted color, this photograph of Mount Rainier National Park was part of a 1916 *National Geographic* feature, "Land of the Best," designed to advocate for an agency overseeing all national parks.

1826-1840

1826 First Permanent Impression

▶ Using a camera obscura, Joseph Nicéphore Niépce of France burns a permanent image of a scene from his window in Burgundy onto a bitumen-covered pewter plate. The black-and-white exposure takes nearly eight hours and fades significantly, but an image remains.

FIRST PERMANENT IMPRESSION

1830s Daguerreotype

FIRST DAGUERREOTYPE PHOTO

DAGUERRE CAMERA

◀ Louis-Jacques-Mandé Daguerre makes the first daguerreotype. In 1839, he publishes details of the new process, which involves iodine vapors, mercury fumes, and salt. Daguerreotypes, which are made on polished, silver-plated sheets of copper, yield images of great clarity, yet further exposure to light makes them fade.

" THE DAGUERREOTYPE WILL NEVER DO FOR PORTRAIT PAINTING. **ITS PICTURES ARE QUITE TOO NATURAL**, TO PLEASE ANY OTHER THAN VERY BEAUTIFUL SITTERS. IT HAS **NOT THE SLIGHTEST KNACK** AT 'FANCY-WORK.' "
—**Lewis Clark, 1839**

1834 Photograms

British scientist William Henry Fox Talbot develops a cameraless technique, pressing plants and other flat materials against paper treated with light-sensitive materials and exposing them to sunlight. In the areas where objects cover the paper, it remains white; the uncovered areas turn black.

FROM TODAY, **PAINTING IS DEAD.**
—**Paul Delaroche, 1839**

1839 Photographic Fixative

Sir John Herschel, son of the British astronomer William Herschel (who discovered the planet Uranus), develops the process of using hyposulphite of soda, or "hypo," to dissolve the silver salts that remain on the film or photographic paper and cause the image to continue fading in light. Hypo then becomes the last step in processing film or paper to fix photographic images, making them no longer light sensitive.

1839 First Photograph of People

▼ Louis-Jacques-Mandé Daguerre photographs Boulevard du Temple in Paris from his window using a camera obscura and his daguerreotype process. The exposure time is thought to be about 10 minutes. Moving objects aren't recorded, but a man getting a shoeshine and the person shining his shoes remain still long enough to become the first people ever photographed.

FIRST PHOTOGRAPH OF PEOPLE

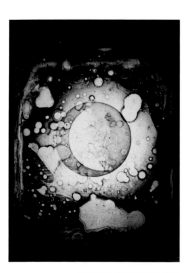

FIRST PHOTO OF MOON

1840 First Photo of the Moon

◀ American physician and professor of chemistry John William Draper captures the first photograph of the moon, a daguerreotype, through a 12-inch telescope, from a rooftop in Manhattan. It takes about 30 minutes to make the exposure. In subsequent decades, more detailed images are taken of the lunar surface, including by Draper's own son, Henry.

1850-1859

PHOTO BY JEAN LOUIS MARIE
EUGÈNE DURIEU

1851 Panoramic Photography

▶ Wanting to show wide expanses and sweeping views of cities and landscapes, photographers line up multiple daguerreotype plates side by side to create a panoramic view of a scene. Early panoramics could be composed from two to as many as 11 plates. The first commercial panoramic camera, the Al-Vista, is made in 1898.

> AN IMPORTANT END AND **AIM OF PHOTOGRAPHY** IS TO IMPROVE THE PUBLIC TASTE, AND TO **ELEVATE AND REFORM ART.**
> —William Crookes, editor of *Photographic Notes*, 1856

1850 Albumen Silver Prints

French photographer Louis Désiré Blanquart-Evrard introduces the first commercially available paper print produced from a negative. Coated with egg white (albumen) and sensitized with silver nitrate, the prints are glossy and finely detailed.

1851 Nude Photography

◀ During this decade, more artists begin to photograph nude people, which they are careful to say are models for painters. And, in many instances, they are. As is the case with the French photographer Jean Louis Marie Eugène Durieu, who provides photographs to the painter Eugène Delacroix, who then uses them as inspiration for his work.

PANORAMIC PHOTOGRAPH OF PARIS, 1856

1851 Wet Collodion Process

Englishman Frederick Scott Archer invents the wet plate process for producing glass negatives. It uses collodion, a recently discovered chemical previously used as a medical dressing that dries quickly, creating a durable, transparent, waterproof film. Many times faster than any previous method, it takes only seconds to create exposures, and it results in clear, highly detailed prints. This process will eventually replace the daguerreotype process.

1853 Tintype Process

▶ Invented in France by Adolphe-Alexandre Martin, the tintype (or, more accurately, ferrotype, because the print surface is made of iron) is a faster, cheaper version of the daguerreotype. The process makes photographic portraits available to the middle and lower classes, capturing images of Civil War soldiers, immigrants, and working people.

TINTYPE PHOTO IN FRONT OF PAINTED BACKGROUND

SARAH BERNHARDT, PHOTOGRAPHED BY NADAR

1853 Beginning of Portraiture

◀ French caricaturist Gaspard-Félix Tournachon, known by the pseudonym Nadar, begins photographing the who's who of French society, using 8-by-10-inch glass plate negatives. He's known for solid backgrounds, dramatic light, and focusing on his subjects' faces, and his work wins praise from the *Gazette des Beaux-Arts*, France's leading art review of the time.

FIRST AERIAL PHOTOGRAPH

> " LANDSCAPE PHOTOGRAPHY! HOW **PLEASANTLY THE WORDS** FALL **UPON THE EAR** OF THE ENTHUSIASTIC PHOTOGRAPHER.
> —**James Mudd,**
> **English photographer, 1858** "

1858 First Bird's-Eye-View Photo

▲ Inspired by interests in aeronautics, journalism, and photography, Nadar climbs into a tethered hot air balloon in Paris and creates the first aerial photograph, capturing the Place de l'Etoile from 1,600 feet above the ground.

1860-1879

1861 Addition of Color to a Photo

▶ Photographer Thomas Sutton, working with physicist James Clerk Maxwell, creates a basic color photo by passing a black-and-white image through red, green, and blue filters and superimposing the three photos on a single screen.

FIRST COLOR PHOTO

> WHY ARE THERE **NO LONGER ANY MINIATURISTS?** FOR THE VERY SIMPLE REASON THAT . . . **PHOTOGRAPHY DOES THE JOB BETTER.**
> – Antoine-François-Jean Claudet, 1865

1865 Flash Photography

John Traill Taylor, photographer, chemist, and editor of *The British Journal of Photography*, develops a safer way to use magnesium flash powder, mixed with compound oxygen in powder form, thus advancing the pursuit of accessible flash photography. It isn't for another 20 years or so, when the high price of magnesium goes down, that flash photography becomes widely used. Contained in a protective holder and ignited by hand, this volatile powder produces a brilliant white flash of light, followed by a characteristic large puff of white smoke.

1869 Pictorial Effect in Photography

▶ British author Henry Peach Robinson publishes a handbook on pictorialism, which embraces photography as an artistic medium. At this time, the photography community is sharply divided between those that believe photographs should be unaltered and used only to document reality, and the pictorialists, who embrace different postproduction techniques to create more Impressionist works of art.

PICTORIALIST PHOTO

1871 Photographic Survey of Yellowstone

▶ The U.S. Geological and Geographical Survey of the Territories commissions William Henry Jackson to photograph the American West in 1870, as part of the Hayden Geological Survey, led by explorer and geologist Ferdinand V. Hayden. Jackson sends photos of Wyoming to Congress in 1871, providing visual evidence of the area's unique features and beauty. These images excite the science community and inspire interest and curiosity all over the country, and a year later Yellowstone, the nation's first national park, is established.

1871 Dry Plate Printing

R. L. Maddox, an American physician, devises a method of preparing glass plates with gelatin emulsion that allows photographers to prepare their plates days or even weeks before using them—a key step toward the invention of photographic film.

1878 First Action Photos

▼ Former California governor and railroad tycoon Leland Stanford wants to prove that all four of a horse's hooves leave the ground at the same time while galloping. So, he commissions Englishman Eadweard Muybridge to provide photographic evidence. Muybridge sets up 12 cameras, all with trip wires and fraction-of-a-second shutter speeds. Muybridge's series of shots confirm Stanford's theory and lead to animation and cinematography.

YELLOWSTONE SURVEY PHOTO

> MANY A COMMONPLACE SCENE . . . REQUIRES **ONLY THE PROPER LIGHTING**, AND PERHAPS **A FIGURE OF THE RIGHT KIND IN THE RIGHT PLACE**, TO MAKE IT BEAUTIFUL.
> –Henry Peach Robinson, 1888

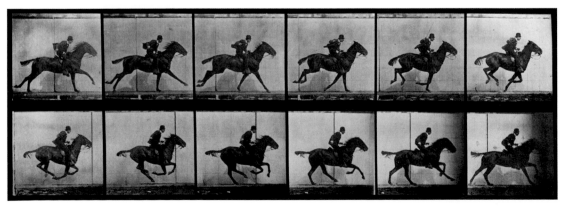

EARLY MOTION SEQUENCE

1900-1909

1900 Brownie Camera

▼ Costing only a dollar, George Eastman's Brownie camera reaches 100,000 in sales in the first year. The box camera comes with a 15-cent removable film container and is so simple to operate that photography quickly becomes a popular pastime.

EARLY BROWNIE CAMERA

GEORGE EASTMAN WITH A KODAK BOX CAMERA

1901 Eastman Kodak Company

▲ The company is incorporated, with George Eastman as its president, 11 years after the business was established in Rochester, New York. Later, the company's name is shortened to Kodak.

1902 Photo-Secession

▼ "Photo-Secession" is a group founded by Alfred Stieglitz that promotes the concept of photography as fine art. They are not opposed to manipulating negatives and prints for creative expression. The group opens a gallery called the Little Galleries of the Photo-Secession, on Fifth Avenue in New York City.

1903 First Photographic Magazine

Influential photographer Alfred Stieglitz begins a quarterly publication called *Camera Work*, which aims to publish the best in artistic photography and includes reviews, poems, and articles written by some of the most prominent thinkers of the time.

" ONLY EXAMPLES OF SUCH WORK AS GIVES **EVIDENCE OF INDIVIDUALITY** AND ARTISTIC WORTH . . . OR CONTAINS SOME **EXCEPTIONAL FEATURE OF TECHNICAL MERIT** . . . WILL FIND RECOGNITION IN THESE PAGES.
—Alfred Stieglitz, on *Camera Work* "

PORTRAIT OF ALFRED STIEGLITZ

1905 First *National Geographic* Photo Series

◄ *National Geographic* publishes its first stand-alone photography series, a photographic tour of Lhasa, Tibet. The Imperial Russian Geographical Society of St. Petersburg presented the images to the National Geographic Society. Later, editor Gilbert H. Grosvenor reveals that he expected the 11-page pictorial would get him fired.

SCENE FROM TIBET, PART OF *NATIONAL GEOGRAPHIC'S* FIRST PHOTO SERIES

1906 First Wildlife Photos in *National Geographic*

▼ *National Geographic* introduces wildlife photography with an article by George Shiras, "Photographing Wild Game with Flashlight and Camera," containing 32 flash-lit photos taken in Michigan's Upper Peninsula. Shiras is the first to use camera traps and flash when photographing animals. Two society board members resign in protest, saying, "wandering off into nature is not geography."

EARLY NIGHT FLASH PHOTO, BY GEORGE SHIRAS

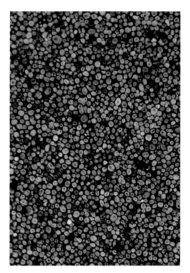

COLORED POTATO STARCH GRAINS

1907 Autochrome

▲ After rwo decades of work, Auguste and Louis Lumière create the first commercially successful color process. They use a glass plate covered with dyed grains of potato starch to make a positive color transparency. The image is made by shining light through the plate.

1909 First Photos of the North Pole

▶ Robert E. Peary, his assistant Matthew Henson, and four Inuit men take photographs to prove they've reached the North Pole after a 37-day dog-sled journey over 400-plus miles of ice. Skeptics immediately question the feat, saying Peary's navigation and reckoning were dodgy and that the round-trip couldn't possibly have been completed so quickly,. Later studies suggest they were at least 60 miles short of the actual pole.

NORTH POLE EXPEDITION PHOTO

AN AUTOCHROME IS EITHER VERY GOOD OR VERY BAD AND **SHOULD BE TREATED WITH THE RESPECT** THE PROCESS DESERVES. A PLATE IS NEVER WASTED IF IT **LEAVES ITS LESSON BEHIND.**
—"Color Photography at Its Best," in *American Photography*, 1915

1940-1949

"AMERICAN GOTHIC," BY GORDON PARKS

1942 Color Negative Film

Kodacolor, the first practical color negative film, is introduced by Eastman Kodak.

1942 "American Gothic" by Gordon Parks

◀African-American photographer Gordon Parks joins the Farm Security Administration's photographic unit. After experiencing overt racism in his first days in the nation's capital, he vows to use his camera to expose inequality and injustice. One night in the FSA's federal offices, Parks meets and photographs Ella Watson, a black woman scrubbing the floor in front of the American flag. With its original title of "Washington D.C. Government Charwoman," Parks calls the portrait "an indictment of America." With its clear suggestion of Grant Wood's iconic painting, the photograph becomes known as "American Gothic."

1942 Xerography Patented

Chester Carlson receives a patent for electrophotography, the technology at the heart of photocopying machines.

> **THE PICTURES ARE THERE,** AND YOU JUST TAKE THEM. **THE TRUTH IS THE BEST PICTURE,** THE BEST PROPAGANDA.
> –Robert Capa, 1937

1944 WWII Photography

▼On June 6, Hungarian-born American war photographer Robert Capa, with his two Contax cameras, is the only photographer embedded within the first wave of Allied forces to land on Omaha Beach in the D-Day invasion of German-occupied France. His photos are an incredible record of the largest seaborne attack in history, one that is said to have been the turning point in World War II.

1946 First Photo From Space

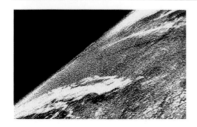

FIRST SPACE PHOTO

◀Researchers strap a 35mm camera to a German V-2 missile. It snaps a picture every second and a half as the rocket shoots 65 miles (105 km) above Earth, revealing a black-and-white wedge of planet framed by the blackness of space.

D-DAY PHOTO BY ROBERT CAPA

EARLY HIGH-SPEED PHOTOGRAPH

1940s First High-Speed Photography

◄MIT engineer Harold E. Edgerton perfects high-speed stroboscopic photography, which freezes movements too rapid for the eye to see. *National Geographic* publishes several of the images, including bullets frozen in mid-flight and stilled hummingbird wings.

1947 Magnum Founded

Robert Capa, George Rodger, Henri Cartier-Bresson, and David "Chim" Seymour form Magnum, the first photographic collaborative owned by the photographers themselves. Moved by what they witnessed in World War II, the founders create the agency as a platform to present their individual visions. Magnum photographers commit to documenting most of the world's major events and personalities, covering industry, society and people, places of interest, politics and news events, disasters, and conflict.

1947 Polaroid Process

▼The Polaroid Company—originally Land-Wheelwright Laboratories—produces a camera with black-and-white film that develops in just 60 seconds. Eventually, Polaroid pares down the processing time to 15 seconds, making the camera even more popular.

1949 First Survey of the Night Sky

MOUNT WILSON OBSERVATORY AT PALOMAR

IMAGE FROM PALOMAR OBSERVATORY SKY SURVEY

◄National Geographic teams up with the California Institute of Technology for the Palomar Observatory Sky Survey, a seven-year project to produce the first photographic map, or sky atlas, of the Northern Hemisphere's night sky. The work is done at the Palomar Observatory in California using "Big Schmidt," a new, 48-inch camera telescope, as it photographically surveys the entire night sky, and results in a comprehensive study of the heavens that leads to the discovery of many new stars and galaxies. Astronomers today still use its findings.

POLAROID PICTURE

1949 Disposable Cameras

The company Photo-Pac invents the first disposable camera. The cardboard camera, which is available at drugstores, is sold for less than $2 and comes loaded with an eight-exposure roll of film.

1970-1979

ALL OF A SUDDEN, YOU BEGIN TO REALIZE YOU ARE **LOOKING AT SOMETHING VERY STRANGE** AND YET VERY, VERY FAMILIAR . . . AND THEN IT'S SMALL ENOUGH WHERE YOU CAN PUT YOUR THUMB UP AND COVER . . . THE ENTIRETY OF THIS HOME PLANET OF OURS.
—**Eugene Cernan, Apollo 17 astronaut, 2012**

SNOW LEOPARD IN PAKISTAN

1971 Photographing Endangered Species

▲ Photographed by Dr. George Schaller in the early 1970s, the first images of snow leopards in the wild include a female *Panthera uncia* perched on a snowy crag in Pakistan's Chitral Valley. *National Geographic* publishes the photographs in its November 1971 issue.

"BLUE MARBLE" SHOT

1972 First Full-View Photo of Earth

▲ With the sun at their backs, the Apollo 17 crew heads for the moon on December 7. Looking back, they photograph the perfectly lit Earth: the famous, awe-inspiring "Blue Marble." Only 24 humans have traveled far enough into space to see the full globe of Earth, and only the three Apollo 17 astronauts saw the full Earth.

"NAPALM GIRL" PHOTO BY NICK UT

1972 A New Era for War Photography

▲ The Vietnam War is sometimes referred to as the first "living room war." The unprecedented access of journalists and photographers and their uncensored reporting brings disturbing scenes from the conflict directly to Americans, into their homes via their TV screens and newspapers. The images make the realities of conflict clear to a generation at home who begin the peace movement.

1974 | International Center of Photography

Photographer Cornell Capa, brother of war photographer Robert Capa, founds New York's International Center of Photography, an influential photography museum, school, and research center that focuses on socially and politically minded images that educate and influence culture.

OXALIC ACID CRYSTALS, FIRST NIKON PRIZE WINNER

1975 | First All-Electronic Camera

PROTOTYPE OF FIRST DIGITAL CAMERA

◀ Steve Sasson, a young engineer at Eastman Kodak, constructs a prototype digital camera. Much larger than a regular camera, it shoots black-and-white photographs at a resolution of 10,000 pixels and saves them to a cassette tape. Only semiportable, it displays its photographs on a television screen. In 1989, Sasson and a colleague create the first SLR camera.

1975 | Photomicrography Celebrated

▲ The Nikon International Small World Competition begins as a means to recognize and celebrate photography through a light microscope. The competition grows and eventually becomes a leading showcase for photomicrography from all scientific disciplines.

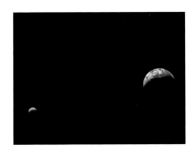

CRESCENT MOON AND EARTH

1975 | First Photo From Another Planet's Surface

▼ The unmanned Russian space probe Venera 9 lands on Venus and takes and transmits the first images successfully conveyed to Earth from the surface of another planet. Because two camera covers don't release, 180-degree images, instead of the intended 360-degree, are captured.

VENUS FROM VENERA 9

1977 | Earth and Moon in One Frame

▲ A month after takeoff, 7.25 million miles (11.6 million km) from Earth, NASA's Voyager 1, a robotic space probe on a one-way exploratory mission into outer space, returns the first image of Earth and its moon together in a single photograph.

PART III
TECHNOLOGY & THE ART

CHAPTER SEVEN

CAMERA BASICS

For many new and experienced photographers, the intangible parts of the photographic process are the hardest. Taking time to self-reflect about voice, approach, and style, as well as to consider creative choices in composition and light, requires a lot of work behind the camera. But all of this careful thought and intention cannot manifest without the camera itself and a photographer's mastery of its functions.

A blessing and curse of the digital age of photography is that it evolves constantly and quickly. Each year, digital cameras become more advanced, with better functionality and more ways to capture, process, and share photos. This means more options for solving visual problems and making photographs that tell the story you want to share. It also means that photographers must work constantly to stay current with changing technology and be flexible and open to the next evolution of photographic tools.

Without question, different types of cameras have different sweet spots—the situations and conditions for which their design and functions are most optimal. Becoming more familiar with not only the equipment you own, but also other types of cameras available on the market, will help you identify the tools you need to make the most of any situation.

You've identified a story and how you want to tell it. The camera, no matter which one you choose, is your tool for capturing and sharing what you see, and what you'd like viewers to feel. With a refresher on the basics and review of new technology, you can shore up the foundational skills you need to go beyond a basic capture to *making* a photograph that fulfills your storytelling vision.

Just before dawn, the statue of King John I as seen through the Rua Augusta Arch in Lisbon evokes a calm fortitude. This exposure captures the blue hues of available light to maximal effect.

TYPES OF CAMERAS

Cameras come in different sizes and price points, with decent options to meet each circumstance and style. Each one has its advantages and disadvantages, plus price differences will likely factor into your selection.

▶ FOR MORE
ON SMART-
PHONE PHO-
TOGRAPHY,
SEE PAGES
224-5

▶ FOR MORE
ON LENSES,
SEE PAGES
268-9

The digital age has revolutionized picturemaking and made it so that we can make hundreds of photographs without pausing to change film or batteries.

The different types of cameras available on the market today work in much the same way cameras have for centuries, but with improved speed, quality, accuracy, convenience, and range. They also vary in size, shape, and portability.

Most types of cameras have a sweet spot—a set of circumstances in which that particular camera is optimal given its particular characteristics and functions. Understanding the sweet spot of the equipment you have is a shortcut to knowing when, where, and how you can make the most of the situation at hand.

SMARTPHONE

There's no question—smartphone cameras continue to improve in quality and functionality. Newer models have built-in lens options, and loads of apps offer a wide variety of creative capture and editing tools. Sharing to social media is possible in just a few steps, and in certain circumstances, this alone may be worth giving up some features of a more complicated camera.

Perhaps best of all, having a camera in your phone means you have a camera with you almost all the time. These tend to work best close to the action and with lots of available light. When it comes to convenience, a smartphone camera cannot be beat.

POINT-AND-SHOOT

In terms of function and quality, these run the gamut. Some are built to fit in a pocket and make quick, automatic exposures, while some feature robust zooms and manual control options. The benefit is convenience; the cost is a noninterchangeable lens and sometimes quality.

Needless to say, as smartphone cameras keep improving, point-and-shoot cameras continue to fall out of favor. Nevertheless, they're still the choice of many travelers and have paved the way for compact cameras built to capture action and adventure.

MIRRORLESS

Mirrorless cameras typically offer large, high-quality sensors without the bulk and heft of DSLR bodies. The mirrorless functionality means that there is no optical viewfinder. Instead, the electronic viewfinder (EVF) lays important information atop a projected, live view of the scene. Depth of field, exposure, and histogram are all visibly responsive as the scene is reframed or settings are adjusted. Some quality mirrorless cameras have a fixed lens—often a 35mm—whereas others can accommodate a multitude of lenses. Also, capture is typically silent because there is no physical shutter or mirror bumping around inside, making them a great choice if you'd

like to be discreet. They can fit in a small bag, can be held at the hip, and their quietness helps keep a subject at ease. These advantages make mirrorless cameras the first choice of many professionals, especially street photographers and journalists who travel light. One downside: Their unique batteries are expensive but rechargeable, and they tend to drain down quickly, so be sure to have extras charged up and at the ready.

DSLR

DSLR bodies tend to have large sensors, but their quality and functionality vary greatly. Their optical viewfinders draw less power, meaning a longer battery life, and their bodies are designed to be used with interchangeable lenses.

A professional DSLR has the same, if not more, bells and whistles as a high-end mirrorless camera body, but with a little more heft and bulk. The robust DSLR build makes them able to host a wider variety of interchangeable lenses. Their optical viewfinders draw less power than the EVF of a mirrorless camera, meaning longer battery life and no delay while framing, as the view is reflected up to the eyepiece with a mirror. For now, most DSLRs autofocus more quickly than their mirrorless counterparts, and they handle moving subjects better, making them the cameras of choice for sports and landscape photographers, whose priorities are autofocus speed and focal length versatility.

ZOOM IN

▶ Take a look at the camera you have and consider which circumstances it's best suited for. The next time you make a photograph with it, try to maximize the opportunity by tapping into its strengths.

WHY I LOVE THIS PHOTO

This image was captured on a smartphone, the only camera photographer Matt Propert carried on his 1,300-mile, three-month trek, where every extra ounce was an added burden. The Appalachian Trail melts away into the soft, misty light of Nantahala National Forest. The lichen-covered, gnarled trees frame the path that leads your eye through the center of the image, guiding your attention up through the branches and then back through the scene, taking in the textured, leafless woods of early spring. Timeless in its mood, this photograph evokes an immediate sense of place, the emptiness yet beauty of a solo hike, and the wondering and mystery of what lies around the next turn in the trail.

—SUSAN BLAIR
Director of Photography,
National Geographic Books

Taken with a smartphone in 2018 on the Appalachian Trail, this image shows the Nantahala National Forest in North Carolina.

THE LENS

The lens determines how the camera will read the scene, and the caliber of the lens is the first factor to determine image quality.

▶ FOR MORE ON TELE-PHOTO LENSES, SEE PAGES 270–71

▶ FOR MORE ON WIDE-ANGLE & FISH-EYE LENSES, SEE PAGES 276-7

The function and importance of a lens remain relatively constant—the lens is the eye of the camera and the gateway to picturemaking. Its job is to take in available light, then focus and deliver the image to the sensor. It does this simple but critical job using a series of shaped glass elements that work in concert to focus an image.

Focal length measures the distance, in millimeters, between the camera's sensor and the optical center of the lens, which is the point at which light rays coming through all the internal elements converge to form a sharp image. The farther the distance (the more millimeters or the "longer" the lens), the larger the subject will be in the frame of the image. Although long lenses vary in build and arrangement of elements, they are collectively known as telephoto lenses.

Any lens with a focal length of 85mm or more is typically referred to as a telephoto. Lenses with a short distance between the optical center and the sensor—ones that have a focal length of 35 or shorter—are known as "wide-angle"

In spite of his impressive proximity to these gelada baboons, this photographer is using a long lens to fill the frame for a portrait featuring just the animals' faces.

A glass ball refracts light, inverting the scene behind it. Refraction also occurs within the camera lens, though lens elements are shaped and grouped to repeat the effect and right the image that reaches the sensor.

for their broad angle of view. Lenses with focal lengths between 35 and 85 are commonly referred to as "normal" or "standard" for their similarity to the angle of view of the human eye. With "prime" lenses, or those with fixed focal lengths, the only way to change the size of the subject in the frame is to change the distance between the camera and the subject. "Zoom" lenses, however, have varying focal lengths, allowing photographers to vary the degree to which a subject fills the frame.

In addition to focal length, it is important to be familiar with the maximum aperture the lens can achieve. The wider the aperture, the more light the lens will let into the camera. A lens that has a maximum aperture of f/1.2 is capable of letting in a lot of light and is considered a "fast" lens. Most zoom lenses have a maximum aperture that varies as the lens is zoomed in and out. For example, a Nikon 18-55mm gradually shifts from a maximum aperture of f/3.5 at 18mm to f.5.6 at 55mm. The maximum aperture, along with quality of glass, determine the caliber of the lens.

Because the lens is your image's entry point into the camera, it makes sense to invest in the best lens you can afford.

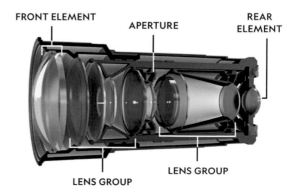

FRONT ELEMENT   APERTURE   REAR ELEMENT

LENS GROUP   LENS GROUP

The glass elements within a camera lens work in concert to refract, reflect, and focus an image before it reaches the camera sensor.

SMARTPHONE PHOTOGRAPHY

Each generation of smartphone cameras evolves and improves, meaning the most powerful camera you have may be the one in your pocket.

By using a smartphone to make this image, the photographer was able to capture a casual, authentic portrait in this neighborhood setting in Guatemala City.

▶ FOR MORE ON HIGH DYNAMIC RANGE, SEE PAGES 318-19

▶ FOR MORE ON SMART-PHONE EDITING, SEE PAGES 378-9

The term "professional photographer" may conjure up visions of a figure carrying bags of gear, large camera bodies, and multiple lenses, whereas "smartphone user" may evoke an image of a young person holding a phone slightly overhead, taking a selfie. But each year, new smartphone technology makes the cameras they contain more powerful, more capable of variety and versatility. Now more than ever, smartphone cameras have made possible the capture of stunning, high-quality imagery. Add to this countless apps with potent and trans-formative editing capabilities, and the potential for fantastic photography is currently in most people's pockets.

To start, the most important camera is the one you have with you. Through their ubiquitousness and availability, smartphone cameras are now the recorders of news as it happens, and of content created from within the heart of the action.

SMARTPHONE CAMERA QUALITY

The quality of smartphone cameras has improved exponentially over the past few years, and to date, nearly matches that of many DSLR cameras. Most current models have sensors of anywhere from 12 to 40 megapixels, and front- and back-facing cameras with double, triple, and even quadruple lens setups—meaning you can shoot super wide, and in an instant, frame more tightly with an excellent optical zoom. Newer phone cameras work well in low light with reduced noise and are capable of wide apertures as low as f/1.5 for dramatic portraits.

Smartphone autofocus technology has begun to rival that of DSLRs, with phase-detection and laser autofocus functions—both use complex analyses that offer accurate focus within a fraction of a second. Most models have built-in high dynamic range (HDR) capability, creating a single, comprehensive frame from three different exposures, as well as panoramic and video capabilities. And many have the option to set focus, aperture, and shutter speed manually, and even offer a RAW file format setting, either through the native camera app or a third-party app.

You could fill a camera bag with accessories that make smartphone photography even more sophisticated. Portable chargers extend battery life. Phone stands, rods, and handles combine with Bluetooth remote triggers to allow photographers to make pictures remotely or capture themselves in action. Clip-on lenses offer even

more variety to angle of view, some with unique filters for special effects. There are LED attachments and even a new line of compact instant printers. And a plethora of third-party photography apps offer the ability to edit your photographs right in the palm of your hand.

Perhaps the greatest advantage of smartphone photography is the ability to share your work with the world instantly through a variety of means and social media platforms. But remember, just because you can instantly publish your work doesn't mean you should. It's wise to edit and thoughtfully consider any photograph before sharing. Smartphone cameras greatly simplify the flow of imagery from concept to community, meaning that more photographs are being made and shared than ever before.

Having a smartphone in hand and ready to make photographs means catching a potentially fleeting scene, like these birds silhouetted on a wire overhead in Tokyo's Shimbashi area.

| # ASSIGNMENT

Human figures and thorn trees make stunning silhouettes against the vivid sand dunes at Namib-Naukluft Park in Namibia.

FINDING THE
SWEET SPOT

Camera sensors vary in how they handle ranges of light, and angles of view vary between lenses, whether fixed or changeable. Becoming familiar with a camera's sweet spot will allow you to respond quickly and effectively to any situation, and with the right tool for the job.

ASSEMBLE YOUR CAMERAS—smartphone, DSLR, or point-and-shoot. Choose a static scene with steady and consistent light. From the same spot, make a few photos with each camera. As you frame, note the angle of view of the lens of each camera. As you review the images, compare the range of light of each camera.

PICK ONE SCENE AND ONE CAMERA, then make photographs of the subject from different distances. How close should you be to optimize the angle of view? If you are using a zoom lens, make one photograph standing at a distance from the subject, and zoom in to fill the frame. Make a second by zooming out, but this time, move closer to the subject to fill the frame. Which image do you prefer? Why?

CAPTURE VARIATION IN LIGHT. If you have only one camera, make pictures of a scene in bright light and very low light, and compare the range of light in the final images. Which scenario is handled best by the camera you have?

Think about these results and start to form an idea of which camera and lens might be best suited to specific circumstances and why.

CHAPTER EIGHT

TECHNOLOGY &
THE IMAGE

Photography employs both creativity and logic. A person's creative impulses help direct the content, composition, and emotional intent of the photograph. And a logical mind helps operate the camera based on the assessment of factors in the scene.

Photographers see stories and make creative choices about how best to relay those stories to viewers in photographs. But what the camera sees is equally important to how a story is conveyed. And so, the mechanical side of picture-making must be second nature—a reflexive response to both vision and circumstance—to allow the creative act to proceed seamlessly and successfully.

Advancements in digital photography might make it tempting to rely on technology to automate picture capture, to ask the camera to automatically produce well-exposed images with minimal intervention. But a thorough understanding of exposure, focus, and the camera itself allows photographers to have more control—to interpret and translate the look and feel of a scene in a deeper way rather than to merely document what objects were where.

Experienced photographers know that successful, impactful photographs require complete collaboration between the brain's creative and logical impulses. Mastery of the principles of photography allows for creation of images that are more than memories—they can be powerful objects of art.

This dramatic portrait of a red fox in Norway makes use of both shadow and the low, late-day sunlight coming from behind the animal to evoke wildness and mystery.

EXPOSURE

Understanding the basics of exposure is critical to the creation of an image, but mastery of nuanced exposure leads to creative control of mood and tone.

► FOR MORE ON APERTURE & DEPTH OF FIELD, SEE PAGES 236-7

► FOR MORE ON SHUTTER SPEED, SEE PAGES 240-41

At the heart of photography is exposure—the amount of light that reaches the sensor. Too little or too much light and there is no picture. Within the range of light that produces an image with visible details, there is a lot of latitude and room for preference, so much so that "proper exposure" is a fairly subjective term.

EXPOSURE RANGES

There is the exposure that allows for all of the elements in the frame to be lit and fully visible, but there are also viable options on either side of that exposure that create a particular tone or mood.

Some photographers prefer exposures that flood an image with light, producing blown-out skies and bright, vivid colors. Bright exposures with readings toward the plus side of the camera meter tend to imply lightness, heat, optimism, and joy.

Other photographers prefer darker exposures, rich with shadows and partially revealed details. Shadowy exposures with readings that sit on the negative side of the camera meter may invoke aloofness, mystery, weight, drama, or cold.

In this way, exposure is a finessing tool. Photographers can use it to provide more context or to make subtle suggestions beyond the content within an image. Even more sophistication may be added to a photograph with a juxtaposition of exposure and content. For example, imagine flooding a serious scene with light, like a home torn apart by a tornado, revealing damage or expressions of fatigue or sadness, or shrouding a gentle, sweet subject in shadow, such as a sleeping baby in a dark room.

EXPOSURE SKILLS

To master skillful use of exposure to create impact, you must first understand the following factors:

► APERTURE—The size of the opening in the diaphragm of the lens

► SHUTTER SPEED—The length of time light is permitted through the opening.

The exposure of a photograph is determined by the amount of light and its time in the camera. The more light that comes in through the lens (the wider the aperture), the less time the shutter needs to be open to create the image (the shorter the shutter speed) and vice versa.

The inversely proportionate ratio remains the same no matter which one

A long shutter speed blurs the flow of water and also allows for a balanced exposure with a small aperture, keeping most of the scene in sharp focus even in the low light of sunset.

of those factors is changed. For example, if an aperture of f/8 produces a balanced exposure at a shutter speed of 1/125 of a second, that exposure will be exactly the same at f/5.6 and 1/250, or f/11 and 1/60.

All photographers must make these choices constantly, at the same time always keeping in mind that aperture impacts depth of field, while varying shutter speeds can either freeze or blur movement in a frame.

Digital cameras contain accurate light-reading tools that can make exposure calculations automatically, but to have ultimate control over the balance of light and shadow in your photographs, you must master the nuanced relationship between aperture and shutter speed.

LENS OPTIONS

Although you can make a picture of anything with any lens, understanding the difference between types of lenses helps identify the right tool for the job.

▶ FOR MORE ON TELE-PHOTO LENSES, SEE PAGES 270–71

▶ FOR MORE ON MACRO-PHOTOGRA-PHY, SEE PAGES 288–9

The lens determines how a camera registers the scene before you. Telephoto lenses reach far into the distance to pull a subject closer and fill more of the frame. Macro lenses magnify something tiny, providing a look into a world the human eye can barely see. Wide-angle lenses take a broad view of a sweeping vista or a large crowd. Superwide fish-eye lenses bend and distort the world. Tilt-shift lenses correct for perspective problems, allowing architectural photographers to photograph tall buildings without converging verticals. Specialty lenses aside, it makes sense to understand the options and features of the most common lenses. Appreciating the sweet

24 MM

70 MM

200 MM

400 MM

Lenses with different focal lengths have different angles of view. In all four images above, the camera-to-subject distance is the same, but each lens fills the frame differently.

THE BEST LENS FOR THE JOB

SUBJECT OR SITUATION	IDEAL LENS
Flower stamen or insects	True macro lens, 60 to 105mm with short minimum focus distance
General backyard wildlife	Basic telephoto lens, anything from 70 to 200mm
Distant sports, birds, or other wildlife	Super telephoto lens, maybe 300mm or more
Sports subjects at varying distances	Zoom, perhaps a 70 to 200mm
Head and shoulder portraits	Anything from 35 to 135mm, depending on camera to subject distance, preferably a fast lens with wide aperture
Large groups or families	24mm or wider
Landscape or cityscape from nearby	24mm or wider
Landscape or cityscape from far away	Basic telephoto lens, anything from 70 to 200mm
Cramped interiors	24mm or wider, superwide if distortion is acceptable

spot of each gives photographers more control and options in picturemaking.

LENS FEATURES

Regardless of what lens is on a camera, there are some general features to consider. Every lens has a minimum focus distance, which is the shortest distance from the sensor to the subject at which the lens can focus. In macrophotography, a smaller minimum focus distance means more magnification of the subject, which might be desirable when photographing flower parts, insects, or other tiny objects with which you'd like to fill the frame.

The "speed" of the lens refers to the size of the widest aperture the lens can achieve. The wider the aperture, the more light can enter the lens, meaning a faster shutter speed can be used, and therefore the lens is referred to as "fast." Faster lenses—those capable of f/1.8 or wider—tend to be more expensive than others, as their focusing elements are more complex, and the body of the lens needs to be longer to accommodate a wider opening.

What lens you choose depends on the subject matter you plan to photograph, the circumstances, and the desired effect. Most lenses have some flexibility, but there are general situations that make optimal use of each.

Remember that making the best photograph you can with the lens you have is much better than not making one at all. But the more familiar you are with lenses, their angles of view and other properties, the more you will be able to envision photographs as you'd like them to look, and quickly identify the right tool for the job.

TECHNOLOGY OF FOCUS

Elements within the lens work together to focus an image on the sensor, and there are a variety of options as to how that focus is achieved.

The vivid colors throughout the frame and the crisp contrast on this reveler's face in this image made during Mardi Gras create an optimum environment for autofocus, which the photographer used to bring the eyes into sharp focus.

▶ FOR MORE ON CONTROLLING DEPTH OF FIELD, SEE PAGES 238–9

▶ FOR MORE ON THE LENS, SEE PAGES 222–3

One element that is nonnegotiable is focus. When you look at a photograph at 100 percent magnification on your computer, the subject is either in focus or it isn't. Focus can be used creatively. It draws the viewer's attention to what's important in the frame, and its absence can be used to blur and obfuscate distracting elements. Although focus is a matter of light and physics, it is technology that allows us to control it.

A camera's lens has a series of elements or glass layers that work together to focus an image. Everything in the scene that is the same distance from the sensor as the focused subject will also be sharp. This is called the focal plane, and its depth varies depending on the depth of field (controlled by lens focal length and aperture).

Photographers can manually achieve focus of a subject, or the camera can do it automatically. In the case of manual focus, the photographer turns the focus ring on the lens barrel, which moves the necessary elements within the lens.

ZOOM IN

▶ Pick a single subject in an empty field and manually focus on it using your eye and the lens focus ring. Then, let the camera autofocus on the same point. Given the circumstances, which process was more accurate and efficient?

Manual focus is useful in situations where the human eye is more adept than a camera, such as areas with a lack of contrast—a cloudless sky or a still pool of water—or in scenarios with insufficient light, making it difficult to discern between subjects. With autofocus (AF), the camera will move elements in the lens to achieve sharpness for the subject. Today's digital cameras autofocus using either "phase-detection" or "contrast-based," achieving focus by distance and contrast measurements, respectively, within the scene. Some cameras use a combination of the two.

Most cameras feature a variety of focus area modes for different circumstances. With single-point AF, the photographer can choose one point in the frame on which to focus. Dynamic-area AF also focuses on one point but has other focus points active in case the subject moves within the frame. In auto-area AF, the camera does all the work and decides on what point to focus. This strips all control from the photographer; the camera may make the wrong decision about where the interest lies.

There are two ways to activate autofocus in most cameras: single-shot AF and continuous AF. To initiate these, the photographer depresses the shutter button half-way and holds it to set the focus on an object within the frame. With single-shot AF, this focal point is held until the shutter is triggered, even if the photographer reframes. With continuous AF, the camera will continue to adjust focus if either the camera or the subject moves, up until the shutter is triggered—good for tracking moving subjects.

Reindeer footprints create snow sculptures in an all-white landscape in Norway. With very little contrast, a scene like this may be more accurately focused manually.

APERTURE & DEPTH OF FIELD

More than determining the amount of light to pass through the lens, the aperture is a major factor in depth of field, or how much of the image is in focus.

▶ FOR MORE ON LAYER-ING, SEE PAGES 56–7

▶ FOR MORE ON THE TECHNOLOGY OF FOCUS, SEE PAGES 234–5

The aperture is the size of the opening in the diaphragm of the lens. The wider the aperture, the more light enters the camera. A series of f-stops denote aperture sizes. Counterintuitively, the f-stop number gets bigger as the aperture opening itself gets smaller. The standard f-stops, from largest to smallest, are f/1.4, f/2, f/2.8, f/4, f/5.6, f/8, f/11, f/16, and f/22.

But what is the impact of aperture size? Other than the amount of light it lets in (which will ultimately be balanced by shutter speed to determine exposure), the size of the aperture has a direct impact on depth of field. Depth of field refers to the degree to which objects in front of and behind the plane of focus are also sharp.

The larger the aperture, the shallower the depth of field. The smaller the aperture, the greater the depth of field, resulting in all or most of the image in focus. For example, imagine a

This stunning view from China was created with a small aperture, yielding lots of depth of field, with everything from the window frame to the distant mountains in focus.

scene with three men. George is standing in front of David who is standing in front of Tim. If all three of them are in focus, the image has a great depth of field, likely with a small f-stop of f/16 or f/22. If only David is in sharp focus and both George and Tim are blurred, the image has a shallow depth of field, with perhaps an f-stop of f/4 or larger.

Interestingly, the distance that objects remain sharp in front of the plane of focus is much shorter than the distance that objects remain sharp behind the plane of focus. One-third of the depth of field is in front of the plane of focus, and two-thirds is behind. This is useful to remember when composing with layers in an image.

Other factors that impact depth of field are the focal length of the lens and the camera to subject distance, where depth of field decreases the closer you are to the subject. The more you understand depth of field—what determines it and its impact on an image—the more creative control you will have to direct viewers' attention in your photographs.

Making good use of a wide aperture and shallow depth of field, the photographer captured only this man's hands in focus. His cane and sweater fade into softness.

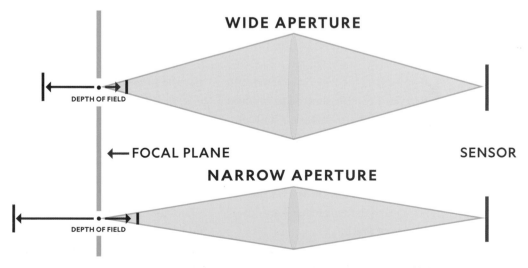

WIDE APERTURE

DEPTH OF FIELD

← FOCAL PLANE   SENSOR

NARROW APERTURE

DEPTH OF FIELD

A wider aperture has a shorter depth of field, and a smaller aperture has a greater depth of field. In both cases, the range of focus is situated one-third in front of the focal point and two-thirds behind it.

CONTROLLING DEPTH OF FIELD

Multiple factors determine depth of field, all of which should be considered in choosing the lens best suited for the circumstance at hand.

This lone tree in a field of lavender in southern France is far enough away from the camera that the photo's depth of field begins well in front of the tree and extends beyond it into the distance.

▶ FOR MORE ON LANDSCAPES, SEE PAGES 152-3

▶ FOR MORE ON PORTRAITS, SEE PAGES 112-13

Knowing all the ways in which depth of field can be controlled enables photographers to dictate which elements in an image are in focus, and in turn, direct viewers' attention. In addition to aperture, the focal length of the lens and distance from the subject at which the lens is focused have an impact on depth of field.

Longer lenses have shorter depth of field. Specifically, a large aperture on a long lens has a shorter depth of field than the same aperture on a wide-angle lens. In this way, a long lens may be focused on a subject in the distance, leaving the foreground and background soft, while a wide-angle lens not only captures more of the world, it also keeps more of it in focus.

Further complicating the depth of field story, the camera's distance from the subject in focus affects how much territory will also be in focus in front of and behind it. At the same f-stop, focus-

DEPTH OF FIELD AS A FUNCTION OF APERTURE

DEPTH OF FIELD AS A FUNCTION OF FOCAL LENGTH

DEPTH OF FIELD AS A FUNCTION OF FOCUSING DISTANCE

Aperture, focal length, and camera to subject distance all impact depth of field. A long lens at close range with a wide f-stop has the least depth of field; a wide lens focused farther with a small f-stop has much more.

ing on a subject close to the camera will yield a shallower depth of field than focusing on a subject farther away from the camera.

PUTTING IT ALL TOGETHER
A longer lens at a large aperture, an 85mm at f/4 for example, focused on a subject close to the camera will have very little depth of field—perfect perhaps for a head-and-shoulders portrait made at a distance of about 10 feet. A wide-angle lens with a small aperture, perhaps a 20mm at f/16, focused on a point in the distance will have greater depth of field—just right for a notable building or monument.

There are many creative ways to put depth of field to use in an image, but there are some tried-and-true applications. Landscapes are typically served well by wide-angle lenses and small apertures, resulting in lots of detail in focus well into the distance. Portraits, on the other hand, are very effective with longer lenses and/ or wide apertures—keeping the subject's face sharp, while allowing the background to fade into softness. A general rule in portrait photography is that the eyes should be the sharpest part of the frame, so place the point of focus squarely on your subject's eye for an impactful image that will grab the viewer's attention.

ZOOM IN

▶ Stand in one place and focus on a distant subject. Use two different focal lengths at f/5.6. Compare depth of field. Next, use one lens at f/8, making photographs at various distances from the subject. Compare depth of field.

SHUTTER SPEED

Shutter speed is the agent of movement in a photograph, used to freeze fast action or animate motion with a soft blur throughout the frame.

▶ FOR MORE ON TRIPODS, SEE PAGES 280-81

▶ FOR MORE ON PANNING, SEE PAGES 308-309

The shutter speed controls the length of time the curtain in the camera remains open, allowing light to reach the sensor. It is fully adjustable, and you can select the shutter speed or have the camera make the selection in a full or partially automatic mode.

Shutter speeds are measured in seconds or fractions of a second and are indicated in the camera's informational displays. Common shutter speeds include, from slow to fast: 1 second, 1/2 second, 1/4, 1/8, 1/15, 1/30, 1/60, 1/125, 1/250, 1/500, and 1/1000 second. Most digital cameras also allow for shutter speeds in between and beyond these as well.

CREATIVE USES OF SHUTTER SPEED

Shutter speed works in concert with aperture to determine the exposure of the image. But ultimately, shutter speed is a creative tool to illustrate time in a photograph.

A fast shutter speed—something like 1/500 or more—freezes fast action like a runner mid-stride, a dog leaping to catch a Frisbee, or droplets of water flying from a sprinkler on the lawn. Freezing moving elements captures a view of a moment that would otherwise be fleeting.

A slower shutter speed—around 1/30 or slower—adds the dynamic element of motion to a still frame, by softly blurring anything that moves, like flowing water, prairie grasses rustling in the breeze, or a dancer's skirt during a spin. At slower shutter speeds, a stabilizer—like a tripod or any sturdy surface that can support a camera while it's framing the subject—is needed to prevent camera movement, unless the photographer chooses to pan, which is another technique that illustrates motion by freezing the subject and blurring the background.

PRIORITIZING SHUTTER SPEED

Photographers should carefully consider the nature of a subject before committing to a shutter speed setting or allowing the camera to do so. For particularly fast-moving subjects or if your intention is to blur motion, prioritize your shutter speed when making choices to determine exposure.

ZOOM IN

▶ Pick a moving subject and play with the depiction of movement, freezing the action with a fast shutter speed or allowing it to blur with a slow shutter speed. Which contributes best to the story of the image?

A tripod and a slow shutter speed render this kingfisher mid-dive as an abstract blue smudge, but the context and pointy beak provide enough detail so that the story of the image is clear.

CONTROLLING SHUTTER SPEED

The key to using shutter speed as a creative tool to illustrate movement is to understand its role in exposure and balance it accordingly.

A slow shutter speed captures the busy pace of this street scene in Kolkata, India. The fastest moving elements—the train, a cart with passengers, and a rushing pedestrian—add artful blur.

▶ FOR MORE ON USING FILTERS, SEE PAGES 290–91

▶ FOR MORE ON EXPOSURE COMPENSATION, SEE PAGES 254–5

In any photograph where time or movement is central to the theme of the image, shutter speed is a photographer's best creative tool, and because of its role in the exposure equation, the aperture should be set to balance it. Shutter speed and aperture are inversely proportional—that is, the longer the shutter is open to let light into the sensor, the smaller the aperture needs to be, to restrict the amount of light coming through the lens. The opposite is also true—the shorter the shutter speed, the larger the aperture needs to be.

OPTIMAL SHUTTER SPEEDS		
SLOW SHUTTER SPEEDS	AVERAGE SHUTTER SPEEDS	FAST SHUTTER SPEEDS
Use 1/60 or slower to blur subjects in motion, but anything slower than 1 second may blur motion beyond recognition.	Use 1/125 to 1/350 to freeze subjects that are still or not moving very fast, or to blur motion of fast-moving subjects.	Use 1/500 or faster to freeze fast-moving subjects. Shutter speeds of 1/1000 or more will require a lot of ambient light.
1/4 second	1/60 second (still subjects)	1/500 second
1/8 second	1/125 second	1/1000 second
1/15 second	1/250 second	1/1500 second
1/30 second	1/350 second	1/2000 second

If one pairing of shutter speed and aperture results in the exposure you like and you want to change the shutter speed, you'll move the aperture in the opposite direction to compensate. For example, if f/8 at 1/125 yields the correct exposure but you'd like to freeze some action, you will move the shutter speed to 1/500 (two stops down) and move the f-stop to f/4 (two stops up).

ADJUSTING FOR OPTIMAL SHUTTER SPEED

You will encounter circumstances where there is too much or too little light for the shutter speed you'd like to use, and not enough aperture options to compensate. Imagine you want to blur a waterfall in the middle of the day. You'll need a slow shutter speed for the job, perhaps 1/30 or slower. You try f/22, but there's still too much light. Ideally, you'd return to the scene at dawn or dusk when less light would prevent overexposure, but what if you can't? First, be sure the ISO is set as low as your camera will allow. If the scene is still too bright for a slow shutter speed, try a neutral density filter to block more of the light, or adjust the exposure compensation function.

Speeding up or slowing down shutter speed to freeze or animate movement can produce dramatic results, but to use it to its fullest potential, you must understand the nature of exposure and everything that influences it.

A fast shutter speed freezes this Colorado skateboarder in midair at the peak moment of his trick. Great composition places the subject well above the horizon for a clean background.

Part of a story on "Teenage Brains" in *National Geographic*, this photograph shows a 12th grader waiting at a stoplight in downtown Austin, Texas.

WHY I LOVE THIS PHOTO

This image is an excellent example of how a challenging exposure situation can be used to the photographer's advantage. It's a seemingly ordinary moment, but the combination of good technical choices makes this a powerful photo by Kitra Cahana. The use of available light in an otherwise very dark setting helps create mood—it's dramatic, quiet, and mysterious at the same time. The shallow depth of field of this portrait integrates the teen into the landscape in which she is traveling. This choice also gives context for how the photo is made (the portrait is a reflection in the vehicle's mirror), but as a viewer, I'm taking in the entire scene—the blurred nightlife, the cars rolling through the intersection, and the focused gaze of the teen out into the street. Where is she going? What is she thinking?

—JILL FOLEY
Photo Editor, National Geographic Books

ISO SENSITIVITY

When there isn't enough available light for your chosen aperture and shutter speed combination, look to ISO to "buy" more light.

▶ FOR MORE
ON AFTER
SUNSET, SEE
PAGES 312–13

▶ FOR MORE
ON LOW
LIGHT, SEE
PAGES 86–7

Photographers use aperture and shutter speed to create exposure, giving priority to the settings that will best serve the image. But when available light doesn't support those choices, ISO—the third part of the exposure equation—comes into play.

Put simply, ISO refers to the sensor's sensitivity to light. The higher the ISO number, the brighter the images will be. Adjusting the ISO is most useful when the scene doesn't have enough light to produce a viable exposure with the aperture and shutter speed of choice. In this way, think of ISO as a way to "buy" more light. For example, imagine photographing a horse galloping along the beach at sunset. In an effort to freeze the horse in mid-stride, you select a shutter speed of 1/500, which requires an aperture of f/4 for a decent exposure. But, say you'd like more

Bumping up the ISO to 800 or higher makes an image in low light possible without introducing blur or losing depth of field because of slow shutter speeds or overly wide apertures.

depth of field than that produces. Enter ISO. By adjusting the ISO up to about 800 or 1,000, you can now use a shutter speed of 1/500 at an aperture of f/8 or f/11.

But raising ISO comes with a cost. If set too high, the image will be grainy or full of noise. This may be effective in some situations, perhaps a darker scene with a lot of mood. And sometimes, it's worth accepting noise to make an image possible. In general, ISO should only be raised when your preferred settings won't work with the available light.

Every camera has a base ISO—its lowest native ISO setting, and the setting at which the highest-quality image with the least amount of noise is created. This should always be your starting point unless you need to buy more light. As you become familiar with the amount of light your camera requires at specific apertures and shutter speeds, your selection of ISO will become second nature, and something you can do before you begin working in a given situation.

The most common ISO settings are as follows:

A high ISO allows detail to be seen even in the shadows of this Buddhist monk's hands as he lights candles in a dimly lit monastery in Bhutan.

COMMON ISO SETTINGS

ISO SETTING	COMMON USES
100	Bright daylight
200	Bright daylight
400	Cloudy day or indoors in a bright room
800	Very cloudy day, dusk, or indoors
1600	Evening or indoors
3200	Indoors or nighttime
6400	Nighttime or star photography

Many cameras can go even higher, but the noise at these settings may be unacceptable for your goals. The doubling of each ISO number equals one stop and can be integrated into the exposure equation. For example, if your camera is set to ISO 200 and you'd like to use an aperture of f/8 and shutter speed of 1/500 but the exposure is a little too dark, you can bump the ISO up to 400 and buy one more stop of light.

When in doubt, use the lowest ISO setting you can to ensure quality and reduced noise. But, keep in mind that sensors are becoming more capable of handling low light and high ISO numbers, so don't be afraid to experiment in pursuit of your creative vision.

METERING

Directed by the photographer, a camera's internal metering system can evaluate light in a scene in a variety of ways for maximum control of exposure.

EVALUATIVE/MATRIX METERING

CENTER-WEIGHTED METERING

SPOT METERING

Evaluative or matrix metering assesses light in the entire scene by breaking it into zones. Center-weighted metering evaluates the center of the frame, and spot metering reads a single point for reflectivity of light.

▶ FOR MORE ON ISO SEN-SITIVITY, SEE PAGES 246–7

▶ FOR MORE ON EXPO-SURE, SEE PAGES 230–31

A light meter is used to measure the brightness of an object or a scene. If set to an automatic mode, the camera will designate settings for ISO, aperture, and shutter speed based on its meter reading. Alternatively, a photographer can select these settings manually, consciously deciding which areas of the image should dictate the exposure to tell the story in the most compelling way. Most photographers use the camera's internal meter to interpret light in the scene, but it's also possible to use a separate, accessory light meter. Light, and the way it plays in a scene and on different objects, can be com-plex and varied. As a result, meters have continued to evolve, adopting better methods of registering light, giving photographers greater control over how to analyze the scene.

MATRIX OR EVALUATIVE METERING

Matrix (Nikon) or evaluative (Canon) metering works by dividing the scene into several zones, each of which is ana-lyzed for dark and light areas within. Exposure suggestions are based on an average of these areas. Some camera models will give more priority to the zone that contains the point of focus.

The aim of multi-zoned metering is to give the final image an overall balanced exposure, which can be a challenge when there are areas of extreme light or extreme shadow.

CENTER-WEIGHTED METERING

Center-weighted metering evaluates the center of the frame for exposure, ignoring the corners, regardless of where the focal point is. This option works best for portraits or landscapes, when the main subject is in the center or nearly fills the frame.

SPOT METERING

Spot metering evaluates light on a single point, calculating exposure based on the focal point (which is determined by the photographer manually or by autofocusing on that point), and ignores everything else in the scene. Spot metering is very effective for emphasizing the focal point of the image with exposure. It works well with a small subject that has a vastly different reflectivity than the rest of the scene, like the bright moon against dark sky, or the face of a child backlit by the sun at the beach. Some models of DSLRs offer multi-spot metering, which allows for analyzing more than one small point, then calculates an exposure based on an average value of those points.

Regardless of which metering mode you employ, such detailed information about how the camera sees and interprets the light in a scene allows photographers to harness the power of exposure for maximum effect.

Spot metering for the yellow centers of these daisies ensured that they were exposed properly as the focal points of the image. The petals are slightly overexposed, bright white frames against a dark backdrop.

RANGE OF LIGHT/ HISTOGRAM

The histogram analyzes the amount of information in the brightest and darkest areas of an image, along with all the areas in between.

▶ FOR MORE ON EXPOSURE CHALLENGES, SEE PAGES 256-7

▶ FOR MORE ON TYPES OF CAMERAS, SEE PAGES 214-15

The camera works similarly to the human eye—light comes through the lens and lands on the sensor, which processes the scene in front of the camera, recording it as a picture. The camera, though, lacks the nuanced interpretive capabilities of the human brain—for now at least!

The term "dynamic range" is used to describe the range of light, or the array of various tones of brightness between the darkest and brightest areas of the image. And although camera sensors have a narrower dynamic range than the human brain can register, advances in technology are rapidly increasing

These two photographs have peaks at the two extremes of the histogram, with a lot of information in the highlights (left) and shadows (right). Both are exposed properly, given the context of each scene.

their sensitivity to the subtleties of light in a scene. To help photographers analyze the range of light in a situation they wish to photograph, many cameras will display a histogram. Learning to read a histogram helps not only as you are taking a picture but also later, as you are editing it.

HOW TO READ A HISTOGRAM

A histogram is a graphical representation of information in the various tones between pure black and pure white in a photograph. The darker tones are displayed on the left side of the graph and the lighter tones are on the right. The middle of the histogram represents the mid-tones in the image.

The tonal range of the image is represented by a curve, the bell of which indicates where the majority of information in the photo resides. If the histogram indicates a lot of information to the far left or far right of the graph, visible detail is likely lost in either dark shadows or blown-out highlights, respectively.

Although the histogram is an indicator of exposure, it's not the whole story. A sharp peak to the left or right of the histogram is typically interpreted as underexposure or overexposure, but it's important to remember that the graph is simply reporting where the most pixels are located in the range of light.

For example, in a photograph of a child playing at the beach that has been exposed for the child's face, the sky may be totally overexposed, resulting in a sharp peak to the right. In a photograph of a white ceramic vase sitting on a brightly lit white backdrop, the histogram

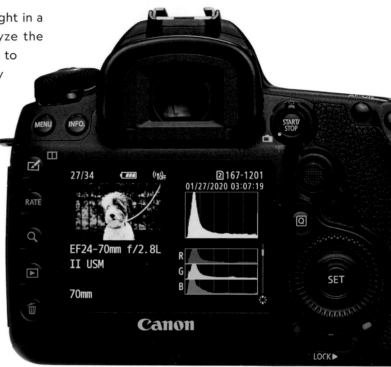

This LCD screen shows a typical histogram for a photograph with a lot of information in the shadows. The RGB histogram scales at bottom indicate the brightness and density of the primary colors in the image.

may also show a sharp peak to the right, but this image is properly exposed.

Most DSLR cameras can display the captured photograph with its histogram beside it in the LCD screen. Many cameras with electronic viewfinders (EVF) can display a histogram for the scene as the photographer is framing it, providing information in real time as creative decisions are being made.

A lot of valuable information can be mined from the technology and tools available in a digital camera. But remember that a photographer's first and best tool is vision. Rely on your eyes to make creative choices, and then refer to the camera's adjustments and guides to help achieve technical success.

CAMERA MODES

Most cameras have a variety of modes, ranging from fully automatic to fully manual, with some great efficiency options in between.

Having the camera set and ready to go for the circumstance enabled the photographer to capture this fleeting and powerful moment, juxtaposing young and old in stunning window light.

▶ FOR MORE
ON WHITE
BALANCE,
SEE PAGES
258–9

▶ FOR MORE
ON MACRO-
PHOTOGRA-
PHY, SEE
PAGES 288–9

All cameras have a variety of exposure modes. Some of these are fully automatic, giving the camera full control of settings, whereas others are partially automatic, giving photographers control of one or two exposure elements, and then the camera sets the rest to balance exposure.

To learn the nuances of exposure, practice in a fully manual mode. But for efficiency on the fly, don't overlook some of these shortcut modes that calibrate settings to your creative choices:

AUTO Fully automatic, the camera selects ISO, aperture, shutter speed, white balance, and flash. This setting is fine for quick snapshots if you're unsure of what settings you need, but most of the time you will want more control. Usually designated by AUTO on the mode dial.

─── **ZOOM IN** ───

▶ Consider the types of circumstances in which you most frequently make photographs, and think about which setting is most useful for these. Leave your camera set there as a default.

PROGRAM The camera sets the aperture and shutter speed, while the photographer sets the ISO, white balance, and flash option. Usually P on the mode dial.

PORTRAIT A fully automatic mode where the camera selects a wide aperture for shallow depth of field—effective for portraits with soft, blurred backgrounds. Some cameras have facial-recognition technology in this mode, automatically focusing on the face in the frame. Usually designated by a portrait icon on the mode dial.

SPORT OR ACTION A fully automatic mode where the camera selects a fast shutter speed to freeze moving subjects. Some cameras may even set an increased fps (frames per second) rate, or adjust the autofocus to continuous AF in this mode. Usually designated by a running figure icon on the mode dial.

MACRO Usually found on point-and-shoot cameras, this mode adjusts to focus on objects close to the camera for magnification, such as flowers, insects, or other small subjects. Not usually found on a DSLR on which the MFD (minimum focus distance) is determined by the lens attached. Usually designated by a flower icon on the mode dial.

LANDSCAPE A fully automatic mode where the camera selects a small aperture for great depth of field. This works well for broad scenic views. Usually designated by a mountain icon on the mode dial.

APERTURE PRIORITY A partially automatic mode where the photographer selects the ISO and aperture, and the camera adjusts the shutter speed for proper exposure. This is a great choice when aperture and depth of field are a priority in the photograph, such as with portraits , which often benefit from shallow depth of field, or landscapes, which usually benefit from greater depth of field. Usually designated by an A or Av on the mode dial.

SHUTTER PRIORITY A partially automatic mode where the photographer selects the ISO and shutter speed, and the camera adjusts the aperture for proper exposure. This is a great choice when photographing fast-moving subjects whose action you'd like to freeze or blur, especially in variable lighting conditions. Usually designated by an S or Tv on the mode dial.

MANUAL The photographer sets each parameter including ISO, aperture, shutter speed, white balance, and whether to use a flash. This mode allows for the most control in picturemaking. Usually designated by an M on the mode dial.

Different brands and models of cameras may have slightly different mode options, or they may represent them a little differently, so pull out your manual to learn the options on the camera you have. Note that many smartphones currently have these options and more, giving you the chance to stay in a completely photographic mindset no matter what camera you have on hand.

EXPOSURE COMPENSATION

Exposure compensation allows photographers to maintain creative control of exposure, even when working in an automatic mode.

▶ FOR MORE ON CAMERA MODES, SEE PAGES 252-3

▶ FOR MORE ON CONTROLLING DEPTH OF FIELD, SEE PAGES 238-9

When working in an automatic mode or one of the priority modes, the camera is doing all or a portion of the setting selection based on its internal light meter and what it deems as the proper exposure. But because exposure is a matter of personal preference, photographers may want to override what the camera has decided and push the exposure in one way or another.

ADJUSTING EXPOSURE

To this end, most DSLR and mirrorless cameras have a useful feature called exposure compensation. This function is usually accessible by a button or dial on the top or back of the camera, indi-

-2   -1   0   +1   +2

EXPOSURE COMPENSATION SETTINGS

By varying exposure compensation under or over the camera's normal exposure setting, a photographer can tweak the resulting image to highlight anything. In this case, trees, castle, or sky get different emphasis depending on the exposure compensation setting.

A camera might underexpose this image in response to the bright white snow, but the photographer can select an exposure compensation of +1 or more to overexpose the image, exposing for the bird.

cated by a box with + – signs within. The function allows the photographer to tweak the exposure up or down in an automatic or partially automatic mode, without adjusting any other settings.

Imagine photographing a child at the beach, and depth of field is the priority for the image. You'd like a shallow depth of field, so you pop the camera into A (aperture priority) and set the aperture to f/5.6, letting the camera select the corresponding shutter speed as light changes with passing clouds. As you work, you decide you'd like the exposure to be a little brighter. By activating exposure compensation, you can adjust the exposure as you wish with a push of the button or turn of the dial. If you select +1, the camera will adjust to consistently "overexpose" the captures by one stop, no matter which aperture you choose.

INCREASED CONTROL

Exposure compensation is displayed as –1.0, –0.7, –0.3, 0.0, +0.3, +0.7, +1.0, where +1.0 is one stop lighter than the optimal exposure as selected by the camera. Typically, by using this function, the exposure can be compensated from three full stops under the optimal, to three full stops over, in steps of roughly one-third. A word of caution: Always remember to return the exposure compensation to 0.0 after a session, or you may risk the first exposures of your next session.

Exposure compensation affords photographers the freedom to work in a fully or partially automatic mode and to quickly override the camera to tweak exposure to personal preference. Understanding this function and its potential adds an element of temporary control back into a conveniently automatic mode.

EXPOSURE CHALLENGES

In scenes that contain both very bright and very dark areas, a photographer must make a choice about exposure, and compensate with context, composition, and framing.

Documenting a cooking school in China, the photographer had to choose between the bright flames and the darker areas, which contain more important content. Exposing for the faces of the students made the most sense.

▶ FOR MORE ON USING FLASH, SEE PAGES 292-3

▶ FOR MORE ON ISO SENSITIVITY, SEE PAGES 246-7

Regardless of a photographer's proficiency, some scenes and situations will present exposure challenges. These scenarios occur when the range of light in a scene exceeds the sensor's latitude of sensitivity, or when the disparity of light in different areas makes balance nearly impossible. Unless you're able to add or remove light from a scene, these situations require making a choice about what to emphasize in the

frame and what can be sacrificed or handled with a change in composition. A thorough understanding of the camera's functions and limitations, as well as potential solutions, will help in these thorny circumstances.

Because extreme light challenges highlight the camera's limitations in both analysis and capture, they will be most problematic when working in automatic or partially automatic

TRICKY EXPOSURE SITUATIONS

SITUATION	EXPOSURE CHALLENGE	SOLUTION	RESULT
Snow-covered ground on a sunny day	Underexposure: Camera meter will attempt to average exposure; bright white turns to gray.	Increase exposure with exposure compensation, or by manually adjusting ISO, aperture, or shutter speed.	Snowfield will appear bright white as it does to the eye; some detail in trees and shadows will be apparent.
Person on a beach surrounded by bright sand and sky	Underexposure of person will occur.	• Expose for person by increasing exposure with exposure compensation, or by manually adjusting ISO, aperture, or shutter speed. • Expose for sand and sky.	• Person will be a strong focal point, properly exposed surrounded by washed-out sand and sky. Pay attention to composition to balance and capitalize on white negative space. • Person will be silhouetted. Pay attention to shapes and separation of dark objects for impact.
Lit person against a dark background (e.g., dark building, water, darkened theater stage, or cliff face)	Overexposure of person will occur.	Decrease exposure to prevent washout of the person by using exposure compensation, or by manually adjusting ISO, aperture, or shutter speed.	Person will be well exposed; detail may be lost in dark surroundings. Compose to balance and capitalize on dark, negative space.
Landscape beneath hazy bright sky or with sun in the frame	Underexposure of landmass beneath sky will occur.	Expose for landmass by increasing exposure with exposure compensation, or by manually adjusting ISO, aperture, or shutter speed.	Landmass will be properly exposed with washed-out sky above. Pay attention to composition: Raise horizon to reduce sky and balance white negative space.

modes. With small subjects against extremely light or dark backgrounds, the spot-meter function will serve best to indicate proper exposure for the subject, ignoring input from the rest of the frame.

Exposure challenges can be most easily managed, however, by manually adjusting settings, which gives photographers ultimate control over exposure of their images. The degree to which you adjust the settings will depend on the circumstance. Your best bet is to experiment and get a feel for the results you prefer. Practice and regularly review your results, and soon, you will begin to assess and make choices in extreme lighting situations as a matter of course. Over time, you may begin to prefer the creative control that working in a manual mode allows, and the practice will help you gain confidence in your picturemaking, no matter what light challenge you are given.

WHITE BALANCE

White balance is a quick way to compensate for undesirable color casts created by varying light sources. When the color of light doesn't help a photograph, white balance will correct it.

▶ FOR MORE ON COLOR OF LIGHT, SEE PAGES 74–5

▶ FOR MORE ON GLOBAL ADJUSTMENTS, SEE PAGES 364–5

Remember that different light sources emit light of different hues. The human brain can correct for those differences, but the camera doesn't. The camera registers the color of the light, and the cast on everything it touches.

For example, a lamp with an incandescent bulb casts a yellow hue onto the white wall beside it. The brain registers the wall as white, and so we "see" it that way. The camera is more literal—it captures the true color of the wall as lit by the lamp. In addition, all the other objects in the scene will appear with the same color cast, altering their true appearance relative to the version of white that the camera has recorded—something that is actually blue might appear green in the photograph, for instance.

The same holds true for other types of light, either artificial or sunlight that is altered by cloud cover or time of day. Sometimes the color of light is important to the story or mood of an image, but when it isn't, there is a tool to correct it.

LIGHT COLOR CORRECTION

White balance is the mechanism by which the camera can autocorrect for the color of light. It's used to indicate which color in the frame should register as white, and after that adjustment, all the other colors are corrected

TOO WARM   DAYLIGHT   TOO COOL

In these three images made in consistent light, a change in the camera's white balance setting altered the color cast noticeably.

Different types of light bulbs, as shown here, have different color temperatures, which ultimately affect the look of their surroundings. In a gallery, a consistent color temperature is critical in lighting art.

accordingly. White balance can be set in advance of capture to adjust the way the image is recorded or it can also be done during post-production editing.

Most DSLR cameras have preprogrammed white balance settings that can adjust for color shifts in shade, fluorescent lighting, incandescent or tungsten lighting, and more. The function compensates for a particular color cast by adding the opposite color to the image. For example, fluorescent bulbs emit green-blue light, so the white balance setting will add a slight magenta cast to the image. This corrects the green-blue tone to white. Most cameras also have an automatic white balance setting (AWB), which is set according to what type of light the camera detects.

ASSESSING YOUR SOURCE

If your light source is consistent, it's a good idea to set the white balance for the circumstance before choosing the other camera settings. Especially outside, the color of light can shift

quickly and frequently. Although it's recommended to make the best picture on capture, don't miss opportunities while making this particular adjustment. More than most other adjustments, white balance is very easily correctable in the editing phase.

COLOR TEMPERATURES		
KELVIN	LIGHTING CONDITIONS	COLOR CAST
10000	Clear blue sky	
6500	Cloudy sky	
5500	Daylight/Midday sun	
4000	Moonlight/Fluorescent	
3500	Morning/Evening sun	
3200	Tungsten bulb	
2500	Sunrise/Sunset	
2200	Streetlight	
1900	Candlelight	

ASSIGNMENT

A scene like this one along the Mekong River at dusk leaves a photographer
with many creative choices, all of which influence the story being told.

CREATIVE
EXPOSURE WALK

Take a walk with your camera and identify a scene with variable areas of light. Make a photograph with the camera in a fully automatic mode and matrix or evaluative metering (if your camera has it). Study the image in the playback screen and notice how the different areas are exposed as a result of the camera's assessment of the scene. Observe which areas are very bright, very dark, and exposed properly.

ONE BY ONE Then, select different areas of the frame and adjust the camera's controls to properly expose each in subsequent photographs. Use different methods to change the exposure, including adjustments in aperture, shutter speed, ISO, and the exposure compensation function. If you're using a smartphone, tap the area of the screen for which you'd like to expose the image.

As you expose for different parts of the image, note how the lighter or darker areas of the image are impacted. How does a different exposure change the feel or story of the image? Think about which settings you prefer, and why.

EXPLORE POSSIBILITIES With each exposure adjustment, note how the camera's meter assesses the image. Switch from matrix or evaluative metering to center-weighted, then to spot metering, observing how the meter assesses the exposure of the frame. Review each photograph with the histogram function display on the back of the camera, if possible.

CHAPTER NINE

CHOOSING YOUR
EQUIPMENT

One of the questions most asked of professional photographers is, "Which camera should I buy?" The truth is, there is no easy answer to that question and no one-size-fits-all piece of equipment. The choice you make should be based squarely on two things: (1) your goals as a photographer and (2) your budget.

When considering your photographic goals, it is critical to understand your own photographic inclinations—that is, what appeals to you visually, what kind of photographs you most enjoy making, and what techniques and styles contribute to your overall voice as a photographer.

Accessibility, usability, and portability are all important factors to consider when purchasing equipment. You likely won't use gear that is frustrating to operate, or that cannot be carried easily, so keep comfort and mobility in mind.

Before making an investment in new equipment for young photographers, make sure that they are making the most of whatever they currently use—most likely a smartphone. Remember that young people typically have active, on-the-go lives, full of variety and adventures. If someone feels burdened by cumbersome equipment, their creativity may be stifled and they may not make photographs at all.

Equipment is important, but it's not a substitute for the reflection, hard work, and time that go into identifying your unique voice and making photographs with impact. With a strong sense of what you're trying to say and a mastery of composition, exposure, and moment, you can make powerful images with whatever camera is available.

To portray Vessel, architectural centerpiece of New York City's Hudson Yards, the photographer has used its stairwell honeycomb as a dramatic frame around visitors and the Hudson River beyond.

CAMERA BODIES

Central to your photographic practice is a camera body. Pick the one that will give you freedom to make photographs you'll love for years to come.

Photographer Tim Laman, who often works in remote and wet locations, needs a camera body that can handle long lenses, have fast and accurate focus, and be stowed in a pack as he hikes many miles into the jungle.

▶ FOR MORE ON RANGE OF LIGHT/ HISTOGRAM, SEE PAGES 250–51

▶ FOR MORE ON PREPARING FILES FOR PRINT SERVICE, SEE PAGES 380–81

At the heart of any photographic kit is a camera body. Whether it's a smartphone, a point-and-shoot, a fixed-lens, mirrorless, or a DSLR with interchangeable lenses, the camera body is the item that will set the tone for what you do and how you do it as a photographer. Whether purchasing a first camera or an upgrade, it's important to think about the type of photography you most enjoy, and set yourself up for success with the right equipment.

SIZE & TYPE

If you love landscapes, you'll want a camera body that uses interchangeable lenses and has a sensor that can handle a wide range of light. If you want to make large prints for display, a camera that produces large, detailed files is important. If street photography is your thing, you may want something small, light, and discreet that you can easily carry and pull out for quick use. Size and weight are important considerations, as the camera body should feel comfortable in your hands. If you frequently use a tripod, however, the size of the camera body may not matter as much as having a decent bag to help transport it.

PERFORMANCE & FUNCTION

Making photographs in low light or of the night sky requires a camera with an excellent sensor and low noise at high ISOs. Street photographers like cameras with speedy and accurate autofocus. If you value being able to operate your camera remotely, or having quick, wireless access to the images you've made for instant sharing via smartphone, near-field communication (NFC) is a must.

RESEARCH & DEVELOPMENT

Read reviews and speak with other photographers and experts at photo houses to help you decide which brand and model might be best for you, keeping your own needs and preferences in mind. Consider your equipment kit as a work in progress, and as such, you'll want to choose and commit to a brand that you can grow with, add to, and be able to use for a very long time.

These young people in Tokyo have small point-and-shoot cameras they can keep in a pocket or on a light, decorative chain. Their cameras include features like live view and zoom lenses.

—— **ZOOM IN** ——

▶ Identify other photographers who make the same kind of photographs you most love to make. Conduct a survey about which camera brands and models they prefer and why.

CUSTOMIZING YOUR CAMERA

Many camera bodies can be customized to meet your needs for intuitively accessing common functions. Make your camera a personal extension of your vision.

▶ FOR MORE
ON TYPES OF
CAMERAS,
SEE PAGES
214–15

▶ FOR MORE
ON CAMERA
BODIES, SEE
PAGES 264–5

Photographers think of a camera as an extension of themselves—an arm or hand that can capture images as they visualize them. To this end, it's ideal to have a camera that feels intuitive as you make creative decisions. There is often more than one way to control a particular setting, and many cameras come with undesignated buttons that can be assigned to the functions a photographer accesses most. Each brand and model is a little different with regard to which controls can be customized and how, so consult the manual for specifics.

Consider streamlining the operations of the camera body to what feels most intuitive. For example, you may want to

Different photographers have different preferences for how they access controls and what feels most intuitive for use. Many cameras allow you to customize access to most functions.

A customizable setting on the mode dial, as in U1 and U2 on the Nikon DSLR shown here, is particularly handy when you use a certain combination of settings frequently and want to return to them quickly.

reassign the dials designated to control aperture and shutter speed, or perhaps you'd like a shortcut to setting white balance. Some photographers prefer the "back button focus method," which is when they reassign autofocus to a button on the back of the camera instead of the shutter button. Many DSLRs have empty slots on the mode dial (listed as U1 and U2 on Nikon, or C1, C2, and C3 on Canon bodies, for example), which can be programmed to your most commonly used settings, such as ISO 400, f/8 at 1/125, with white balance for daylight. No matter what you've been photographing, as soon as you get back into a familiar setting, you can flip to U1 and have your settings return to whatever you've programmed them to be.

A data feature that is commonly customizable is the ability to add your name and copyright information into the metadata of the image file as it is captured. This assures your name is attached to each image file regardless of where it goes next. Another proprietary feature is the ability to customize the file names of the images. For example, John Smith may want his image files to be named "JS0001, JS0002, JS0003 . . ." and so on as the camera continues to produce photographs.

Features on the viewfinder and LCD displays also can typically be customized. For example, you might choose to add a grid for composing, to dictate the orientation of an image on playback, or select which capture information is displayed alongside it.

Customizing your equipment is about eliminating roadblocks in your creative process. Get to know your photographic habits, consult your manual, and consider the ways you can make your camera work for you.

LENSES

A lens is the front line of picturemaking and is worth the most significant investment you can make.

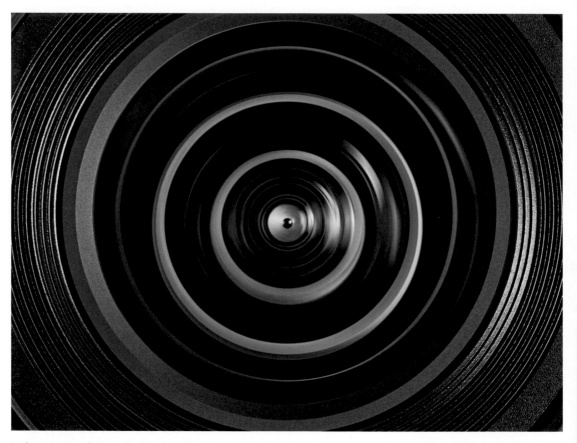

Light must travel through a lens barrel with up to 20 glass elements per lens on its way to being focused on the sensor. Quality glass is critical to preserve the integrity of the image and the accuracy of its focus.

▶ FOR MORE ON LENS OPTIONS, SEE PAGES 232-3

▶ FOR MORE ON ZOOM LENSES, SEE PAGES 278-9

The lens is the eye of the camera. Although the sensor is responsible for the quality of the image produced, the quality of the lens will determine the purity of light coming through. With as many as 20 glass elements to pass through, images will be as sharp as the flawlessness of the glass.

In general, there are three classes of lenses based on focal length: wide, normal, and telephoto. Wide lenses have shorter focal lengths, anything from 20mm to 35mm. These typically have a short minimum focus distance (MFD) and lots of depth of field, even at wider apertures. Lenses with a focal length between 50mm and 80mm are considered "normal" lenses for their angle of view, which is closest to that of the human eye.

The term "telephoto lens" is generally used to describe any lens with a long focal length. These typically have long MFD and shallower depth of field than wider lenses at the same aperture.

Prime lenses are those with a fixed focal length, whereas zoom lenses have variable focal lengths. Although the optical quality of zoom lenses has come to rival that of prime lenses in the past few years, it is also true that it's nearly impossible to find a zoom lens as "fast" as a prime lens—that is, with as wide a maximum aperture, thereby letting in the maximum amount of light possible.

MAKING THE MOST OF YOUR LENS

Many photographers believe that lenses are more important than camera bodies. Lenses often last longer than camera bodies, too. If you can only afford one lens, the best bet is to invest in a high-quality zoom that offers flexibility in focal lengths appropriate for your needs, is made of great glass, and has the lowest aperture range available.

It's often a good idea to consider lenses compatible with your camera body but made by a different company. You may also find that it is possible to find high-quality lenses offered by lesser known manufacturers, and even sometimes for slightly lower prices.

ENHANCING LENS OPTIONS

It's also possible to extend the reach of the lens you currently have by using extension tubes and teleconverters. Extension tubes bring the end of the lens closer to the subject, in spite of the MFD, allowing for greater magnification of smaller subjects. Teleconverters add a magnifying lens between the camera body and the existing lens to increase overall focal length. This can reduce sharpness unless the added glass is high quality, so be sure to weigh the advantages of a teleconverter versus buying a longer, better lens.

Read reviews and talk with other photographers to make sure you are investing in the best and most appropriate option for your photographic practice.

LENS FOCAL LENGTH
IN MM AND ANGLE OF VIEW IN DEGREES

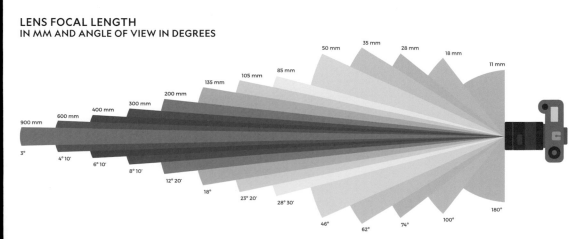

This graphic demonstrates the way angle of view shifts with the focal length of a lens. As focal length increases, angle of view narrows. Wide-angle lenses have a broad view (blue), and telephoto lenses fill the frame with a distant object (pink).

TELEPHOTO LENSES

A good telephoto lens allows you to fill the frame with something far away.

▶ FOR MORE
ON TRIPODS,
SEE PAGES
280–81

▶ FOR MORE
ON AFTER
SUNSET, SEE
PAGES 312–13

Like binoculars and telescopes, telephoto lenses make a distant subject seem closer. With a relatively shallow depth of field even at smaller f-stops, photographers can fill the frame with faraway objects and isolate important elements with focus.

A true telephoto lens is one whose physical length is shorter than its focal length, but the word has come to describe any lens with a focal length longer than a normal lens. The most common telephoto lenses have a focal length between 70mm and 200mm. Any lens with a focal length of 300mm or more is considered a "super-telephoto" lens. The use and parameters of these are the same as other telephotos, but with a greater magnification of distant subjects. Many super-telephoto lenses are quite long, heavy, and can add unwieldy bulk and torque onto the camera body. These may have handles with mounts on the barrel of the lens that can attach to a tripod or body harness for added support.

This image of a colorful building in Japan appears to have been made from an adjacent building with a telephoto lens, which allows the tiny figure to be seen among the colorful doors.

The longer the lens, the trickier it becomes to achieve sharp focus. Even with a tripod, a telephoto lens requires a shutter speed of about 1/250 or faster to keep the image sharp, meaning it requires a lot more light than a wider lens to make a reasonable exposure. Plan ahead with stabilization and wind-blocking tools if you intend to use a telephoto at night.

Telephotos come in prime and zoom varieties. As usual, lenses with fixed focal length tend to be faster, but the zoom offers the flexibility of multiple focal lengths in one lens. Telephoto focal lengths can be divided into three general groups:

SHORT TELEPHOTO LENSES (85MM TO 135MM)

▶ Ideal for portraits or candids at a slight distance, like at a wedding or other event
▶ Typically compact, lightweight, and can be handheld

MEDIUM TELEPHOTO LENSES (135MM TO 300MM)

▶ Great for sporting events when standing on the sidelines
▶ Ideal for travel and some wildlife photography

SUPER-TELEPHOTO LENSES (300MM AND LONGER)

▶ Essential for wildlife or sporting events at a significant distance
▶ Require stabilization and lots of light for fast shutter speeds to avoid movement blur

A telephoto lens yields a type of distortion known as lens compression, which is the phenomenon of background elements appearing larger and closer in a photograph than they really are. An example is a cityscape with an unusually large moon on the horizon. The long focal length

Great framing and a telephoto lens allowed the photographer to capture the distant pitcher through the arms of the batter. The telephoto's shallow depth of field further emphasizes the focal point.

magnifies both the foreground (the buildings) and the background (the moon). As you move away from the buildings, they become smaller in the frame. But the distance between the camera and the moon doesn't change (relatively speaking) nor does the distance between the buildings and the moon. The effect is a flattening, or compression, of the layers in the photograph. The result is the moon looking closer and larger.

The physics of the creative effects of telephoto lenses can be confusing, but experimentation and practice will reveal the ways a telephoto lens fits into your kit and rounds out the way you tell a story in pictures.

MACRO LENSES

Macro lenses reveal the smallest elements of a scene, and offer the potential for visually arresting photographs made from an intimate perspective.

▶ FOR MORE ON MACRO-PHOTOGRAPHY, SEE PAGES 288-9

▶ FOR MORE ON LENS OPTIONS, SEE PAGES 232-3

Macro lenses bring small objects into focus from a very short distance and make them large enough to fill the frame. Photographing small details in this way can add depth and dimension into a well-rounded photographic story.

Macro lenses come in many focal lengths with the most typical being around 50mm, 100mm, and a telephoto, around 180mm. Macros with longer focal lengths require a greater distance between the camera and the subject. This may be an advantage when trying not to cast a shadow on the subject with the camera, or if the subject is particularly skittish, like a butterfly. But as with telephotos, a long-length macro may require extra light and the support of a stabilizer to prevent motion blur with a very shallow depth of field.

CLOSE-UPS

Macro lenses can focus at extremely short distances. A true macro should also perform with minimal distortion, high sharpness at its closest focusing distance, and magnification of at least 1:1, where a one-inch object is projected at one inch on the camera sensor. For even more extreme close-ups, you can try an extension tube, which is a glassless cylinder that fits between the camera body and the lens, allowing more magnification of the subject while maintaining the minimum focus distance (MFD).

The quality of a macro lens is extremely important to a successful image. True macro lenses are corrected for optical aberrations that can occur when focusing at close range, and those corrections hold even when the lens is focused to infinity. For this reason, macro lenses are most often prime, or fixed focal length, as zoom lenses typically lack the quality of construction, minimum focusing distance, and aperture variation required to actually magnify a small subject to a 1:1 ratio.

Although optimized for magnification in close quarters, modern macro lenses are useful for many aspects of general photography with quality glass and wide aperture settings. A prime, 50mm lens makes a lovely choice for both a still life or portrait as well as a photo that fills the frame with the stamens of a lily.

ZOOM IN

▶ Look at a common household object in a new perspective. What textures, contours, or other details are revealed with the use of a macro lens that might otherwise be missed?

A macro lens offers an uncommon perspective on this flower's seed head. Although a broader view might reveal the whole fuzzy sphere, this lens brings sharp focus on the blossom's core.

WHY I LOVE THIS PHOTO

By choosing to shoot with a wide-angle lens, photographer Ami Vitale pulls us right into the middle of this jam-packed scene. With the spout as a focal point, what is central to the people in this image becomes central to us as viewers. The photographer guides us to what is important and then allows us to explore the surrounding layers. The distortion at the outer edges of the frame is our indication of the wide-angle lens. This lens choice allows us to see an enormous amount of activity in such a tight space. A longer lens, used from a farther distance, would have removed us from the crowded moment and made for a less intimate photograph. Here, we aren't observers. Instead, we're forced right inside the frame—eye level with the waterspout as it fills the jug before us.

—REBECCA HALE
Studio Photographer, National Geographic

Women collect water at a well built by the Northern Rangelands Trust and the Nature Conservancy at Kenya's West Gate Community Conservancy.

WIDE-ANGLE & FISH-EYE LENSES

Wide-angle lenses allow you to get a lot of the scene into one frame, but understanding their look is key to managing distortion.

▶ FOR MORE ON ZOOM LENSES, SEE PAGES 278-9

▶ FOR MORE ON ADVEN-TURE, SEE PAGES 142-3

If you're forced into cramped quarters and just cannot get everything you'd like into the frame, you need a lens with a wider angle of view. Wide-angle lenses are versatile lenses with expansive fields of view. They typically come in focal lengths from 10mm to 35mm as well as in a variety of zooms. These lenses offer stability and great depth of field, allowing photographers to hand-hold a camera at even slower shutter speeds.

Although excellent lenses in a variety of circumstances, like a small room or a large crowd, wide-angles also come with a few drawbacks. Because these lenses see so much of the scene, objects are small within the frame. Filling a frame—or even making a subject stand out—requires proximity. But proximity is

A sphynx cat comes in close to check out the wide-angle lens. The distortion of the cat's face works well to enhance its jewel-like eyes and the peculiar nature of its face.

A fish-eye lens adds a curve to the scene and makes the woman in this lily pond at Kew Gardens in Surrey, England, look tiny. The lens's effect is pleasing in this whimsical context.

tricky, as a wide-angle lens will also alter proportions, exaggerating the foreground and diminishing the background. If tilted up or down, the vertical lines in the image will appear as if they're converging—a phenomenon known as "the keystone effect." The key with a wide-angle lens is to find the right distance for the particular perspective of your subject, and to position objects within the frame wisely. Anything placed on the edge of the frame of a wide-angle lens will be distorted.

A fish-eye lens has an extremely wide angle of view—up to 180°, with a focal length of 12mm or even shorter. Although these lenses will definitely distort the image, they produce dramatic photographs that accentuate the curvature of Earth by bowing the horizon. Fish-eye lenses are popular with adventure photographers who value speed and depth of field, and are often photographing from the heart of the action.

A wide-angle can be a great workhorse lens once you understand it. These are typically lightweight lenses that have a minimal profile when added to a camera body, making them very portable and convenient for packing in a kit.

ZOOM IN

▶ Stand in a small room and look through a normal lens or smartphone and notice the parameters of the frame. Stand in the same spot with a wide-angle lens. How much more of the room can you see? How do elements at the edges of the frame look?

ZOOM LENSES

With multiple focal lengths in one lens, a zoom is the most versatile lens in any gear bag. If you can only have one lens, make it a zoom.

A zoom lens allows the photographer to focus in on one item among many, such as one echinacea bloom in this broad field full of them.

▶ FOR MORE ON THE SENSOR, SEE PAGES 216–17

▶ FOR MORE ON LOW LIGHT, SEE PAGES 86–7

A zoom lens is the utility player on your photography equipment team, freeing you from the expense and weight of owning and carrying multiple lenses. Zooms come in a variety of focal lengths, allowing photographers to change visual proximity to a subject without taking a step. The versatility of zooms makes them ideal for travel, when every extra pound counts.

Zoom lenses typically cover specific classes of focal lengths. For example, a telephoto zoom might be 70mm to 300mm, whereas a wide-angle zoom might cover 17mm to 35mm. All-purpose zooms can cover as much as 18mm to 200mm.

ZOOMS & LOW LIGHT

One disadvantage of zoom lenses is that they tend to be slower than prime lenses, with typical maximum apertures of f/3.5 or f/4, limiting their usability in low-light situations. Some excellent

With a good zoom, the photographer can choose how many subjects—in this case, flamingos—to include in the frame by changing the focal length to include many or just a few.

zooms are available with very low maximum apertures. But, these tend to be heavy and expensive due to the number and quality of glass elements within that make such wide apertures possible at varying focal lengths.

The zoom lenses that can be added to a camera body are optical zooms, meaning they use a series of elements that move back and forth within the barrel to transition between focal lengths, and magnify an object to fill the frame for capture on the sensor plate. A digital zoom means that only the center portion of the sensor plate is used to capture an image—equivalent to cropping a photograph—which ultimately reduces its resolution. Most smartphone and point-and-shoot zooms use digital zoom technology as a function of their size. Although optical zoom may produce higher quality imagery

than digital zoom, it is important to note that as sensors continue to increase in megapixel potential, digital zoom imagery will only continue to improve.

One final precaution about the wonderfully efficient zoom lens is that it should not be a substitute for positioning yourself wisely and creatively within the scene. Zooming in shouldn't mean you don't move around to explore the best possible angle and perspective or get as close as you possibly can. In the end, the less space between you and a willing subject, the better the final image will be.

For a practical first acquisition, consider the focal range that will best suit your practices, and purchase the best quality zoom you can. You will likely continue to use it even after your kit grows to include other specialty lenses.

TRIPODS

Keeping your camera supported and steady requires a stable foundation, and one of a variety of tripods is the right tool for the job.

▶ FOR MORE ON ACTION, SEE PAGES 302–303

▶ FOR MORE ON ATHLETIC EVENTS, SEE PAGES 144–5

Any kind of photography that requires a slow shutter speed also requires stabilization of some kind to prevent movement of the camera while the shutter is open. Although there are many ways to support and stabilize a camera using steady foundations, a tripod is the tool designed for this purpose, and is a part of most professional photography kits. Landscape photographers use tripods to make stunning scenic photographs at dawn or dusk with long shutter speeds that allow water to blur and the softest pastels to be captured. Sports photographers use sturdy tripods or single-leg monopods to support heavy super-telephoto lenses that focus fast to capture action at a distance.

MAKES & MODELS

Although the three-legged build of tripods hasn't changed over the years, they do vary in size, materials, and fea-

A tripod that is sturdy but lightweight is perfect for a predawn hike to capture the sunrise from a mountaintop in Nepal.

tures, with a model to suit nearly every preference and budget. Many are made of aluminum or carbon fiber for lightweight durability, and even lighter plastic models are suitable for small cameras. Most have adjustable, telescoping legs capable of standing firmly on uneven surfaces and extending to heights that exceed what a photographer can reach alone. When combined with a remote trigger, these allow for a wider variety of angles and perspectives. Some have bendable legs that can be wrapped around tree branches or signposts, and some collapse to a quarter of their size for travel.

TRIPOD HEADS

The element that secures the camera to the tripod is called the head. Some heads are highly technical with a variety of features, like levels for keeping the horizon straight, multidirectional controls for smooth panning and switching easily from horizontal to vertical, and quick-release mounts for speedy transitions. Heads come in many builds and sizes to accommodate everything from a smartphone to a large DSLR with a long lens.

A monopod is a stabilizer with one leg instead of three. Although it isn't able to stand alone, the trade-off is that it is quicker to set up and move. These are popular with wildlife and sports photographers who value support for long lenses and mobility.

As you consider a tripod, try to balance your need for one with the bulk and effort it adds to your portability. If you frequently need stabilization in the field or in areas where long shutter speeds can make or break a photograph, find the model of tripod that will suit your style and let it keep your work steady.

A tripod base and a remote trigger can produce a wildlife photograph that might never be achieved by holding the camera. This red fox came in for a closer look in Kamchatka, Russia.

OTHER ACCESSORIES

A camera is all you need to make a photograph, but these accessories can add logistical, technical, and creative punch to any photo session.

There are accessories for nearly every aspect of picturemaking, from stabilizers to supercharged battery packs. Get to know the options, and prioritize those best suited for your photographic habits.

▶ FOR MORE ON BACKUPS, SEE PAGES 358-9

▶ FOR MORE ON USING FILTERS, SEE PAGES 290-91

You have everything you need within you to make the best photograph possible with a simple camera. But there is a wide array of accessories, ranging in purpose from efficiency to artistry, that can enhance the photomaking experience. Although adding too many gadgets could weigh you down and potentially hamper your flow, exploring the available tools and accessories will help you discover new avenues of creativity as well as expand your understanding of what can be achieved with a camera, and how.

Here are a just a few of a photographer's many options:

SPARE BATTERIES AND CHARGERS— Whether a smartphone or DSLR, just about every camera today is powered by a rechargeable battery, making these among the most important accessories. Most batteries can be charged from inside the camera, by plugging it in to a power source, but having a separate charger and extra batteries allows you to continue making pictures while one battery is recharging. (Mirrorless cameras drain batteries quickly, so be sure to have several charged up and ready to go.)

SPARE MEMORY CARDS—These ensure the security of precious image files while you're still in the field. Many cards are capable of holding thousands of images, but swap them periodically to avoid having all your photos on one card. Separate used cards from unused cards in a holder, and be careful not to reformat any until the images are in at least two other places.

MEMORY CARD READER—This allows you to transfer image files from a card to a hard drive without plugging the camera into the computer, which drains its batteries.

CAMERA STRAPS—When moving around on the job, these prevent you from dropping the camera. Straps vary from the standard type that hang from the neck, to wrist straps, and even complex harness systems that secure a camera to your body while evenly distributing its weight.

GEAR BAGS— Ranging from traditional shoulder bags to backpacks, messenger-style or rolling bags, most have configurable padded inserts to protect and separate gear.

DIFFUSERS AND REFLECTORS—These allow the photographer to make the most of available light, softening and reflecting it to enhance a subject. There are many options for lightweight and collapsible diffuser-reflector combo discs. Although it's useful to have someone else hold one, in a pinch it can be leaned against your camera bag or even held by the subject in the case of a head-and-shoulders–style portrait.

REMOTE SHUTTER RELEASE OR REMOTE TRIGGER—For the operation of a camera from a distance, and without disturbing its stabilized state, remotes are often used by wildlife photographers who set up a camera and step away from the scene, or by astrophotographers making long exposures of the night sky, who need to avoid even the slightest bit of camera shake. Remote triggers can be tethered or wireless, using infrared or Bluetooth technology. There are even apps that allow control of your camera from a smartphone. Different models work with different cameras, so be sure to research compatibility before purchase.

FILTERS—Transparent layers of glass most commonly screwed onto the front of the lens, these add enhancing and creative effects to images on capture. They also protect the front element of the lens from debris and scratches.

OFF-CAMERA FLASH—When used skillfully, adding an off-camera flash to any photographic effort can turn an average photograph into something special.

ZOOM IN

▶ Make a list of accessories you'd like to add to your kit. Prioritize them and try adding one at a time as your budget permits. Use each item to its full potential, and identify how best to carry your accessories safely and efficiently.

ASSIGNMENT

A hiker photographs an iceberg graveyard in a fjord in Scoresby Sound, Greenland, where ice meets water for a reflective photographic opportunity.

THINK ABOUT WHAT YOU WANT, KNOW WHAT YOU NEED

If you are considering upgrading or purchasing a new camera system, first examine the imagery you have been making with whatever camera you currently have.

PICK YOUR 10 FAVORITE PHOTO-GRAPHS and put them together in a set you can review at once. Note what these pictures have in common. Do you love the soft colors of low-light sunsets over landscapes? Do you gravitate toward photos of the bustle and busyness of strangers on a city street? Do you prefer stunning portraits with shallow depth of field, or are you a wildlife photographer at heart? Find the common thread between the photographs that most define your work as a photographer thus far.

NEXT, CONSIDER WHAT TYPE OF CAM-ERA AND OTHER EQUIPMENT might help you improve the way you make the pictures you love. What will give you room to grow in technique and skill? Make a list in order of priority. Do you require a camera body that can use multiple lenses for travel or portraits? Do you need a long lens to focus on wildlife or sporting events? Be honest with yourself—don't overreach on equipment you won't use yet.

CONSIDER YOUR BUDGET, AND START RESEARCHING brands and models online. Ask photographer friends, and read reviews. Think carefully about what you are willing to carry, and what will excite and inspire you to grow most as a photographer.

CHAPTER TEN

BEYOND
THE BASICS

As you continue to make more photographs, you'll notice a few things begin to happen. First, the tenets of photography will become your default and you'll begin to *see* in pictures. Light will be one of the first things you notice each day, and you'll recognize compelling composition in ordinary scenes. Next, the function and control of technology will become second nature, an extension of yourself. You'll pick up the camera and adjust its controls to make a photograph with the same ease as adjusting the seat in your car or adding toothpaste to your toothbrush. You won't need to think about these steps—they will be part of your daily process.

Once you achieve that level of instinct with the basics, you can begin to explore new tools and techniques to add layers of creativity to your work. As you begin to play with new ways of doing things, it's important you not lose sight of your standard for what makes a great photograph. There is no substitute for solid application of the basics—photographs should be sharp, well exposed, and thoughtfully composed. But within those parameters, there are ways to enhance the elements of a great photograph and turn it into something truly unique and special.

As you stretch beyond the basics to realize your artistic vision, remember that in addition to successes, you will have failures, false starts, and dead ends. These are not wasted moments or frames. They are the foundation on which you will build an understanding of your photographic voice.

A subject carrying a light moved through the scene during this long, stabilized exposure.
Only the densest part of the Milky Way and the walker's light are bright enough to appear in the frame.

MACROPHOTOGRAPHY

Photographing the very small details in the world around you requires the right lens and special attention to technique, but the results are well worth the effort.

▶ FOR MORE ON MACRO LENSES, SEE PAGES 272–3

▶ FOR MORE ON CONTROLLING DEPTH OF FIELD, SEE PAGES 238–9

Macrophotography is essentially an in-depth, up-close look at the world. By filling a frame with the smallest details, photographers can give stature and prominence to things often overlooked. Although you might see an insect with your naked eye, do you see the colorful pattern of its wings, or the small, complex joints of its leg? Textures, patterns, and exquisite design reveal themselves upon magnification.

There is beautiful order in the very small, and macrophotography gives photographers a way to direct viewers' attention to it.

To capture small subjects with impact requires some specialized equipment. The ideal is a macro lens capable of focus at close range so that a tiny thing can be magnified to at least 1:1, which means the image of the object projected onto the sensor is the same size as the object

Water droplets on strands of spiderweb look like strings of party lights. Shallow depth of field produces a "bokeh" effect—the rounded blur of out-of-focus points of light.

in real life. In some cases, even more magnification is desirable, and some macro lenses can magnify up to 5:1, or five times life-size. This type of magnification is ideal for capturing the eye of an insect or the tiny reflection in a drop of dew.

Macro lenses come in fixed focal lengths from 50mm to 200mm, and both ends of this range have advantages. A shorter macro lens means more depth of field, which is critical in this type of photography. A longer macro lens, however, means a greater working distance, which is the distance from the front of the lens to the subject at which it will still magnify the subject 1:1. This is useful for skittish subjects that won't tolerate a lens at close range.

It's vital in macrophotography to master depth of field. Depth of field refers to the range in front of and behind the point of focus that is also sharp, and this range is greatly reduced at a short camera-to-subject distance, something inherent in macrophotography. The best work-around for a dramatically shallow depth of field is a change in composition that puts more of the scene's important elements within the plane of focus. For example, photographing a grasshopper in profile instead of head-on will put its entire body in focus, rather than just its eyes. For proper exposure when working with limited depth of field, subtle adjustments to focal length and aperture require corresponding adjustments to shutter speed. This may in turn require stabilization, and possibly the addition of light. An even more complex solution to the macro depth of field problem is called focus stacking, which involves some heavy postproduction work.

A macro lens allows the photographer to nearly fill the frame with the head of this adult male blue dasher dragonfly, giving prominence to its eyes, which are in sharp focus.

To be sure, macrophotography has more technical considerations than many other general areas of photography, and that is the price to be paid for exposing the divine loveliness of tiny treasures existing within every realm. But in addition to images that will amaze, the deeper grasp of depth of field required for macrophotography will serve you well in all areas of your photographic work.

ZOOM IN

▶ Notice how the order of things at the macro level mirrors that of life at standard size, and how composition, texture, pattern, shadow, and highlights work together to create tone and impact with even the smallest details.

USING FLASH

Good use of flash can make an image possible, or can make an already decent image great, but the key is to move it away from the camera.

▶ FOR MORE
ON DIREC-
TION OF
LIGHT, SEE
PAGES 78-9

▶ FOR MORE
ON EXPO-
SURE, SEE
PAGES 230-31

Most people who grab snapshots on automatic mode have a minimal understanding of flash. Flash is built into their cameras and is automatically activated when the light is too low to take a picture in a given scene. The results are typically fairly poor—harsh light and subjects looking as if they were caught unaware, red-eyes wide, surrounded by a sea of black. Alternatively, the skillful addition of flash into picturemaking can make an otherwise impossible image doable and can make a good image special.

Remember that light shining directly on a subject from at or behind the camera—the sun behind the photographer, for example—produces a fairly flat, uninteresting look. As with available light, the key to great use of flash is to get it away from the lens, and if possible, to light the subject at an angle. At a minimum, this will eliminate the dreaded "red-eye" effect, but it will also illuminate your

Adding to the light coming from the speleologists' equipment, flash emphasizes the scientist in yellow and creates visual tension with other illuminated elements, including the waterfall.

In this unusual portrait of a horse, the flash is balanced with an exposure for ambient light, making the subject pop as the focal point of the image.

subject in a more natural way and add opportunities for more creative results. This requires an investment in an external flash unit that can be activated by triggering your shutter. If within your budget, start by thoroughly researching the speedlight (external flash) options compatible with your camera body.

In most cases, flash is something photographers add into an existing exposure equation, to enhance or draw special attention to a subject. It's another tool with which to direct the viewer's eye. Adding flash into an image may seem a little intimidating and is definitely easier once the principles of exposure are second nature, but the rewards of doing so can be great. It's helpful to think of flash as icing on an already perfectly baked cake—the heat (amount of light coming through the aperture) and time (shutter duration) made the cake good, but the icing (flash) will make it delicious.

There is much to learn about the ways flash can be added to photography. Thankfully, the digital revolution has made experimentation much less expensive and mysterious than in the film days, so play liberally with off-camera flash to explore its parameters and impact.

ZOOM IN

▶ Look at the two images on these pages and note which elements are illuminated by flash, and try to determine where the flash is coming from. Great use of flash should make an impact without being obvious.

FILL FLASH

Fill flash adds a sophisticated punch to an already balanced exposure. Building your photograph from back to front will demystify the steps to getting the look right.

▶ FOR MORE ON ISO SENSITIVITY, SEE PAGES 246-7

▶ FOR MORE ON BRIGHT LIGHT, SEE PAGES 84-5

An understanding of the relationship between aperture and flash will help you to confidently use flash as an accent in an otherwise balanced exposure. Fill flash is a subtle addition to a photograph that makes a subject pop by defining its edges and filling in unwanted shadows. It is especially useful when the subject is underexposed because of a strong backlight, and as with every image, balance is key to an appealing exposure.

BUILDING A PHOTO

Think about building a photograph in layers. Imagine making a portrait of

The photo on the left is made only with available light, leaving the girl's face slightly in shadow. On the right, a small amount of fill flash illuminates her and helps her stand out in the photographic frame.

─── **ZOOM IN** ───

▶ Bring a friend to a shady spot and make a portrait with ambient light. If a touch of flash could make your subject stand out, begin by adjusting your settings for the background. Then, use a flash and continue to fine-tune settings until you have an illuminated portrait with a natural feel.

your friend in the woods on a beautiful autumn day. Start by finding the camera settings for the background—something that will perfectly expose colorful leaves on trees as they are illuminated by sunlight filtering through. The scene is mostly in shade, so perhaps you choose an ISO of 400. You'd like your friend to be in focus, with the trees blurred in the background in soft blocks of color.

GIVING THE TECHNIQUE A TRY
You select f/5.6 to achieve this look with a shallow depth of field. At that aperture, the meter indicates that the shutter speed needs to be 1/200. Make a photograph to check it out. Notice the well-exposed color in the background, but that your friend, although sharp, is mostly in shadow from the leaves above her. Fill flash will give her a little glow and make her stand out.

Have an assistant, buddy, or family member hold the flash, perhaps with a small softbox or other diffuser in front of it, slightly to your left, up high, and pointed down at your subject. Then, at a distance of six feet, say you try the flash at full power. The background looks good, but your friend is way overexposed. Your options are:

▶ Step down the aperture to f/8 or f/11.
▶ Turn the flash to half or quarter power.
▶ Have your helper move the flash farther from the subject.

Any of these options will work. Turning the flash power down will also save its batteries, and so you opt for that. The flash still looks a little "obvious," so maybe you have the person holding the flash take a half step back. Understanding the relationships between these functions, you make slight adjustments with each frame. You end up with a lovely, balanced exposure in which the friend you are photographing subtly glows against a colorful, soft background of autumn foliage.

Fill flash also works well for portraits made in bright sun, when a subject has strong shadows under nose and brow. Similar to using a reflector, subtle flash can fill in shadows and make your subject stand out in the scene.

BALANCING SHUTTER SPEED, APERTURE & FLASH
The key to having the background well exposed in your autumn portrait is to make sure your shutter speed is in balance with the aperture, which is in turn balancing the flash.

Crafting an ambient light exposure is like baking a cake, while adding the flash for emphasis is like applying icing. As you begin to try this technique, you'll quickly realize that shutter speed plays the same role as always—it balances with aperture to properly expose for ambient light. The difference here is that shutter speed shares aperture's attention with the flash power.

Adding fill flash is as simple as remembering the equation of exposure. Doing so successfully adds a layer of sophistication that will make any photograph stand out.

STUDIO FLASH

In studio photography, it's common for all light in the exposure to come from flash, giving photographers endless opportunities for creative lighting effects.

► FOR MORE ON COLOR OF LIGHT, SEE PAGES 74-5

► FOR MORE ON APERTURE & DEPTH OF FIELD, SEE PAGES 236-7

In a studio setting, exposure is entirely created by flash, managed with ISO, flash power, and aperture. The shutter speed needs only to be the same speed or slower than the flash to sync with it. In the case of most speedlights, that may be as fast as 1/250, but many studio flashes have slightly slower sync speeds.

SETTING SHUTTER SPEED

Sync speed is listed in the flash manual, but generally, setting the shutter speed to 1/60 is a safe bet. As long as the ambient light in the room is not bright enough to expose at 1/60, there will be no impact on the image. To test this, set the ISO and aperture you intend to use with the flash. Adjust the shutter speed to 1/60 and take a picture *without the flash*. If the frame is completely black, you know you'll be creating all the light in the image with flash.

In this situation the duration of the flash effectively becomes the shutter speed, recording an image only for the fraction of a second it is illuminating the scene. Most studio photographs are made with relatively low ISOs—400, 200, or less, depending on the power of the flash. After selecting an ISO, balance the power of the flash with the aperture required for the desired depth of field.

STUDIO STROBES

Although a speedlight is suitable for a completely controlled setting, most studio photographers use studio strobes, which are typically more powerful, have a quicker recycle time, and produce multiple exposures with a more consistent color temperature. In most professional studios, multiple strobes are used at once, with a variety of stands to hold them, and modifiers to shape their light. Some photographers work with continuous lights, which remain on throughout the session, allowing them to see the way light falls on a subject. But most strobes are flashes that fire remotely when the camera's shutter button is pressed. The results can only be seen on playback.

Photographs made in a controlled space are typically more creative than documentary, more art than everyday life. A studio is a photographer's playground—where if you can dream it and light it, you can photograph it.

ZOOM IN

► Have a friend sit in a chair in low light. Play with an off-camera flash in different positions, with varying apertures and modifiers. Make methodical adjustments until you find settings that produce an exposure you like.

With two flashes—one placed in front and to the left of the subject, the other directly to the right—very little light falls on the backdrop, creating the effect of a singular element in the frame.

CREATIVE FLASH

Imaginative use of flash and long shutter speeds provide opportunities for creative photographs that bend reality in informative, artistic ways.

► FOR MORE ON SHUTTER SPEED, SEE PAGES 240–41

► FOR MORE ON AFTER SUNSET, SEE PAGES 312–13

Flash can give you one more tool for infusing photographs with unique creativity. Just as a slow shutter speed captures motion, slow curtain sync can illuminate that motion. "Slow curtain" refers to the length of time the shutter (or curtain) is open, and "sync" refers to the point in the shutter period at which the flash fires. In this technique, the shutter speed is set to allow some ambient light to reach the sensor and to stay open long enough to capture movement.

The default mode for all flashes is "front curtain sync," where the flash is triggered at the beginning of the time period when the shutter is open. The effect is a lit image of the subject frozen at the beginning of its path of motion, and a blurred continuation of that motion in front of them.

It can be effective to freeze action while still implying motion, though longer exposures create *advancing* ghost trails. A more natural look is achieved with

At a Day of the Dead festival in Mexico, the pop of a flash freezes this dancer amid a colorful smudge created by the slow shutter speed and her movement trail, infusing the photograph with vivid energy.

"rear curtain sync," where the flash is triggered at the end of the time period when the shutter is open. The result here is the opposite—a subject lit and frozen with a ghost image trailing off behind.

Another playful technique is to have the flash fire more than once within a shutter period, creating multiple images within one frame. Imagine a situation where even a shutter speed of 10 seconds will not fully expose the image—perhaps on a beach well past sunset. Use a wide-angle lens and set the camera on a tripod with

one of the longest shutter speeds available. Activate the shutter and have a friend move to several spots within the framed scene. At each one, manually fire the flash using the "test" button on its back. The result is several lit, frozen images of your friend in one photograph.

These techniques require attention to the balance of aperture and flash power as well as trial and error to get right. But once the required settings are clear, worlds of possibility and expression are available with the push of a button.

In a photograph created by firing a flash hundreds of times while the shutter was open, every stage of legendary golfer Bobby Jones's swing is captured in a single frame.

BLUR EFFECT

Blur infuses an image with a sense of movement, the emotion of which is determined by how it is captured and woven into the story of the photograph.

▶ FOR MORE ON USING FLASH, SEE PAGES 292–3

▶ FOR MORE ON WATER, SEE PAGES 310–11

By nature, blur indicates motion in an image, as the subject is moving fast enough to create multiple impressions on the sensor during the time the shutter is open. When used intentionally, blur provides context about subjects— their action, trajectory, and speed, and when used well, this technique can infuse a photograph with a sense of energy and speed or calm and hypnotic continuity, depending on the subject and the nature of its movement.

To be more than an abstract smear, a photograph using blur should have an anchor point, something that is sharp and steady in the frame, to set the foundation for the situation. It is the contrast between what is still and what is moving that illustrates motion and defines its speed. A sharp element can

A slow shutter speed turns the swirling skirts of these Brazilian dancers into a brightly colored blur. The women's faces anchor the image—if the shutter were any slower, the image would be pushed into abstractness.

ZOOM IN

▶ Sit and observe something in perpetual motion—like waves on the seashore or a mobile hanging in a child's room. Slow your shutter speed to animate the movement. How much is just enough?

Twilight is a perfect time to use a slow shutter speed to dramatic effect. Movement of the sea is blurred to a soft white blanket, but the exposure preserves the moodiness of the sky above.

be created with a pop of flash that hits the subject during an extended shutter period, leaving the subsequent motion to add a soft ghostlike blur. Alternatively, a stabilized camera can hold focus on a still element in the frame, while a slow shutter speed permits blur from the motion of anything moving in the scene. This is very effective when objects are moving around a stationary subject—a swirling river of action around a central focal point.

Using a stabilizer on a city street at night yields an opportunity for creative use of shutter speed and blur. Cars dissolve into streaks of headlights and taillights while stationary buildings glow in illuminating reflections. Consider varying shutter speeds in this setting—too short and the blur may look like a mistake, too long and the image may be simply abstract without defined emphasis on urban hustle and bustle. Water turns milky white when blurred in an otherwise still frame, transforming fountains and rivers into softly textured, contrasting elements.

There is an art to adding just the right amount of blur to an image, and to get it right, it is important to consider what the blur is intended to suggest.

WHY I LOVE THIS PHOTO

Is this a truck stuck in a fast-moving, muddy river? At first glance, it looks like it. The magic of photography for me is being clever with technique to create a photograph that at first looks like something else. This is probably a common scene in sheep country: an old truck surrounded by passing sheep. Photographer Andy Mann chose a slow shutter speed, though, to make this everyday scene look special. Photographers often shoot many pictures as an event plays out, which is smart in a situation like this, with crazy sheep chaos all around. Then, when the shoot is over, the photographer can select the ideal frame. Notice how seeing the whole tire helps anchor the truck to the ground instead of it floating in a sea of sheep. We only see it because in this particular shot, there is a gap between the sheep right at that point.

—MARK THIESSEN
Staff Photographer, National Geographic

In Nelson, New Zealand, an abandoned truck becomes a metaphorical log in a fast-moving river of sheep.

WATER

Dynamic and hypnotic, water adds a powerful element to any photograph. Its movement in a frame should complement the mood of the scene.

▶ FOR MORE ON USING FILTERS, SEE PAGES 290–91

▶ FOR MORE ON SHUTTER SPEED, SEE PAGES 240–41

Water of any kind adds so much character to a scene, regardless of whether just one of many layers in the frame, or the focal point of the photograph. Its fluid nature leads to ever-changing textures, shapes, colors, and reflections. Utterly responsive to its environment and never appearing the same way twice, water is without question one of the most dynamic components of any photograph. It's up to the photographer to make the most of it as an artistic element.

REFLECTIONS

When still, water is as reflective as glass. Some reflections may enhance an image, such as the mirroring of colorful autumn leaves along a shoreline. Other reflections—bright sun or a washed-out, empty sky—may result in a blown-out image, distracting from the point of interest in the photograph. Often, reframing is all that is needed to eliminate an unwanted glare. A polarizing filter will help diminish reflections, and a graduated neutral density (ND) filter can help balance radically different exposures above and below water's horizon line.

With moving water, photographers must decide whether to freeze the action or let it blur into a smooth, milky softness, making appropriate use of shutter speed either way. Freezing water with fast shutter speeds is quite effective in the case of kinetic scenes where big waves, froth, or splash illustrate energy, power, and force. Swift or consistent movement is often best illustrated and enhanced with a slow shutter speed, where the resulting white blur feels calming, soft, and serene.

Protecting gear around water is always a challenge. Most gear can take a little external moisture, but be sure to dry it with a clean cloth as soon as possible.

The more dynamic the scene, the more opportunity photographers have to make unique photographs. With water as a subject, the variety of photographic choices and interpretations mean it will never be captured in quite the same way twice.

The better you understand the available tools and how to use them to their full potential, the more impact you can creatively mine from one simple scene.

ZOOM IN

▶ Find a place with moving water and make two photographs with varying shutter speeds—one fast and one slow. How do the different appearances of water influence the mood of each frame?

For this image of Shays Run waterfalls in West Virginia, a small aperture and slow shutter speed create a velvet ribbon of white without overexposing the deep, rich greens of the surrounding foliage.

THE NIGHT SKY

Long exposures made of the night sky may reveal clusters of stars that add a magical element to any photo made after dark.

▶ FOR MORE ON ASTRO-PHOTOGRA-PHY, SEE PAGES 332-3

▶ FOR MORE ON SPECIAL-IZED FUNC-TIONS, SEE PAGES 376-7

Astrophotography refers to making photographs of celestial bodies in the night sky. It can be highly technical, using complex equipment, but it's also possible to get some impressive results by applying basic rules of composition and an appropriate exposure formula.

The night sky varies depending on your location, time of year, and time of night. Some stargazing apps offer detailed information on moon phase and time of its rise, and where to focus the camera to reveal the galactic core, or densest section of the Milky Way. Locations with little to no light pollution are best for photographing the night sky, as is a moonless night. Clear skies allow for the best array of stars, but partly cloudy nights can deliver some lovely results with soft, glowing clouds parting to reveal windows full of stars.

With shutter speeds of 20 seconds or longer, stabilization of your camera is

Planning and positioning are critical to achieve an image like this one, where the tip of a South Korean pagoda meets the center of a circle of star trails created by multiple long exposures throughout the night.

essential. A wide-angle lens with very wide aperture is best for gathering tiny points of light; something like a 20mm lens at an aperture of f2.8. Manually set the focus to infinity (typically marked with "∞" on the lens). Some photographers recommend focusing on a distant horizon during the day, then marking the focus ring and lens barrel for easy repositioning in the dark.

The following is a list of settings that provide a good place to start. Try these, review the results, and adjust as necessary:

▶ Manual mode
▶ RAW format
▶ ISO 2500–6400 (as low as possible to minimize noise)
▶ Center-weighted metering
▶ White balance on auto
▶ Wide-angle lens at f/2.8
▶ Shutter speed anywhere between 10 and 40 seconds, depending on focal length (wider lenses need shorter shutter speeds)

These settings should yield photographs full of stars. If you're pointed at the Milky Way's galactic core, you'll notice colorful clusters in the areas most filled with celestial bodies. To add more depth and context to your star photographs, look for compositions that use silhouetted elements like trees or mountains to frame the sky.

If you're interested in star trails, you'll need to leave the shutter open for a longer period of time, perhaps five minutes or more. Dropping the ISO will make longer shutter speeds possible. An alternative method is to set up in one spot and make a series of 20- to 40-second exposures over a period of a few hours, then stack them into one image using specialized editing software in postproduction.

Areas with little to no light pollution and other interesting elements in the landscape make great star photographs even better. In this one, made in California's Death Valley National Park, the mountain silhouettes and the dry lake bed add a compelling pattern to the frame.

Astrophotography feels like magic the first few times you experiment with it, as extended shutter speeds reveal forms and details that your eyes cannot register. The deeper you go into photographing the night sky, the more you will discover subtle adjustments—in the camera and later in editing—that will produce imagery that inspires you to look at your favorite locations in an entirely new way.

HIGH DYNAMIC RANGE (HDR) PHOTOGRAPHY

When a scene has too great of a range between the darkest and lightest tones, the camera may not be able to capture them all in one image. HDR photography offers a multi-image solution.

▶ FOR MORE ON TRIPODS, SEE PAGES 280-81

▶ FOR MORE ON SPECIALIZED FUNCTIONS, SEE PAGES 376-7

No matter your skill level or quality of your camera's sensor, some circumstances will make a balanced exposure nearly impossible. Scenes with such broad tonal range between the lightest lights and darkest darks prohibit any camera from capturing them all. The result is an image with too much contrast—dark black shadows and blown-out highlights—both void of detail. There is a solution, though, and that's high dynamic range (HDR) photography.

HDR photography is the practice of making multiple frames of the exact same scene, exposing for different tonal areas, and then combining them into one image with a balanced exposure. The goal is a natural-looking image that appears the way the human eye

This image of a Japanese garden in Brooklyn was made by combining multiple frames with different exposures—a technique that preserves details in the shadows without blowing out more reflective parts of the scene.

With exposure set for the sun, a single photograph would have left the foreground bushes and trees dark. Combining multiple frames exposed for the snow, greens, and sky yield a balanced image.

registers the scene, without areas at the extreme edges of a histogram.

There are a few ways to achieve HDR in a photograph. Photographers can make varying exposures manually, combining them later in postproduction with special HDR software, or they can select the auto-bracketing feature included on most DSLR cameras. With one push of the button, this feature makes several photographs at multiple exposures in rapid succession for later merging on a computer. Some modern cameras have in-camera HDR functions that capture, bracket, and combine images into one photograph, which is then written to the memory card. Although this function is highly convenient, most photographers prefer more control, opting for combining exposures themselves in editing.

The following are a few best practices for making a successful HDR image:

1. To achieve perfect alignment between frames, use a tripod and a remote trigger to eliminate any movement.

2. Make the exposures within a few seconds of each other, to decrease the chances that something within the scene moves or changes.

3. To alter the exposure between frames, only change the shutter speed. Changing ISO or aperture could alter other elements in the scene, like overall brightness, noise content, or depth of field.

4. Using autofocus runs the risk that the camera will focus on a different element between frames. Manually focus on one area in the frame and maintain that through each exposure.

5. Last, don't overdo it in editing. Avoid eliminating all shadows and contrast, which will flatten the image and make it look unrealistic.

BLACK-AND-WHITE

More than just a novelty, a black-and-white photograph should serve the story of a scene, as it does when it's created with intention and thought.

This photograph of a villager crossing a rope bridge in Peru uses black-and-white to bring out textures and the lines of his journey, illustrating the region's tradition of building with local materials.

▶ FOR MORE ON DEFINING COMPOSITION, SEE PAGES 42-3

▶ FOR MORE ON CONVERSION TO BLACK-AND-WHITE, SEE PAGES 372-3

Black-and-white photographs often elicit emotional reactions within viewers, and they tend to have a tried-and-true poignance and popularity. Perhaps it's the sense of history that black-and-white intrinsically evokes, or perhaps the eye is guided more deeply into the frame, focusing on elements of composition, texture, and tone without stopping at the vivid colors of real life. Regardless, no matter what advances technology brings, black-and-white will always have a place in the appreciation of photography.

Although digital imaging means we don't have to commit to color or black-and-white for 24 or 36 pictures by loading a roll of film into the camera, it's important to note that intention and vision set apart a good black-and-white frame. Most digital cameras can be set to capture in black-and-white, which helps put the photographer in a colorless mindset—envisioning the scene in

——— ZOOM IN ———

▶ Pick a photograph you've made locally that you think might be served by black-and-white. Return to the location to remake a version in black-and-white or convert your existing image. How does the absence of color change the photo's impact?

black-and-white, with attention to contrast, patterns, shapes, and shades. A more common practice is to capture in color and convert later in post-process editing. The advantage of this is that the original color image is still available after conversion.

THE STRENGTH OF BLACK-AND-WHITE

Whether on capture or conversion, it's wise to consider the role color plays in a scene before deciding to make an image black-and-white. If color is a key element in the story, or provides visual weight that balances the frame, the photograph may not be as strong without it. Black-and-white works best when the lack of color accentuates compositional elements in the image. Strong shapes silhouetted against a contrasting backdrop, or detailed textures and patterns are some examples. When used well, black-and-white can calm the impact of distractions in the background and add a focused poignance to the subject. But removing color can also complicate an image and confuse the brain, which uses color to help define elements in a busy scene. And so, black-and-white should be chosen with careful attention to all layers of the frame and to the story of the photograph, rather than just as a filter to place atop it.

Some compositional and technical considerations serve black-and-white photographs in particular. Negative space helps separate and define one element from another when both are in shades of gray. Simple backgrounds work well, but in busier scenes, search for angles where contrast helps the subject stand out, or use a shal-

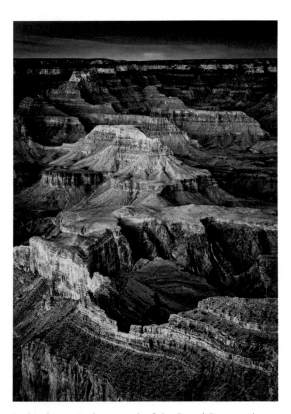

In this dramatic photograph of the Grand Canyon, the photographer has eliminated the famous reds and browns, calling attention instead to the variation in shades and textures of this natural wonder.

low depth of field to direct focus. Darker tones add visual weight and drama to black-and-white images, so keeping the ISO at its lowest possible setting helps minimize noise in these areas.

Black-and-white brings with it an artful regard to almost any photograph. Be sure not to rely on its long tradition of honor in photography, and instead, make good use of an opportunity to grab the viewer's attention in an intentional, meaningful way.

ASSIGNMENT

A slow shutter speed turns marathoners into a river of color as they pass beneath the Kennedy Center in Washington, D.C., setting the movement against the solid stone structure above them.

LIGHT MOVES, NIGHT MOVES

Shutter speed experimentation allows for tremendous photographic creativity. What you'll need: a friend willing to run, dance, or swing for your photos.

BLUR In low light, choose a shutter speed of 1/15 of a second or slower. Select the appropriate ISO and aperture or choose S or Tv mode (shutter priority), and have the camera set the aperture for you. Use stabilization and focus in advance on the spot where your friend will run, swing, or dance past the camera. Then, slow the shutter speed, and notice the blur created by your subject in motion, while the background is relatively sharp.

PAN Using the same set of shutter speeds, hold the camera and have your friend run or swing past you. Make several exposures panning the camera to track her as she moves. If you move at the same speed as your subject, the effect should be that she is relatively sharp while the background is blurred.

LIGHT PAINTING After dark, stabilize your camera and have your subject stand perfectly still. Try a small aperture and a long shutter speed—f/22 and 15 seconds or more. While the shutter is open, enter the scene with a flashlight and "paint" her with light. Exit the frame before the shutter closes. Note how you can invisibly enter and exit the scene if you keep the light off until you're ready to paint with it.

SPECIALTIES

Once you have a good grasp on some of the more advanced photographic techniques, you may want to explore merging your newfound skills with other passions. Perhaps you are a pilot and want to fly with a camera, or maybe you're a scuba diver and want to use your new photography aptitude to document the wonders that exist beneath the waves. Without question, photography offers a dynamic way to share your unique perspective, including your varied interests and expertise.

When specializing in a particular field of photography, it's important to understand what to expect from the subject and its environment and be able to look in the right places to anticipate the most impactful moments. Advanced knowledge of your subject—whether it be weather phenomena, microscopic organisms, or celestial bodies you admire in the night sky— will also prepare you for a thorough investigation of equipment required to tell its story.

And even if you have no experience with a particular specialty but find it intriguing, go ahead and experiment. Photography is an experiential process, and by documenting your own exploration, you introduce viewers to one of their own. Let your investigation and learning be evident in the photographs, and as you discover, allow your revelations to influence their tone. When a photographer succeeds at capturing a subject intimately known or the process of getting to know more, a photograph is more than a mere picture *of* a subject, it becomes an illustration of the journey towards a relationship with, and a true understanding of the subject as well.

A distillation of color patterns in the scarlet macaw's plumage may compel you to take a closer look at the structure of feathers.

STORM CHASING

Experiencing a coming storm feels like witnessing the very edge of change, and a photograph that truly captures the transition from calm to chaos can be extraordinary.

Regions with wide-open spaces are fantastic landscapes for photographing storms. Here, above the sagebrush fields of Cody, Wyoming, at twilight, lightning illuminates a large thunder cloud from within.

▶ FOR MORE ON CAMERA MODES, SEE PAGES 252–3

▶ FOR MORE ON LENS OPTIONS, SEE PAGES 232–3

Even a dull landscape is utterly altered by the weird and wonderful light of a coming storm. The leading edge of a weather system is dynamic and transformative, often sudden and sharply defined in extreme cases. Being in the right place with the right photographic equipment can forever preserve a sight that has the potential to be extraordinary but fleeting.

Professional storm chasers travel thousands of miles during a storm season, working with weather experts to purposely put themselves in the path of something dramatic and exciting. It's thrilling and potentially dangerous when a supercell materializes, but sometimes an investment of miles and time amounts to nothing.

As a beginner, be on alert for storms that develop nearby. A location with access to wide-open skies, a large body of water, or other elements that reflect atmospheric changes is a great place to set up when severe weather is imminent. Seek compositions and exposures that accentuate these effects. Storm light can be ephemeral, so check camera settings and results quickly and often.

If you're committed to a certain aperture or shutter speed, consider a priority mode and let the camera keep up with exposures to match changes in available light. If it's missing shadows or highlights you'd like to emphasize, use exposure compensation to make quick, overriding adjustments. Stay present and connected to the environment. Whatever you feel—excitement, uncertainty, fear—convey the mood in your photographs. Consider the reactions of those around you by documenting expressions of concern or resolve, wind in someone's hair or clothes, or open umbrellas and raised raincoat hoods to protect against the elements.

Most professional storm chasers carry both wide-angle and telephoto lenses to cover whatever circumstances they find. Wide-angles are a good choice for their breadth and speed when the weather is close by and makes a distinct impression on one part of a broader landscape. A telephoto brings a distant, dynamic element within photographic reach. A polarizing filter deepens the richness of dramatic skies. A waterproof case protects gear not in use. Additional technology like a NOAA weather radio and GPS keep photographers abreast of developing conditions and the best routes for travel and setup.

A storm often refreshes a landscape, and after the dark, there can be bright light, rainbows, and wet surfaces rich with textures and reflections that make a place more spectacular than before.

Storm scenes often feature a broad dynamic range. The sky surrounding this Kansas tornado ranges from bright white to almost black.

UNDERWATER PHOTOGRAPHY

Photographs made underwater can grab a viewer's attention, whether made at depth with complex equipment or right at the surface with the camera you already use.

▶ FOR MORE
ON WHITE
BALANCE,
SEE PAGES
258–9

▶ FOR MORE
ON TYPES OF
CAMERAS,
SEE PAGES
214–15

Nothing transports viewers to another realm quite like photographs made underwater. From the organisms of a unique ecosystem to the way light bends, an underwater image can evoke a variety of concepts and emotions, from speed and grace to optimism, mystery, and calm.

In addition to specialized camera equipment, underwater photography requires extreme comfort in the water. For photographers seeking quality images of species that call for patience at depth, advanced scuba training is essential. And perhaps more than in any other circumstance, making photographs underwater requires second-nature control of the camera.

Underwater cameras are available in various levels of sophistication and price points. The most elaborate have heavy-duty, watertight housings with lens-

Photographs made just beneath the water's surface include a range of light and reflections that may challenge your camera, so play with angles and composition when exposure is difficult to balance.

───── **ZOOM IN** ─────

▶ Fill the bathtub with water and find a way to waterproof the camera you currently use. Add an object and wave your hand to create bubbles and waves, making pictures as you do. Examine how these differ from photographs made in air.

specific ports that contain regular DSLR setups with accessible buttons and controls. There are some very good underwater point-and-shoot cameras, but although these create high-quality image files, photographers have limited control of settings. Small and adaptable, adventure-type cameras are rugged and waterproof, but with their superwide-angle lenses, proximity to a subject is key. Many smartphones are waterproof to a depth of about 30 feet, and for a short period of time. A better bet is an underwater case made for your specific model.

The physics of light in water creates unique challenges for underwater photographers. Water distorts and changes light unlike any other medium. In addition to refraction—the bending of light as it breaks the water's surface—the spectrum of light is absorbed as it descends. Within the first 10 feet, reds, oranges, and yellows are swallowed up, giving everything a green-blue cast. The only way to see true colors at depth is to add light from an underwater flashlight or flash. Some color correction can be done, however, with white balance adjustments in postproduction editing.

If you're not ready to make the plunge into scuba certification and an advanced underwater photography kit, consider working just below the surface with some simple waterproof accommodations for the equipment you already have. Aquatic creatures aside, the cusp of water and air is one of the most dynamic places on Earth to make photographs. At this interface of mediums everything changes, from how animals respire and move to how gravity and light behave. With the wave of a

To reveal the actual color of objects in a photograph made at a depth of more than about 10 feet, scuba gear and an introduced light source are usually required.

hand, prismatic droplets launch into air and bubbles shimmer like underwater jewels. Dip below and look up at a liquid mirror, at once reflecting what is beneath and distorting the world above. Try to split the view and catch the cross section of a wave. Add a model into the mix—a swimmer with flowing hair, a dog paddling by, a child with goggles and a goofy grin—for a portrait like no other. Show your audience what weightlessness feels like in a photographic tableau of color, shape, and texture that rivals any work of art.

AERIAL PHOTOGRAPHY

Getting above the scene allows for photographs with patterns and textures that provide a completely different perspective on a familiar landscape.

▶ FOR MORE
ON LAND-
SCAPES, SEE
PAGES 152–3

▶ FOR MORE
ON CAMERA
MODES, SEE
PAGES 252–3

From above, familiar places look completely different. Known streets become lines in a maze, rivers and streams look like branching trees, and acres of pines become lush carpets of green. As you travel and photograph great landscapes, look for ways to get up higher.

GETTING IN POSITION

If you're flying in a commercial jet, take-off and landing are your best opportunities to capture aerial views. Reposition yourself in your seat to keep the horizon straight, and have your seatmate hold up a dark blanket or sweatshirt behind you to help avoid reflections. If you have access to a pilot with a small plane or helicopter, open the window or request removal of the door for unfettered views.

Shutter speed should be at least 1/350 or faster to avoid blur, and shutter priority mode is a good choice here. You'll likely be strapped in tightly, so have gear assembled and in hand for takeoff, with spare batteries and memory cards at close but secure reach. Consider wearing a tightly fitting hat under your headset to keep hair away from your eyes and lens, and keep your camera strap around your neck at all times.

More popular than ever, drones allow photographers to get a camera in the air while standing safely on the ground. Modern drone technology allows for remote vision and flight control via smartphone, even when the unit is out of view. Drone use is heavily regulated in urban areas, and most countries prohibit it around airports and other high-security locations. In the United States, use of a drone for commercial purposes—like a paid photographic assignment—requires a Remote Pilot Certificate from the FAA. The test for certification requires highly technical knowledge.

Even without the benefit of flight, your location photographs will be served by getting up above the scene. Find roof access to a tall building, climb a tree or water tower, or even stand on a stepladder for a different perspective on a lovely table setting, swimming pool, or holiday parade. Once nearly impossible, getting a bird's-eye view of places you've known only from the ground has never been easier.

ZOOM IN

▶ Identify a place that might have a particular order to it—a town with intersecting streets or a manicured garden—and find a way photograph it from above it. Note how an aerial view adds to the story of a place.

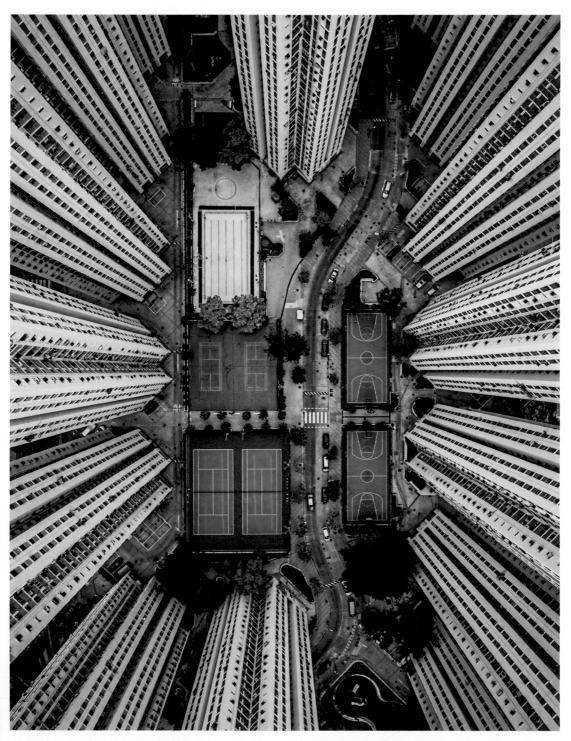

Photographed from high above an apartment complex in Hong Kong, the aerial view of the city's geometric patterns and design makes for a dizzying and dramatic image.

ASTROPHOTOGRAPHY

From simple exposures of the night sky to highly complex telescopic photographs of deep space, astrophotography lets you capture the stars.

▶ FOR MORE
ON WIDE-
ANGLE &
FISH-EYE
LENSES, SEE
PAGES 276-7

▶ FOR MORE
ON EXPO-
SURE, SEE
PAGES 230-31

Photographing celestial bodies can be as simple or as complicated as a photographer chooses. At its most basic, you will need a camera with a wide-angle, fast lens, a tripod, and a solid exposure equation—something like ISO 2500, f/2.8, and a long shutter speed of anywhere between 10 to 40 seconds. Research in advance the moon's phase and rise and where to look for the Milky Way's galactic core. Then, choose a location with very little light pollution. Together, these factors will help you capture details in the night sky you cannot see with the naked eye.

Common types of astrophotography include Milky Way panoramas, auroras, meteor showers, star trails, constellations, and night landscapes. Photographing star trails involves a much longer exposure of five minutes or more. An alternative method is to set up the camera in one spot and make a series of exposures over several hours that can then be stacked into one final photograph in postproduction editing.

This exposure of a green meteor above India's Sky Islands required lots of advanced research and planning, including scouting out a good vantage point and developing a complex time-lapse procedure.

For a much more technical foray into deep-sky imaging, you'll need a greater understanding of space and some sophisticated gear. The following is a list of equipment professional astrophotographers typically use:

APOCHROMATIC REFRACTOR TELESCOPE—
A telescope with excellent contrast and color correction, perfect for capturing details in celestial bodies

EQUATORIAL TELESCOPE MOUNT—
A mount for a telescope designed to compensate for Earth's rotation, which follows the smooth arc of a celestial body across the night sky

DEDICATED ASTROPHOTOGRAPHY CAMERA—
Used in lieu of a standard DSLR, this is a highly technical camera lacking a display and controls on its body, which is controlled by astrophotography software on a computer

REMOTE SHUTTER CONTROL AND INTERVALOMETER—
An intervalometer allows for preprogrammed, timed shutter releases for time-lapse photography

LIGHT POLLUTION SUPPRESSION (LPS) FILTER—
Designed to suppress artificial lighting emissions

SPECIALIZED ASTROPHOTOGRAPHY SOFTWARE—
Editing software specific to image stacking and other postproduction processes unique to astrophotography

SPARE POWER PACKS FOR THE CAMERA—
These prevent the camera's battery from dying when in use for several hours, sometimes in cold temperatures

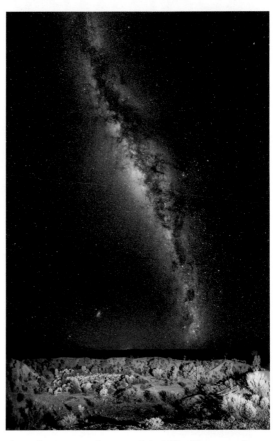

The galactic core—the part of the Milky Way most dense with stars—is revealed in detail well beyond what the naked eye can see in this astrophotograph made in Australia.

DEW HEATER—
A heating unit designed to prevent moisture from collecting within the telescope

TELESCOPE LENSES AND EYEPIECES—
An array of specific lenses and eyepieces to meet photographers' preferences

If you love the night sky and are enamored by the idea of seeing into deep space via your camera, some research, investment, and practice can help you boldly make photographs of places where few humans have gone before.

PHOTOMICROSCOPY

To capture life at the tiniest level, make use of a microscope for a photographic celebration of the unseen—but divine—order of things.

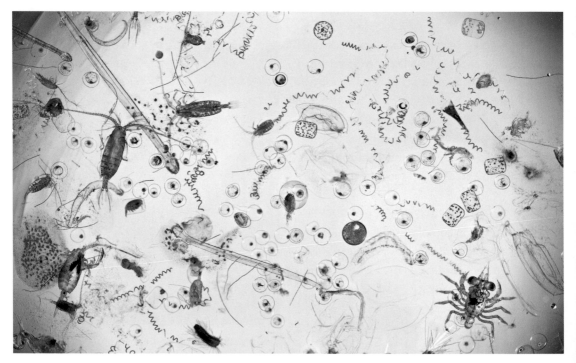

Photographed under a microscope, a splash of seawater reveals a myriad of planktonic species and the teeming diversity of life existing in even a single drop.

▶ FOR MORE
ON CON-
TROLLING
DEPTH OF
FIELD, SEE
PAGES 238–9

▶ FOR MORE
ON CAMERA
MODES, SEE
PAGES 252–3

Photomicroscopy offers a view to an ever present but otherwise unseen world. At its most basic definition, photomicroscopy is high-magnification photography where the camera makes pictures through the use of a microscope. Part science and part art, it can reveal the carefully crafted nature of nearly everything around you. To begin photographing the elemental makeup of things, insect wings, plankton, granules of sand, and onionskin all make great subjects.

Almost any digital camera can be used with almost any microscope, though a DSLR with a removable lens is the best bet. The camera is typically coupled with a vertical photo tube on the microscope that magnifies any vibration, so a remote shutter trigger is advised.

Depth of field is extremely narrow when photographing through a microscope. Anything to be photographed must be prepared into thin slices and mounted on a glass slide. For thicker samples, a series of images with multiple focal planes can be focus-stacked later in postproduction editing software.

Once under the microscope, the subject should be lit evenly and sufficiently for the camera's sensor. Microscopes have two types of lighting: transmitted light, which passes up through a transparent sample, and reflected light, which comes from above an opaque sample. The addition of a polarizing filter reveals a rainbow of colors in many chemicals under the microscope, as polarized light changes the refractive index of the crystals within them.

Not all DSLR cameras are able to meter through a microscope adapter, so manual mode is recommended, with adjustments to shutter speed to find just the right exposure.

In addition to a DSLR with macro lens and remote trigger, a typical gear list for photomicroscopy is:

TRINOCULAR MICROSCOPE— A microscope with two eyepieces and a separate camera port
C MOUNT— Used to mount the camera on the microscope. Some also have optics to fit the image onto the camera's sensor
FIBER-OPTIC LIGHT— Provides additional lighting to the microscope's built-in light
MICROSCOPE SLIDES— To mount samples
COTTON BUDS— For positioning samples and keeping slides otherwise clean
CLOTH BACKDROP— Placed beneath the sample for a clean background

Photomicroscopy is perhaps easiest in a lab or other setting already equipped with microscopes and the accessories required for examining the tiniest elements in the world. This specialty offers a way to preserve and share visions that, in the past, were only available to scientists.

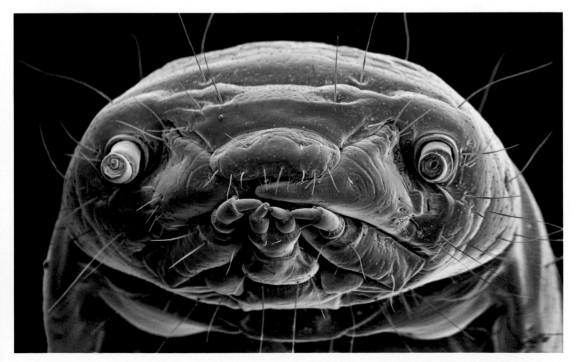

Made with a scanning electron microscope and a highly technical process, this photograph reveals the face of a mealworm magnified more than a thousand times.

In far eastern Nebraska, the striated formation of a mothership supercell looms over the township of Imperial.

PANORAMIC PHOTOGRAPHY

Almost as good as being there, a well-crafted panoramic photograph offers a sweeping view that a single frame cannot usually capture.

▶ FOR MORE ON SPECIALIZED FUNCTIONS, SEE PAGES 376-7

▶ FOR MORE ON PANNING, SEE PAGES 308-309

A panorama, stemming from the Greek words for "all view," is essentially a broad, comprehensive rendering of a scene. Panoramic photography refers to the seamless combination of images—either automatically in the camera, or with special software in postproduction—to form one, sweeping photograph.

There are three basic types of panoramic photographs:

▶ Wide, single-row panoramas that show up to 180° or more, created by a stitched series of adjacent images

▶ Multirow panoramas that show a view wider and taller than normal, created by two or more stitched series of adjacent images made at more than one level

▶ Spherical panoramas, also known as "planets," capturing 360° field of view, stitched and converted to a square spherical image

Creating a panoramic image is a two-step process: the capture, followed by combining two or more photographs into one broad image. Although typically created with horizontal frames, many professional photographers recommend vertical captures to assemble a single-row panorama, as the final result

Consistent exposures and focus settings are critical for capturing fantastic, sprawling landscapes like this series of sandstone structures at Canyonlands National Park in Moab, Utah.

includes more sky and foreground, with less resolution lost to cropping.

While moving along a consistent plane, a photographer pans across a scene, making pictures from one end to the other, keeping the horizon level, and overlapping each frame by 20 to 50 percent—crucial for the successful alignment in the stitching phase of the process.

PANORAMIC BEST PRACTICES

To ensure consistent exposure and focus, working in manual mode is recommended, as is manually focusing on a distant point. An aperture of at least f/8 is best for depth of field that keeps as much of the scene as sharp as possible. A normal lens is a smart choice (something in the 35mm to 85mm range), as wide-angle lenses may distort or vignette at the edges of each frame, and telephoto lenses have a too-narrow field of view. Other considerations include avoiding moving elements in the scene, removing any lens filters (these may cause color inconsistencies at the edges of each frame), and ensuring smooth panning from side to side, whether hand-holding the camera or using a tripod with a movable head.

There are specific panoramic equipment kits, expensive but designed for the job, with special tripod heads that rotate around the stationary lens opening, making precise captures of an entire scene, easily combined later in postproduction. There are many software programs for panoramic stitching, and it can also be done in more comprehensive programs like Photoshop. Most smartphones and many DSLRs have panoramic functions that will either capture a panorama in one smooth move, or will stitch multiple frames together in-camera, saving the panoramic image onto the memory card.

Regardless of how a panorama is captured and rendered, a large image of an expansive view is a good way to represent any magnificent natural area.

INFRARED PHOTOGRAPHY

Always present, infrared light reveals itself with a specialized filter, and sets all living things aglow in a photograph.

With a camera converted to infrared photography through the removal of its internal IR filter, normal shutter speeds become possible, meaning moving subjects can be captured with only IR light—as in this photo of giraffes.

▶ FOR MORE ON USING FILTERS, SEE PAGES 290–91

▶ FOR MORE ON PATTERN & TEXTURE, SEE PAGES 34–5

Beyond the visible spectrum is a realm of long-wavelength light called infrared, where warm and cool subjects produce bright and dark tones, respectively. Infrared (IR) photography is the practice of making exposures using only infrared light. Depicting landscapes with surreal colors and black-and-whites with super high contrast, the distinct effects of IR photography look highly graphic and like fine art.

ALL ABOUT INFRARED

Infrared light, though invisible to the human eye, is always present, and readable to an unaltered digital camera sensor. To preserve the color fidelity of a regular exposure, modern digital cameras come equipped with IR cut filters to block IR and UV light from reaching the sensor. Accessory IR filters added to the front of a lens take advantage of imperfections in the built-in cut filters, allowing IR wavelengths to pass, while

This infrared photograph renders the leaves on the trees as a ghostly white canopy over the rows of graves at Arlington National Cemetery in Virginia.

blocking all other light. The external filters look nearly black, and indeed, block so much visible light that they require a very long shutter speed and tripod in the height of midday sun. Older digital cameras have weaker versions of the IR cut filter (or none at all), making these great candidates for IR photography.

As the infrared exposure result looks similar to black-and-white, you should make the same compositional considerations. Look for contrast between adjacent elements and allow for negative space between subjects that reflect similarly. It's also effective to use varying textures in close proximity to one another.

One of the most spectacular things about infrared light, and therefore photographs created by exposing for it, is that more of it is reflected back from living things. Trees, grass, flowers, and skin all appear bright white in the frame—a sugarcoated world from science fiction. Inanimate objects like stone and concrete and even water tend to absorb more IR light, making them darker in the frame.

The best conditions for IR photography are sunny, summer days when there are lots of living things in view. The result is a photo glowing with life that lends a new, artistic appearance to your environment.

ZOOM IN

▶ Do an internet search on infrared photography to see the range of artful ways this photographic specialty can be used, and try to envision a familiar natural area captured using only infrared light.

THERMOGRAPHIC PHOTOGRAPHY

A thermal imaging camera allows you to photograph one aspect of a subject you've never seen—its heat signature.

▶ FOR MORE ON SMARTPHONE PHOTOGRAPHY, SEE PAGES 224-5

▶ FOR MORE ON FRAMING, SEE PAGES 52-3

A thermal image, also known as a thermogram, is a visual representation of the radiation emitted by an object as a function of its temperature relative to its environment. Put more simply, a thermal camera is one that can interpret heat from an object in the form of infrared light. By registering the temperature of an object rather than its reflected light, a thermal camera essentially makes it possible to see in the dark.

As a very basic explanation of how a thermal camera works, it records an image using a small array of sensors known as microbolometers. These sensors absorb the thermal radiation (heat) reflecting off an object. Microbolome-

This thermal photograph of a boy using a smartphone illustrates how the heat from his finger remains on the device's screen long enough to be captured by the camera.

ZOOM IN

▶ Note that thermal imaging reduces a scene to a small range of colors—from bright red in the warmest areas to blue in the coolest—making successful composition about placement and framing of objects.

Made with a technical imaging tool, creative framing and placement of warm subjects makes for an artful photograph of a crowd from behind.

ters react in a way that can be electrically measured. This measurement is subsequently interpreted into an image revealing halos of color representing the temperature, or thermal signature, of the object.

Advanced thermal cameras are extremely expensive and are often used for animal research and rescue operations in scenarios where atmospheric conditions, like smoke, obscure vision. Thermal signatures offer an advantage over aerial photography in the scientific study and mapping of mountainous terrain as they illustrate the way the landscape is absorbing solar radiation, which varies with

moisture, evaporation, and even wind direction. For a more practical and affordable alternative, pocket-size thermal cameras, and even thermal imaging attachments for smartphones, are now available for everyday thermographic photography.

Sometimes used in mechanical and electrical applications to detect structural defects, areas of heat loss, and plumbing issues, there are creative opportunities in the ability to make photographs of the heat you've never seen. Thermal imagery offers one more variation on photographing the complex world around you, in a way at once both informative and artistic.

TIME-LAPSE PHOTOGRAPHY

Time-lapse photography manipulates life's progression by compressing processes and giving the course of change center stage.

Similar to a long exposure, a time-lapse photograph can illustrate the passage of time by combining several consecutive exposures into a single composition—in this case, lights from moving vehicles.

▶ FOR MORE ON STORING IMAGES, SEE PAGES 212–13

▶ FOR MORE ON BLUR EFFECT, SEE PAGES 304–305

You've likely seen a clip of a flower blooming, wilting, and then dropping to the ground before your eyes. A natural process that normally takes days or weeks appears to happen in a matter of seconds. Rather than running a video camera for the duration of a blooming event, the effect was likely created with time-lapse photography and hundreds of images made at regular intervals over a period of time. Like an old-timey photo flip book, the images are viewed in rapid succession, allowing you to witness and appreciate change in a way that bends time.

While cinematography strings together a high volume of still frames at a very fast rate to illustrate movement, time-lapse photography captures still frames at a much slower rate, for subsequent playback at a faster rate. The result is that photographs taken during events that normally take hours or days can be viewed in their entirety in just seconds. Think of the tide rising and dropping around the posts of a pier, or the lights of a city snapping on as the sun rapidly sets. Sequences of photographs like this tell the story of how nature transforms a landscape or how an entire community responds to the end of a day.

You can set yourself up for time-lapse photography with just a few simple additions to a basic camera kit. A tripod holds the camera in place for the duration of an event to be photographed, and an intervalometer is a programmable device for automated, repetitive triggering of the shutter. Many modern DSLRs and smartphone cameras have an intervalometer or time-lapse feature, so be sure to investigate your current camera before investing in one. As many—possibly hundreds or thousands of frames—will be made during the event, it's important to be sure the camera's memory card has the capacity for a high volume of image files, especially if they will be captured in RAW (they should be!).

A successful time-lapse compilation involves some advance planning. Evaluate the event for composition, and anticipate the nature of the transformation. The duration of the event should determine the length of the session. Calculate your rate of capture on the pacing of the change you are trying to illustrate, then program the intervalometer or camera's time-lapse function to meet those calculations. Be sure to set the camera in manual mode for consistent exposures throughout, and lock it into manual focus on the point of interest in the scene. Many photographers design a little blur into each frame with a shutter speed of under 1/100 for a smoother look on playback. Be sure to run a test of a shorter version of the time lapse before starting your planned session.

After capture, you'll have hundreds of files or more to push through postproduction editing and rendering into the final time-lapse composition. Software can facilitate your workflow by making edits and exporting efficient and accurate.

For compelling time lapses, consider scenes that have contrasting static and dynamic elements—an anchoring, stationary element will amplify the effect of the change you want to illustrate. The flow of traffic along a city boulevard lined with skyscrapers, a stadium filling with thousands of people before a game, and the transition of shadows across a field as the sun moves through the sky are great examples of how common, everyday scenes animate with the passage of time.

One photograph can illustrate multiple positions of a moving subject with multiple images made over a period of time and stacked together, as in this composition of a BASE jumper in Switzerland.

ALWAYS LEARNING

In an endless cycle of expansiveness, photography can influence your interest in specialized ways of examining the world, as exploration can inspire you to make photographs.

▶ FOR MORE ON IDENTIFYING STORY, SEE PAGES 24–5

▶ FOR MORE ON CHOOSING YOUR EQUIPMENT, SEE PAGES 262–3

One of the most fulfilling things about photography is that it is an active, creative means to explore, learn, and experience more of the world. A camera is a fantastic tool for thoughtful study—to examine more deeply the things and places with which you are already familiar, and to venture out into an entirely new field.

Of course, you could read entire books and take countless workshops on any of the specialties discussed here. The introductions in the previous pages are meant only to ignite your interest and inspire you to explore further in your study of the world with a camera. When you merge your passion for photography with intrigue for other special techniques, the only thing limiting your photographic development is the depth of your curiosity. And so, curiosity and the photographic process are

This window frames the view of Namib-Naukluft Park in Namibia, but the lacy curtains become a canvas for shadow, light, and texture, illustrating that sometimes the frame is the view itself.

By photographing the world in ways others might not easily see, you create community as you share your view of life. Connecting with other photographers doing the same will expand your own vision.

locked in a dance: You learn to make better photographs to share your fields of interest, and you enjoy your interests more because of a desire to make photographs.

BECOME AN EXPERT

If you find a specialty that speaks to you, connect with other photographers already doing the work. Engage in discussions about prime locations, and stay current on relevant issues in the field, advancements in equipment, and associated technology. Set goals for equipment acquisition and make plans for your next photographic quest. Become an expert in the subject and infuse your picturemaking with the deep knowledge that will set your work apart.

In digital photography, and especially in some of the more highly technical specialties, there is an after-capture component in the art of making a photograph. Sometimes it's only through these postproduction processes that the elements most important to the photographer can be coaxed into deeper focus, or teased out to be seen at all. Combine this concept with a picture of the stars, plankton, heat, or some other facet of the world that couldn't be experienced without the work of a camera, and it makes the whole process seem a little like magic.

No matter the realm or equipment required to capture them, remember that great photographs always begin and end with the vision of the photographer. No bells or whistles can substitute for thoughtful composition and awareness of light in consideration of the story and subject. Let your passion for making pictures that will stir viewers guide you while expanding your skill set to reveal a part of the world they may never otherwise see.

ASSIGNMENT

A diver encounters a school of bigeye kingfish in Baja, Mexico, in an underwater photograph that uses light and shadow to invite a brief visit to another realm.

DIVING DEEP INTO A SPECIALTY

Pick a photographic specialty you're interested in exploring, and identify three photographers who work within that specialty. Study their websites, follow their social media accounts, and examine their work. Try to identify the techniques or equipment they might use to make photographs that illustrate the world in a new way.

RESEARCH Commit to learning everything you can about the specialty that interests you. Do in-depth research online or from books, watch tutorials, and become an "armchair expert" in this branch of photography. Begin to experiment within this specialty, making use of equipment you have.

PLAN Consider your budget and the bare minimum equipment necessary to dive deeper into this specialty. Plan to expand your kit with the tools you need to improve and advance.

CONNECT Look for online communities of other photographers working in the same specialty and communicate through social media feeds dedicated to the medium. Consider a joint project with another photographer, and create a body of work you can present locally.

Committing to a photographic specialty is a great way to continue developing your voice as a photographer, helping you to further identify styles and mood that appeal to your aesthetic.

EDITING

Potential. An important part of photographic vision is realizing an image's potential. To be sure, planning for a great story and executing a photographic idea begin with camera in hand. There is the active, uncompromising search for great light and optimal composition. There is the presence and confidence required when pushing the button. But in addition to these crucial steps, photographers with vision go into every situation considering even the final steps of the process, not only making the best captures, but doing so in a way that will allow for the best polishing and broadcast.

This is not to say that photographers should lean on technology to make corrections and fill holes that were left when making an image. It is important that you always capture the best frame you can, doing as much work as possible in-camera, working within the specific circumstance and your understanding of the scene. But a photographer's final vision for an image is realized in the back half of picturemaking.

The following pages are a guide to the postproduction editing process, from the critical eye you must use in examining the work, to the logistics of workflow, backing up, selection, and enhancement. This is a jump start to the evolution of your style as an editor—something you will likely develop over many years to come.

Beyond that, sharing your work is critical and perhaps the most challenging part of the entire process. It requires follow-through, savvy, continued vision for presentation, and the guts to put yourself, by way of your work, out there. Finish the process of making great photographs by realizing their full potential and sharing them with waiting eyes.

Good postproduction editing perfected this photograph of the crescent moon moving across the evening sky in Tehran, Iran.

WORKFLOW

The steps from camera to sharing your work may be the most intimidating part of picturemaking, but designating a space for an organized workflow will set you up for success.

Meet Hopper, the hero of the editing chapter. This image will be your frame of reference throughout the postproduction discussion and will be used to illustrate various editing techniques.

▶ FOR MORE ON IMAGE SELECTION, SEE PAGES 360-61

▶ FOR MORE ON BACKUPS, SEE PAGES 358-9

Many new photographers excel at capture only to balk when it comes to editing. Even the word "editing" is a little confounding, as it encompasses so many steps in the process of finishing the work. Where the capture of an image is mostly objective—the light dictates a certain range of exposure options, the camera functions in a particular way—the editing process is largely subjective, calling for decision making, judgment, and quality control on the part of the photographer. After the files are transferred from the camera, cataloged, and backed up, it's time to select the best of the work. The selected frames are enhanced, polished, and exported to the platform of choice. Throughout, photographers must be methodical and discerning in determining the most effective way to share their original vision. This is a tall order after the effort of capture.

One stumbling block for many pho-

ZOOM IN

▶ Find a space that combines comfort with security—where you won't mind spending a few hours and can walk away from the work without risk of it being disturbed. This will be the place you'll bring your photographs to their full potential.

---

tographers is not having a system in place that makes the process smooth and efficient. Setting up a workflow in advance increases the likelihood of getting the best version of your work from camera to audience.

Whether you are making pictures with a smartphone or DSLR, designing and building your editing workflow in advance means you'll be less likely to reach a dead end with a memory card full of photographs, or worse, lose something special because you forgot it was there. For this reason, it's essential to create an organized, comfortable workspace for your postproduction process, and understand that you will be in it for a while.

For a typical DSLR workflow, you'll need the following:

▶ Your camera
▶ Memory cards with photographs from the day
▶ A card reader—one that reads the type of cards your camera uses and connects to the computer that you'll be using to edit
▶ A computer
▶ Photo-editing software, either native to your computer or specialized
▶ An external hard drive or two, for storing and backing up files

The general flow is to transfer the images from memory card to computer, where you will organize, edit, and store them. Everything is backed up to an external hard drive for security. The final image selections, polished to their full potential,

can be shared as you wish, to social media, a website, or to a lab for printing.

Committing to this process soon after capture will ensure the work is completed and shared while fresh in your mind, as well as safe and secure in an organized system.

IMPORT
Move image files from camera to computer, organize into file structure, and add relevant metadata.

BACK UP
Make sure all image files exist in two places.

SELECTION
Distill set to the most important frames.

POSTPRODUCTION
Enhance selected frames for maximum potential.

BACK UP (AGAIN)
Back up all edits (selections and enhancement adjustments).

EXPORT AND SHARE
Export final frames for printing or sharing.

The fine details of the process may vary with the make and model of your camera, computer, and software, but the general workflow should follow this flowchart, with incremental backups between steps, enhancing only the best images for efficiency.

RAW FILES

Using the RAW file format means you'll have access to every bit of information the camera recorded in the scene.

When a RAW file is imported from the memory card into photo-editing software, the image often looks fairly dull without enhancement.

▶ FOR MORE ON STORING IMAGES, SEE PAGES 212–13

▶ FOR MORE ON PHOTO-EDITING SOFTWARE, SEE PAGES 356–7

To approach capture with an eye toward realizing the full potential of an image, a photographer must record to the memory card as much data as possible. Preserving every pixel the sensor can handle ensures you'll have the most to work with later, with maximum latitude for enhancement. This means choosing the right file type before pressing the button.

Selecting an image file type should be among your initial tasks when you turn on the camera for the first time. This designation will be somewhere in the shooting menu. You'll notice other options including JPEG and possibly TIFF, but for maximum flexibility in postproduction, select RAW and leave it there.

Technically, a RAW file isn't actually an image; it's data collected by the sensor and written to the memory card. As such, RAW files retain every bit of information as originally captured when you

With even minor enhancement, the image begins to come to life. Enhancement is possible and effective due to the maximum amount of information preserved in the file.

shot the picture, but in an uncompressed, uninterpreted format. As a result, RAW files are always large and require a lot of digital space for storage, which is something to consider when purchasing memory cards as well as hard drives intended for permanent cataloging.

Because RAW files come out of the camera without being processed, photo-editing software is required to interpret them, and you'll enhance each file to your preferences before exporting it as an image. Be aware that RAW files typically appear dull at first glance after importing them into your system. This is normal, as they are canvases on which you will work to bring each image to its full, vibrant potential.

Perhaps one of the greatest advantages of RAW files is that they allow nondestructive edits, which means no matter what changes you make in editing, the original information is always available. You can interpret, shift, and alter an image, export that version, and then start over again with the original at any time.

The photo-editing programs bundled with the latest operating systems on both PCs and Macs will handle RAW files, though most photographers prefer more sophisticated programs to interpret and edit their images. Each brand of camera produces a unique, proprietary type of RAW file, and these get more complex with each camera model advancement.

Interestingly, your computer's ability to see different RAW files is a function of its operating system, regardless of your photo-editing software. The RAW readers for files from newly released camera models are bundled in computer operating system updates, so be sure to allow updates as they become available.

With all the effort you've put into planning and making photographs, it makes sense to retain all the information you've captured.

PHOTO-EDITING SOFTWARE

Finding a photo-editing software system you are comfortable with is as important as having the right camera, and it will allow you to organize and finish the story you've started.

▶ FOR MORE ON CUSTOM-IZING YOUR CAMERA, SEE PAGES 266–7

▶ FOR MORE ON OTHER ACCESSO-RIES, SEE PAGES 282–3

To elevate your photographs to the next level, you must commit to learning and using more advanced tools. Beyond the camera, lenses, and accessories, you need a robust computer equipped with photo-editing software. Although the photo programs native to both PC and Mac systems can do a lot, your aspirations to take your work further may leave you wanting more. Professional photo software may sound intimidating, but just like moving to a new town, once you learn your way around, you'll be able to efficiently get where you want to go.

There are many photo-editing programs available, but the gold standard is Adobe, with its suite of applications, including Photoshop and Lightroom.

Photoshop is an amazing, complex, and at times overwhelming program that is the go-to for designers, professional photo retouchers, and other

Different software programs arrange work spaces and adjustment palettes differently, but most offer the same functions and options to make adjustments globally or to specific parts of an image.

digital creatives around the world. Most photographers get by with using—at most—about 10 percent of what the Photoshop software offers.

A more streamlined, photographer-specific program is Lightroom, which allows you to organize, edit, and adjust photographs with an elegant and intuitive interface. Lightroom, like most other photo-editing applications, comes loaded with some powerful features, including:

▶ Corrections to aberrations specific to cameras and lenses
▶ Batch editing of metadata and adjustments
▶ Brush and gradient adjustments
▶ Patching tools
▶ Professional filters and presets that can be imported and customized
▶ Sliding controls for adjustments
▶ Syncing between devices
▶ Slideshow, website, and book templates

Many photographers do the bulk of their adjustments in an application like Lightroom and go to Photoshop for more specific or complex needs. Lightroom is able to accept edits made in Photoshop and save a new copy of the file right beside the original.

No matter which program you choose, organizing thousands of photographs requires a filing system that is intuitive to the way you think about your work. For example, it's useful to organize imagery by location and date in a series of nesting folders. Any professional photo software is customizable to your filing preferences and can feed images into designated folders on import.

When you make a photograph, the camera writes information into the metadata of the image file about the capture, like the date the photo was taken, the focal length of the lens, the aperture, the shutter speed, and anything else you have programmed into the camera's custom settings. All this information travels with the photograph into your computer. Your software will also likely have a host of identifier functions such as GPS and facial recognition, which tag your photos with location information and names of people who appear in them. Other metadata such as keywords, captioning, and contact information can also be added during or after import of photographs. All these identifiers will refine your searches for specific images later on.

When you are making photographs regularly and storing thousands of files, hard drive space will quickly become an issue. Most applications offer the option to create a "referenced" library—one that keeps only the edits (metadata, rating systems, and adjustments) on your computer, while the originals are stored on an external hard drive. This significantly lightens the load on your primary machine and allows for growth of your system by adding more external hard drives over time.

It's important to get set up with a photo-editing system that you feel comfortable with in advance of import. Shop around, talk with other photographers, and see what connects best with the way you work.

──── **ZOOM IN** ────

▶ Do a test project with about 20 images and move it through your new editing program to get a feel for how it works. Explore the organization, keywording, and adjustment options.

BACKUPS

Backing up your work is as important as creating it. Period.

▶ FOR MORE
ON PACKING
TO MAKE
PICTURES,
SEE PAGES
132–3

▶ FOR MORE
ON WORK-
FLOW, SEE
PAGES 352–3

Working in a digital medium makes backing up work simple and quick, and there's no excuse for skipping this critical step. Replicating and storing important files is a matter of a few clicks, and you cannot do it often enough. After capture, and as soon as possible, your image files should always live in at least two places. On location, designate a safe place to keep used cards where you won't confuse them with new ones, and never reformat a card until you are sure that the image files on it have been copied to two separate hard drives at home.

Digital storage space is fairly inexpensive, so invest in a few highly rated hard drives to incorporate into your storage system. Get in the habit of making incremental backups of originals and your entire editing software library anytime you import and edit new work. You can do this manually or ask your editing software to automatically do it for you. Be sure to clearly label hard

When using a laptop, a small external hard drive is essential for storing originals, as is a second to back them up. When working on a desktop computer, look into larger drives for regular backups.

ZOOM IN

▶ Purchase two hard drives and integrate a backup system into your photo-editing workflow before you begin to import any photo projects. Don't ever skip the step of backing up.

Hard drives vary in price point and quality. Some are better for transport; most are compatible with both PCs and Macs. Be sure to read reviews before purchasing one.

drives with originals and backups to prevent confusion for the software and for you, and if possible, keep backup drives in a different location. Cloud storage isn't a practical solution for the backup of all your originals, but it is a good option for high-resolution copies of your most important photographs.

If you're going to be on location for more than a day, consider bringing a portable hard drive. Some wireless, portable drives can read and copy a memory card without using a computer, allowing you to back up the card before storing it safely for transport home. Be sure to

pack the hard drive and memory cards in separate bags for air travel and keep one set in your carry-on.

Backing up work can produce a little anxiety, but redundancy is the best way to ensure that you won't lose the photographs you've worked so hard to create. No matter how many copies you have, and no matter how many places you have them, it never feels like enough. Give yourself peace of mind by making an intuitive backup system an automatic part of your workflow. At the end of the day, backing up your work is as important as creating it.

IMAGE SELECTION

Selecting the best frames from a set of photographs—ones you have poured yourself into making—can be difficult, so take a deep breath and put only your best work forward.

▶ FOR MORE ON IDENTI-FYING STORY, SEE PAGES 24-5

▶ FOR MORE ON BACKUPS, SEE PAGES 358-9

As you put more of yourself into your work, you may begin to lose some objectivity about the photos you make. You may feel a deep connection to the scenarios you photograph, your subjects, and ultimately, the images themselves. But photographers must regard their own work with a highly critical eye when deciding whether an image makes the cut. Of course, that is easier said than done.

Most photographers don't waste time deleting bad frames. Storage is cheap, and your time is better spent seeking the most successful images. Make several passes through a collection of photographs with an eye toward elevating the best frames. Most editing programs use a star rating system that allows you to promote images you like the most. Perhaps on your first pass, you give one star to anything with merit that contributes to the story you're trying to tell. Then filter for just the frames with one star and take another pass. Promote the best of this set to two stars, and so on. Continue in this way until you've distilled the story to 10 frames or

fewer, depending on the body of work. Confirm that each frame makes a totally unique contribution to the whole. Be ruthless, assuaging any anxiety by remembering that demoted photographs still exist; they just aren't making the final set.

Study magazine stories to get a sense for how editors think. Note how each photograph contributes to the whole story, and how typically, no two images do exactly the same job.

As with developing your photographic skills, the art of analytically editing your own work is a constantly evolving process. You'll continue to refine your tastes and critical eye, and you may find that with some space from a project, you can reselect and be a little more ruthless than you were initially. Some photographers never achieve the emotional distance from a project that is required to be discerning, and that's why it helps to enlist the help of an editor or other photographers. Trusting someone else's critical eye might be just what you need to ensure you're putting your best photos forward.

ZOOM IN

▶ When considering photos for a particular story, put your final selections together and review them as a set, making sure each image contributes something unique to the whole. If you have redundant images, choose the best one.

Select images by viewing them in a contact sheet–style grid. Most editing programs will help you group similar photos together. Then review groups one at a time, distilling each down to the strongest images.

ADJUSTING FRAME

Correcting the horizon to make it level and finalizing the frame is an important first step in the editing process and sets a strong foundation for optimizing an image.

This picture of Hopper in front of an apartment building feels off-kilter. The straight lines of the entryway are off level because the camera was not parallel to the facade of the building.

▶ FOR MORE ON HORIZON LINE, SEE PAGES 48–9

▶ FOR MORE ON FRAMING, SEE PAGES 52–3

Once you've made your final selections of the best images within a given body of work, it's time to bring them to their full potential. Remember, you should always make the best images possible in the camera. There are no digital tricks that are a substitute for thoughtful composition and skillful use of exposure. That said, there are almost no perfect captures, and especially when working quickly on site and in the moment, you may find your framing can use a little tweak as you are reviewing and editing your photographic results.

ON THE HORIZON

The horizon is the foundation of a photograph and will anchor the viewer in the frame. Unless the goal of the image is to evoke a sense of chaos or imbalance, a level horizon will usually serve best, and correcting horizon in postproduction is relatively simple. Every photo-editing program has a straightening tool that drops a grid over the frame for adjusting to level.

Most applications also allow corrections for vertical and horizontal distortion, which is useful when the camera's lens plane doesn't match that of the subject or setting. For example, if you're photographing a window and the camera is not perfectly parallel to the wall, the window will turn out to appear bigger on one side than the other. A horizontal distortion adjustment will correct the scene to flush. This feature should be used for only subtle corrections, as too much of it will cause even more distortion.

HOW BEST TO CROP

Most horizon and distortion corrections will require a subsequent bit of trimming to recalibrate an image to its original proportions, and the cropping tool can be used for this. Usually found in the same control panel as the horizon adjustment, you can either crop freehand or set the tool to a specific aspect ratio.

Professional photographers traditionally maintain the same aspect ratio that the camera produces as it first captures the image, but it's possible to alter an image to square, or even to turn a horizontal frame into a vertical. A note of caution that doing so reduces the overall resolution of the final image, and so changing the orientation or zooming in on a subject using the crop tool is not generally recommended unless you are working with a very large digital file.

Cropping can also be used to omit distracting elements at the edge of a frame, such as the corner of an object that doesn't add to the composition or a surface that detracts from the framing you were striving for. But these decisions work best when made with your camera in hand. Try to reserve the cropping tool for subtle

Editing software has different ways of letting you correct your image, leveling it through horizon adjustment and vertical and horizontal distortion, which requires cropping to finish the frame without any white space at the edges.

adjustments and minor corrections. The more effort you put into level, intentional framing of photographs before you make them, the less time you will need to spend correcting.

GLOBAL ADJUSTMENTS

Make global adjustments to the entire image with a light touch, using sliders that can be nudged for incremental changes.

Before adjustments, this RAW file of Hopper looks a little dull. Making global adjustments is the best place to start to bring the image to its full potential.

▶ FOR MORE
ON WHITE
BALANCE,
SEE PAGES
258-9

▶ FOR MORE
ON CONVER-
SION TO
BLACK-AND-
WHITE, SEE
PAGES 372-3

In your approach to postproduction, it's important to keep the truth of an image at heart. Unless a photograph has a purely fine art context, all enhancements and adjustments should be made with a light touch—never changing the facts of the image—merely bringing it to its full potential.

To start, look to global adjustments—those applied to the entire frame—that can correct for a minor error in exposure or enhance the picture's overall look.

These first-round, comprehensive adjustments typically include white balance, exposure, contrast, shadows and highlights, and saturation:

WHITE BALANCE— This is typically in a panel with two sliders, temperature and tint. You can adjust the white balance automatically with the eyedropper tool, clicking on an area of the image that you know should read as white, and the program will recalibrate the rest of the frame.

EXPOSURE— Adjusts the exposure of the image by brightening or darkening the entire frame. The whole numbers on the slider equate to f-stops on the camera. As this adjustment is a good place to start, it's usually found at the top of the adjustment panel. Generally, a move to the right brightens exposure, while a move to the left darkens it.

CONTRAST— Helps define light and dark areas of the image. Adding a touch of contrast will usually make a subject pop against a contrasting background.

SHADOWS AND HIGHLIGHTS— These are two different sliders that influence the brightest and darkest parts of the image. Moving them one way or the other increases or decreases targeted areas.

SATURATION— Modifies the color intensity in the entire image, either boosting it or toning it down. This adjustment should be used very subtly to avoid an unnatural look. Sliding it all the way down gives you a quick conversion to black-and-white, but most photographers prefer a little more control in this rendering.

You can use many other controls either for slight enhancements of particular parts, or for more dramatic changes. With any adjustment, play with the slider to get a feel for its impact. Slide it all the way to one side to direct your eye to the changes it makes, then reset and make incremental movements until you're satisfied. Consistency is key, and if you prefer a certain look in your work, try to use it evenly across all your selects. It's easy to get carried away with changes that enhance a photograph, but remember that less is usually more.

In the images above (clockwise from top left), exposure, contrast, and saturation are all increased by moving the designated sliders to the right, while highlights within the image are pulled down by moving that slider to the left.

ADVANCED CONTROLS

Use advanced controls to adjust ranges of color or tones within an image, leaving the rest of the photograph unaltered.

▶ FOR MORE
ON COLOR,
SEE PAGES
32-3

▶ FOR MORE
ON RAW
FILES, SEE
PAGES 354-5

Taking your adjustments to the next level might include more specific changes applied to a certain range of colors or tones in an image. Unless you're already familiar with what these advanced tools can do, experimentation is the best way to learn how to control them and, in turn, realize exactly how you can manipulate your images.

The HSL panel allows you to target the hue, saturation, and luminance of specific values in a photograph, meaning you can independently control the appearance of different colors in the frame. Hue allows you to shift the shade of a color within its family, perhaps changing royal blue to sapphire, for example. Saturation controls the intensity of a specific color, giving it a more vivid or muted appearance. Luminance refers to the brightness of a color, where an increase makes the color stand out more, whereas a decrease subdues it. Making these types of changes to various color ranges within

The Hue panel of the HSL adjustment control allows you to change a color throughout the frame. Here, the reds have been pushed to magenta and the blues in the shadows pushed to aqua.

By pulling the Lights slider to the right and the Darks slider to the left, the curves on the graph deepen to an effective increase in contrast. A little goes a long way—and this example goes too far.

an image gives you more control of mood using the psychology of color.

USING THE CURVE TOOL

The curve tool is another way to control brightness and contrast within your photographs. The curve in the graph represents different regions in the image, specifically highlights, lights, darks, and shadows. By moving each associated slider, you will see the brightness and contrast of the corresponding tone change throughout the image. You'll also notice the curve in the graph bending one way or another.

Alternatively, you can move the curve line with guides on the bottom of the graph, or pin the curve to points, moving other portions of the graph. For even more specific control, most programs have a selection tool to choose exactly which tone in the image you'd like to brighten,

darken, or change the contrast of. As you move the cursor throughout the image, you'll notice the sliders and curve on the graph changing.

If you're feeling adventurous and in need of more precise control, bring an image into Photoshop where you can create layers for each adjustment, as well as masks for specific elements in the frame, which allow you to either include or exclude them from an adjustment.

Some of these tools might seem daunting at first glance, but explore each adjustment one at a time and watch the image as you do, noticing which areas are impacted. You can undo any alteration at any time in your history panel. And, if you're working with RAW files, all of your edits are nondestructive, which means none of the original image data is overwritten. You can edit the image in a completely different way at any time.

LOCAL ADJUSTMENTS

For adjustments to specific areas or objects within a frame, use local adjustments in the form of gradients and brushes.

A radial filter has been placed on Hopper's nose with a series of selected changes (sliders at right) applied within the solid circle. These gradually drop off toward the dotted outer circle.

▶ FOR MORE ON USING FILTERS, SEE PAGES 290–91

▶ FOR MORE ON EXPO-SURE, SEE PAGES 230–31

Sometimes a photographer wants to lay a particular adjustment over specific areas of an image. Most editing programs have filter and brush tools for applying any adjustment to precisely where you'd like it in the frame.

Similar to a graduated filter you might add to the front of a lens, a graduated filter in your editing program allows you to add any adjustment in a gradient across the frame. You can drag the cursor up or down, from one side to another, or even diagonally across the image, and whatever adjustment you have chosen will wash across it as you have directed. The adjustment will be most intense at the beginning of the gradient, fading to no effect at the end. This can be particularly useful with a bright sky above a dark body of water in the bottom of a frame, when a global exposure adjustment won't work for both. Select the graduated filter and exposure, drag the cursor from top to bottom, and adjust the slider until you see your desired effect.

A graduated filter with a tint adjustment has been initiated at the left edge of the image and dragged past center, with the greatest change at the start of the filter and then trailing off toward the leading edge.

The radial filter works in a similar way with a circle of influence in any part of the frame. Let's say you'd like to bump up the contrast in the center of a photograph of your daughter by the water's edge. You can use the radial filter tool to create a circle around her and adjust the contrast in just that region. Radial filters can be "feathered" for a softer, more graduated effect at their perimeter, which helps to ensure the modification won't stand out as obvious.

For a more exact application of a particular adjustment, select the brush tool to "paint" the effect precisely where you want it. Most brush tools have a masking function, where the brush recognizes and stops at the edges of the object being painted so you don't have to struggle to stay within the lines. Brush tools can also be feathered for a softer, more gradual effect.

Almost any editing program has a spot-removal tool that allows you to eliminate unwanted artifacts from the image. This is helpful when dust on your camera's sensor is visible in a wide-open sky, or to remove blemishes from the face of a portrait subject. Most spot-removal tools have two types of functions. The clone tool exactly matches a sampled area in another portion of the image, and the heal tool blends information copied from the sampled area with the spot to be covered for a more natural correction.

With all adjustments, you can save custom presets of any combination of alterations for quick access to either paint into the image or add with a radial or graduated filter. Any adjustment is most effective if it isn't too drastic in comparison to the rest of the image, so use a light, subtle hand. If viewers can tell which areas have been adjusted, you've gone too far.

WHY I LOVE THIS PHOTO

I have always gravitated toward wildlife and science photography, even before I came to National Geographic. When I first started digital photo editing in 1983, this type of image was very difficult to produce electronically. But now, with the digital tools available, these types of color adjustments are much more commonplace. This image works for me because, first, it is a stunning capture with good detail and interest. Second, the photographer, Keith Ladzinski, converted it to black-and-white, and then added a tint of color, making the image unique to him. The added sharpness and contrast bring out the detail and shapes in the elephant's face, while limiting the distraction of an unimportant background. It also has the effect of holding your interest and keeping your eyes moving around the image.

—CLAYTON BURNESTON
Technical Director, Production Services,
National Geographic Partners

Taken at the Malilangwe Wildlife Reserve in Masvingo Province, Zimbabwe, this portrait of an African elephant has been elevated with the stylized use of black-and-white.

CONVERSION TO BLACK-AND-WHITE

An impactful conversion to black-and-white is much more than adjusting the saturation slider to zero. Take advantage of granular controls to strike just the right tone.

▶ FOR MORE
ON BLACK-
AND-WHITE,
SEE PAGES
320–21

▶ FOR MORE
ON PATTERN
& TEXTURE,
SEE PAGES
34–5

Remember that photography is about recording light—the way it illuminates elements in its path, and the way shadows are crafted in its absence. Without the vivid diversion of color, contrasts between highlights and shadows register as patterns and textures, evoking the other senses in a way that can be deeply impactful. And so, when applied appropriately and well, a skillful black-and-white conver-sion has the power to make a photo-graph extraordinary.

When you've got an image that might look particularly arresting in black-and-white, or better yet, when a black-and-white treatment might take the image from average to special, there are some particulars to consider in a conversion from color. Your editing software likely has a number of black-and-white preset filters—these are essentially collections

With a simple click between filters, you can sample and apply different collections of black-and-white conversions. Here, B&W Soft has been applied. It converts the image to gray scale without sharp contrast between shades.

After a conversion has been applied, the same sliders can be used to make adjustments to contrast, highlights, shadows, and more.

of varying conversion steps that result in different grayscale looks, or ones with varying shades of gray. If you apply any one of these filters, you can see the impact on the image, but also review the adjustments that create the achieved look. From there, you can tweak each adjusted slider to begin to understand its impact, and fine-tune the look you're after.

Many photographers prefer to build a black-and-white treatment in steps specific to the tonality of the image. For example, if an image has lots of shadows important to its mood, contrast and richness in the dark areas are important. If the image is full of washed-out highlights, lightening shadows to reveal their details against a white backdrop is effective. A manual conversion allows photographers to control the way each element plays in the overall composition.

Most programs have a "B&W Mixer" panel, which drops the image into a grayscale setting, but further offers detailed control over the luminance of each individual color channel—a way to precisely determine how each color is converted. Manipulating the luminance of each color yields different black-and-white results—darker skies or lighter trees—and you should play with each to choose a look that most suits your aesthetic and the tone of the scene. After this detailed initial conversion, global and local adjustments can be added to enhance contrast and adjust exposure of different areas, to your preference.

As with any adjustments, don't go overboard on dramatic effects. Make a conversion, tweak the overall impact, and take a break from the image. Come back later and look again—you'll know right away if your edits were the right choice.

SHARPENING

Sharpening can give an image a little extra pop, but careful attention should be paid to how much is just enough.

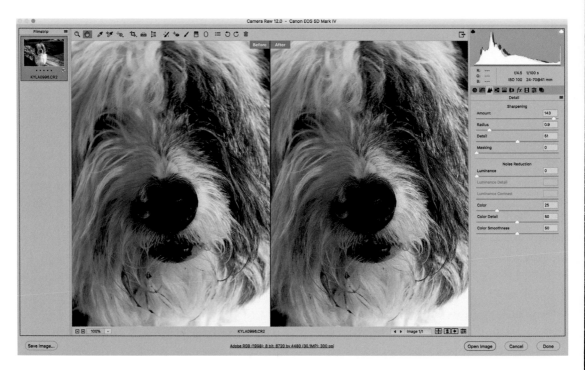

Adjusting the sharpening sliders to the right creates tiny halos of white space around elements of a specified size, here giving the hairs on Hopper's head a sharper look.

▶ FOR MORE ON TECHNOLOGY OF FOCUS, SEE PAGES 234–5

▶ FOR MORE ON PREPARING FILES FOR PRINT SERVICE, SEE PAGES 380–81

Remember that a lack of focus in a photograph is a deal breaker, and there is no fix for a soft image. But most images can benefit from a little digital sharpening, a refining of edges within the frame that gives a subject a little more pop.

The sharpening tool does this by adding empty "halos" of pixels around the edges of everything in the image. These minute gaps enhance contrast between elements, giving everything a sharper look.

THE SHARPENING PANEL

The sharpening panel usually features three sliders, representing "Radius," "Threshold," and "Amount."

The radius setting adjusts the width of the halo added to the edges, and a typical setting is between 0.5 and 1. The threshold setting determines how the edges in the image are identified as a function of differing values between adjacent pixels. The higher the threshold, the more different the pixels need to be for an edge to be identified and

— ZOOM IN —

▶ **Sharpening benefits some images more than others. A landscape washed in a sunset's soft pastels may not improve with sharpening, as the blending of elements adds to the image. A photograph of an exotic bird perched on a branch, however, will likely benefit from a little pop.**

therefore sharpened. A typical threshold setting is about 10. The amount setting controls how much contrast is added to the edges. The higher the value, the more sharpening will be applied. A good starting point for the amount setting is usually about 150.

CONSIDERING THE SUBJECT

The content of the image should influence the choices you make for sharpening settings. A photograph with a lot of small detail can take small radius sharpening at a high amount. An image with larger elements benefits most from smaller amounts of sharpening with a larger radius, perhaps 1 to 1.5.

Sharpening is something that works best when it's very subtle, and you should play with the sliders to see exactly how much each image can take. To do so, enlarge the image to 100 percent in the viewer of your editing application.

Alternatively, most programs have a preview window on the sharpening panel. This offers a full-size look at a portion of the image where you can see the impact of adjustments as you make them. Not enough sharpening, and you won't get the potential definition to make a subject pop. Too much, and the image will look too "crispy," with obvious white lines around edges and a lot of unwanted noise.

WHEN TO SHARPEN

It's important to note that sharpening should be the final step in your postproduction treatment of a photograph before you export the image

file for use elsewhere. In general, if an image will be printed, it can take more sharpening than it can for on-screen viewing. Most programs allow you to export an image at a specific size, with the optimal amount of sharpening for the file's specific application. When exporting your image, select the appropriate sharpening settings, either for printing or on-screen viewing, depending on how you plan to share the photograph.

The Unsharp Mask filter in Photoshop has a slider panel similar to those for other functions. The sample box offers a view of a portion of the image at 100 percent, or full size, allowing you to gauge the impact of each adjustment. Sharpening should be your final adjustment step.

SPECIALIZED FUNCTIONS

Some editing functions, like combining multiple images in one way or another, make certain varieties of photographs possible.

▶ FOR MORE ON PAN-ORAMIC PHOTOGRA-PHY, SEE PAGES 338–9

▶ FOR MORE ON MACRO-PHOTOGRA-PHY, SEE PAGES 288–9

To manifest certain grand visions, some images require merging of more than one frame. Whether combined at their edges or stacked atop each other for various applications, the magic of postproduction editing makes impactful compositing possible. Although automated steps by software handle the most laborious aspects of combining frames, each photograph must be captured with an attention to detail and consistency that the final composition requires. Intention and planning are key to ensure a successful merge.

PANORAMIC PHOTOS

Panoramic photographs, whether one row, multirow, or 360° spherical images, involve the stitching of multiple adjacent frames into one, comprehensive image. Although some cameras can combine a sequence of images immediately after capture, doing so later in editing allows the most control in the final image.

Some key considerations on capture will make for better results, including overlapping frames 20 to 50 percent and maintaining position, focal length, focus, exposure, and a level horizon. Smooth panning and manual camera settings are the best bet here. The trick is to take a matching set of photographs that can merge together into one interesting combination.

There are software programs designed specifically for creating panoramas, but most panoramic stitching can be done precisely and efficiently in Photoshop. After importing the image files, Photoshop has a powerful Photomerge function that makes the procedure as simple as designating the

In this image of scientists collecting samples beneath the Golden Gate Bridge, multiple frames have been stitched together with editing software into a composition that makes artful use of their varying borders.

In this panorama of a forest, the multiple frames have been stitched together seamlessly for a smooth, well-blended final composition.

images to be merged, selecting among automated layout options, and letting the software do the rest.

FOCUS STACKING

Stacking is the sandwiching of two or more images of the same scene. Focus stacking refers to layering identical frames with a slightly different point of focus in each one. The effect is extended depth of field, with elements from each frame in focus.

This is particularly useful in macro photographs made with extremely shallow depth of field. For example, in a photograph of the face of an insect taken head on, focus stacking can make more than just the eyes sharp.

Using an Auto-blend command in Photoshop, the multiple images are combined seamlessly into one final composite image. Auto-blend is also used to create dramatic star trail images, which are composed of a series of exposures made over a long period of time to capture the apparent path of stars in the night sky.

HIGH DYNAMIC RANGE

Photoshop's Merge to HDR and other HDR software applications process two or three images exposed for different parts of the same scene. These are combined to create one composite with a broad dynamic range.

Photoshop and other programs are capable of powerful automation that takes guesswork and tedious blending procedures completely off photographers' hands. In general, it's wise to combine the photographs before making other adjustments or enhancements, but Photoshop takes care of the blending and layer adjustments that make for seamless merging. Understanding the ways a program performs these elegant tasks will help you plan in advance for optimal captures when you want more than the camera can give.

ZOOM IN

▶ Precision and consistency are key in compositions that require special functions to combine multiple photographs. Plan ahead to capture the best assets you can, and let your editing program handle the rest.

SMARTPHONE EDITING

Consider your smartphone a serious camera and give the work you produce with it the attention it deserves, with thoughtful editing and deliberate adjustments.

> ▶ FOR MORE
> ON SMART-
> PHONE PHO-
> TOGRAPHY,
> SEE PAGES
> 224–5
>
> ▶ FOR MORE
> ON BACK-
> UPS, SEE
> PAGES 358–9

Smartphones are becoming the one-camera bands of photography, offering the power to create, edit, and share your work in the palm of your hand. This ubiquitous convenience is both a blessing and a curse.

The blessing is the ease with which smartphones make photography possible. This is also the curse, because often, after a smartphone photographer has captured many frames, the phone is returned to a pocket without another thought to the images just captured.

You likely already have hundreds or thousands of smartphone images somewhere that have not been managed. Don't overwhelm yourself with trying to go back and work with those. Begin with today, and commit to an efficient execution of your new routine going forward.

Your workflow should be similar to that of a DSLR to computer system, complete with incremental backups, selection, enhancement, and sharing. And as with your other work, the sooner you edit, the more likely your photographs will meet their full potential and be seen.

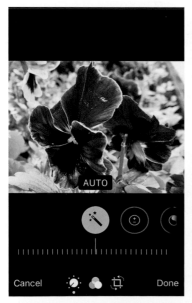

Smartphone editing panels vary across brands, but the adjustments available are generally the same. The iPhone used as an example here features adjustments such as general global enhancement, highlights, and saturation, each with a slider to control the change.

Other adjustments might add a vignette (darkening around the edges of the frame), filter the image for various looks including several versions of black-and-white, or crop the image, allowing for reframing or subtle rotation to level the image.

BACKING UP

Establishing backup for your phone photos is the first priority. Many cloud options integrate automatically with various brands of smartphones. Research a platform thoroughly before committing, expect to spend some money to maximize cloud storage space, and have at least one hard drive backup for your mobile photos. Set up an organized folder system in the destination drive that is intuitive to you for efficient retrieval later.

Regarding photo selection, most phone photo apps have a rating system that uses hearts or stars, as well as options to create specific albums for photographs. Employ both of these tools in an intuitive system that promotes frames you like until your final album has the very best ones.

SELECTING, ENHANCING & SHARING

Enhancing phone photographs is simple and fun, but also easy to overdo. Be true to your style with a consistent look that doesn't pull an image too far from reality. Native phone photo apps are fairly robust and packed with sophisticated editing functions. Hundreds of third-party editing apps vary in effectiveness and interface elegance. Look for apps that offer nondestructive edits, which enables you to always have access to the original captures. The best apps offer the same edit functions as desktop editing programs, with sliders for easy adjustments that you can see as you make them.

Most sharing platforms offer opportunities to enhance or filter images on import. Filtering a photograph more than once can result in an overprocessed look, so make the choice to filter in one place but not another. As you post your work to social media, be sure to add thorough and compelling caption information. The story behind a photograph is almost as important as the image itself.

PREPARING FILES FOR PRINT SERVICE

Taking an image from digital file to print has never been easier, but attention to some specific adjustments will ensure your prints look their best.

► FOR MORE ON GLOBAL ADJUSTMENTS, SEE PAGES 364–5

► FOR MORE ON SHARPENING, SEE PAGES 374–5

Making prints of your photographs remains a classic and sophisticated way to present your work. You can navigate the world of inks, papers, and other technical aspects that go into printing yourself, or you can upload your image, have someone else handle the printing, and have the prints delivered right to your home. It's never been easier or less expensive to get good, professional printing, and many online labs offer a wide variety of print sizes and products. That said, printing is a very different application of a digital image than displaying it on a backlit screen, so file preparation is an important part of the process.

No two computer monitors are exactly the same, so the only way to be sure of how your image is going to look when printed is to calibrate your monitor to match the standard of your cho-

Check the website of your chosen print service for recommendations about calibrating your computer monitor to match their printing equipment so your prints look just as you expect them to.

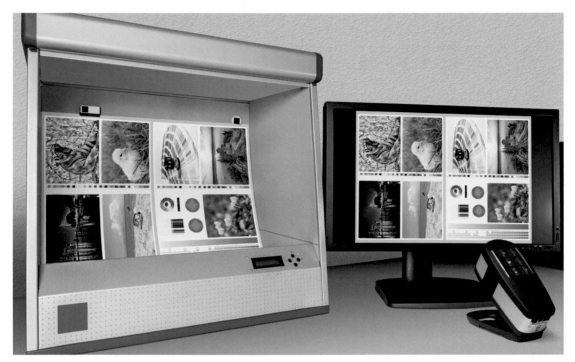

For large prints or images applied on surfaces like glass, metal, or wood, request a proof—a small sample showing how the image will look on the selected medium—before the final product is printed.

sen printer. You can buy a relatively inexpensive calibration kit and speak to a representative at your printing lab for details about the standard that best matches their system.

The factor that will most impact the print quality of your photographs is resolution. Resolution refers to the amount of information per unit of length. In reference to an on-screen image, resolution is measured by ppi (pixels per inch). In printing, the measurement is designated as dpi (dots per inch), as printers create images with millions of ink dots. In both cases, the more information per inch, the higher the quality will be.

Although on-screen applications of an image look good at lower resolution, printing requires a higher resolution. Different types of prints have different minimum resolution requirements, but in general, aim for a resolution of 300 dpi at the dimensions (in inches) of the intended print. You can designate these size parameters on export from your editing software, or you can size the image in Photoshop and export it from there.

The other factor to consider is sharpening the image. To set an image up for successful sharpening, be sure to have your other enhancements where you want them, and make sure an adjustment to contrast has been made to maximize the distinction between different elements in the frame.

Your best bet is to find a photo lab that you like and build a relationship with them. Speak with a technician about the best ways to optimize your photographs for printing on their machines with regard to monitor calibration, resolution, sharpening, and more. Most labs have detailed information like file recommendations and templates on their websites to make sure you get precisely what you want from their services.

WEBSITE PLANNING: A DIGITAL PORTFOLIO

A website is the best way to showcase a portfolio of your work. Keep it simple and be sure to pick only your strongest photographs.

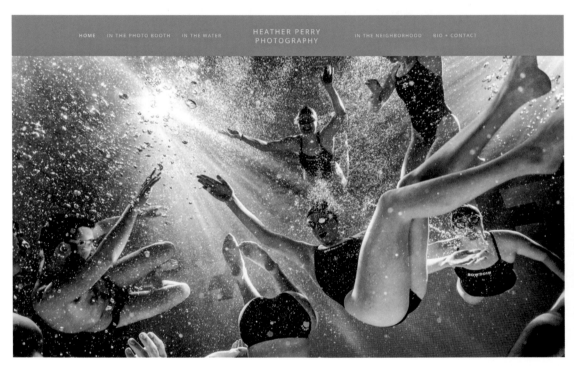

Design your website's home page with a strong image representative of your style and photographic voice and full of impact when presented at full screen. Change this image as your work evolves.

▶ **FOR MORE ON POR-TRAITS,** SEE PAGES 112–13

▶ **FOR MORE ON UNDER-WATER PHO-TOGRAPHY,** SEE PAGES 328–9

The best way to share a focused portfolio of your work is to produce a professional website. Designing and maintaining a clean, easily navigated site has never been easier thanks to many reasonably priced template-based web platforms. The best photography websites feature large, full-screen images with smooth navigation functions, and minimal bells and whistles. You've worked hard to make images with impact, and a good website should let them be center stage without other distractions.

MAKE A BLUEPRINT

Essential to crafting a successful website is planning. Begin with a home page that features one stunning photograph that both represents you as a photographer and makes viewers want to see more.

ZOOM IN

▶ Sketch a map of your future site, complete with home page, three galleries, and a page about yourself. Make a list of your best images for each gallery and consider a simple color palette that will suit your work—neutral colors work best for a photographic portfolio.

Next, plan three galleries, each with a common thread linking the photographs within them. Galleries could be split into specializations like, "Portraiture" or "Underwater," and feature imagery from across many projects that fit into those themes. Alternatively, each gallery could feature a specific story like "Ice Fishing" or "Windmills." Add an "About" or "Bio" page to your site—this is your opportunity to say something about your experience and your approach to photography. And don't forget to include contact information.

Look at your best work with a highly critical eye to further distill your selection to the top 30 images you've made thus far. Keep your galleries tight and succinct—about 10 images each—and be sure no two photographs say the same thing.

Export your gallery images into organized folders for easy access and uploading to your site. Most website platforms suggest an optimal file size for their templates, typically between 1200 and 1600 pixels wide. Following these recommendations will ensure your images load quickly for the viewer. Consider short bodies of text to introduce each gallery and caption information to accompany each image. Choose your words carefully, and don't forget to proofread (or have someone you trust do it). Remember, this is the public face of your work.

Once you've designed your portfolio, it's time to build your site. You'll need to register a domain name in advance—be sure to pick something that incorporates your name and is representative of who you are as a photographer.

INTRODUCE YOUR WORK TO THE WORLD

Be sure to spread the word about your new site and seek feedback from people whose work and artistic sense you admire. Keep your site simple, but update it often as you make more photographs. A website should not be a static portfolio piece; rather, it should be a revolving showroom that represents your style and illuminates your unique photographic voice.

Keep galleries tightly edited with a concise set of strong images that are linked by a particular story or theme. Make small subsets or pairings that illustrate both the cohesiveness and the breadth of your work.

SHARING TO SOCIAL MEDIA

Posting to social media is the fastest way to have your work seen, so craft your photographic presence carefully and tend to it often.

▶ FOR MORE ON IDENTIFYING STORY, SEE PAGES 24-5

▶ FOR MORE ON IMAGE SELECTION, SEE PAGES 360-61

The easiest way to share your work with a broad audience is to publish it on social media. Consider creating pages and feeds on various platforms specific to your photographic work, separate from your personal profiles. Making regular, curated posts will help you establish your presence as a photographer and cultivate a following. Consider arresting stand-alone images with meaningful captions, and small collections of images—maybe five or fewer—to represent larger stories. Be open to sharing anecdotes about the making of a photograph, or thoughts and feelings about the story and why it compelled you to pick up the camera.

ALL ABOUT INSTAGRAM

Currently, Instagram is center stage for sharing photography. The app allows you to publish more than one image at

As you post to social media, remember that many people may be posting imagery from the same events as you—so be sure to apply what you know about what makes a great photograph to set your post apart.

a time, and images can be full-frame or cropped to square. In addition to powerful tools similar to those in your primary editing program, Instagram and other apps have distinct collections of filters that can be added to your images before posting. Skillful use of these will subtly enhance an image, rather than steal focus from the content. Be consistent with your look across your media feeds, selecting images of coherent subjects or tones and treating them with similar edits and filters. Beware of adding too many postproduction layers to any image, and if you know you're going to use a filter in Instagram, perhaps skip an enhancement (or a few) earlier in your editing process.

Some platforms make posting from either a computer or smartphone equally easy, whereas others, like Instagram, require a smartphone for publishing. Many social media sites are linked, or feed into one another in some way, allowing you to publish to one and automatically push to your accounts on other platforms with a single click.

BEING MINDFUL OF AUDIENCE

Be true to yourself and your work, but always consider your audience before posting. Think about who you are trying to reach and why, and try to imagine seeing the photographs for the first time through their eyes. Consider image order, arrangement, and words to accompany each post. And once you've shared, be open to comments and responses from your audience. Let these guide you in future posts.

Some photographers express concern about proprietary issues and the risk of having shared work misappropriated on social media. Although the internet is evolving more quickly than the world can develop rules to govern it, it seems better to have your work seen than not. Each post is a record of your creative ideas, and own-

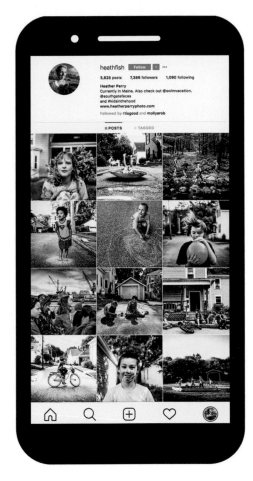

Most great photography feeds have a thread of continuity. Study popular accounts to get a sense of what makes them work, and apply the same principles to your own feed. Maintain a consistent, curated standard.

ership comes with the first time a post is seen.

Be patient and thoughtful as you develop an online presence for your photographic work. When crafted well, your feed as a whole should read like a narrative in your evolution as a photographer. Interact regularly with your peers on the same platforms, and help promote and celebrate their photographic achievements along with your own. Cultivating a positive community around your work will foster your growth as a photographer.

PULLING IT ALL TOGETHER

Throughout both the capture and editing process, being true to yourself and consistent with your style is key to developing your photographic voice.

Wherever you are, strive to make a photograph that conveys your personal experience of being there. If you succeed at this, your image will be unlike anyone else's.

▶ FOR MORE ON ANTICI- PATING COMPOSI- TION, SEE PAGES 64-5

▶ FOR MORE ON AWARE- NESS OF LIGHT, SEE PAGES 70-71

The challenge of the back half of picturemaking is in maintaining continuity in your standards for what makes a good photograph. The discipline required to edit your pictures with an eye to that standard is significant when you've poured yourself into making them. With some edits and adjustments, just because you can doesn't mean you should. The goal is always to make art that represents life, and to bring the stirring content of a photograph to its full, evocative potential.

The more passionate you become for the art and work of making photographs,

the more driven you will be—you'll see in pictures and never want to be without a means for capturing them. Although this kind of obsession gives birth to great photographers, the challenge becomes balancing drive with the equally important goal of just being in the moment. One could argue that cultivating this kind of presence will make you a better photographer, and ultimately, a better human, in the long run.

There's a lot to learn in the art and work of photography, and mastery of the particulars may take years of practice, split-second decisions, and honest assessment of successes and just-misses. You can easily get lost in an endless stream of technology, physics, and details. But remember that photography is about tuning in to the world around you—with open eyes, an open heart, and guts—and then using the tools at hand to craft something that will preserve a moment, and make it known.

Find photographers who inspire you, who make the kind of photographs you want to make. As you study their work, try to imagine how each image was made—assess equipment and logistical considerations, analyze composition and lighting, and think about their approach.

Most of all, reflect on what makes their work distinct. When you look at a photograph, can you tell immediately who made it? This is the mark of voice. Begin and end each day with the study of others' work as you consider the development of your own.

Any professional photographer will tell you that the effort of realizing your full potential is never done. "To see takes time," as Georgia O'Keeffe said. You're taking this time, and you're learning to see. You're thinking in a new way about the tools you have to best express what you experience. Now, trust the process and pick up a camera. Don't think; just see. Go make pictures.

Don't be afraid to make photographs in the moments before or after the obvious action. These frames are where the truth of life is captured and may be the most relatable of all.

—————— ZOOM IN ——————

▶ Take a breath and remember that who you are is inextricably tied to how you see. With this in mind, make photographs that are an extension of how you experience the world.

ASSIGNMENT

A Grand Canyon ranger watches a winter sunrise in a photograph that successfully uses exposure, composition, and moment to fill viewers with an overwhelming sense of place.

PUTTING IT OUT THERE

Often the hardest part of photography is all the post-capture work required to present your vision to the world.

COVER IT Think of a story you can capture and tell through photographs relatively easily and in one day. This can be something you've been meaning to work on, or perhaps a small vignette about a typical day in the life of someone you know. Assume the same goal as a professional magazine photographer, which is to capture more photos than one story needs.

EDIT Design and set up your workflow in advance. Use this system to immediately back up your work and to import the photographs into your photo software. Now, distill the set down to the five best frames that cover the story with quality and variety. Take these photos through your postproduction process to bring them to their full potential. Compose a meaningful caption for each, or a brief statement about your inspiration or context for the project. Add this to the image file's metadata.

SHARE Upload the final five on a platform where friends and other photographers can see them. Create a dedicated gallery on a website, a comprehensive post on social media, prints for display, or even a book or magazine. Spread the word about your project and be open to the feedback you receive.

GLOSSARY

A

aberrations Optical faults that cause a lens to produce an unsharp or distorted image. These can be corrected (and sometimes eliminated) by the optical design of a lens. Stopping down to smaller apertures also minimizes the effect of some aberrations.

angle of view The amount of any scene that a lens "sees," measured in degrees; the shorter the focal length, the greater the coverage. Also called *field of view*.

aperture The opening inside the lens that allows light to pass; this is adjusted in size (except in mirror lenses and a few others) by the diaphragm and is expressed in f-stop numbers, such as f/8. Aperture is a major factor in depth of field.

aperture priority A semiautomatic camera mode where the photographer sets the f-stop and the camera adjusts to the shutter speed required for a correct exposure, based on information from the in-camera light meter. Denoted on the mode dial as "A" or "Av."

aspect ratio The ratio of width to height in an image or image sensor.

autofocus (AF) A tool where the camera will automatically move the elements in the lens to achieve sharpness for the subject. Types to activate include single-point AF, dynamic-area AF, auto-area AF, single-shot AF, and continuous AF.

B

bokeh The aesthetic quality visible in the blurred, or out-of-focus, areas of an image. The term comes from the Japanese word *boke*, meaning "blur."

bounce Flash light of an electronic flash reflected from a wall, ceiling, or other surface instead of being aimed directly at the subject. This produces softer, more diffused lighting. Some flash units have a swivel and/or tilt head that allows the use of bounce flash with the unit mounted on the camera.

bracketing Taking a series of photos, identical except in the exposure for each frame, so as to get at least one ideal exposure.

byte A measurement of digital information.

C

cable release A mechanical or electronic cable used to trigger a tripod-mounted camera without touching it directly, to prevent shake or vibration.

camera trap A system using motion detection or the break of a laser beam to trigger the shutter release; used by professional wildlife photographers.

center-weighted meter A type of metering that evaluates the center of the frame for exposure, ignoring the corners, regardless of where the focal point is; works best for portraits or landscapes when the main subject is in the center or nearly fills the frame.

cloning In digital imaging, copying pixels from one part of an image area and using them to cover other areas to correct flaws such as scratches or dust specks. Cloning can also be used to add more of the same element to the final picture (e.g., more leaves onto a branch).

color temperature A measurement of the color of any given light source provided in degrees kelvin. "Warm" light, such as the light at sunset, has a low temperature, whereas "cool" (bluish) light, as on a heavily overcast day, has a high color temperature on this scale.

composite A photo illustration made by combining parts of multiple images.

composition The placement of objects and elements in the frame.

compression The process used to decrease the size of a digital image file by combining, averaging, or eliminating redundant pixel data.

continuous autofocus (AF) Technique where the camera will continue to adjust focus if the camera or subject moves while the photographer depresses the shutter button halfway and holds it to set the focus on an object within the frame.

contrast The range in brightness present on a subject; the difference between the lightest and darkest parts of an image. A scene with

high contrast includes both extreme highlights and very dark shadows.

D

depth of field The zone or range of apparent sharpness in a photograph. Although only the focused subject (and other objects at the same distance) is truly sharp, the range of acceptable sharpness extends in front of and behind the focused point.

diaphragm The mechanism inside a lens that controls the size of the aperture, using overlapping metal leaves.

diffuser A translucent material generally held between the subject and the light source to soften illumination.

digital zoom A camera function that digitally magnifies the center of a frame.

distortion An optical flaw that causes straight lines near the edges of an image to be bent, either inward ("pincushioning") or outward ("barreling").

dpi (dots per inch) The density of information produced by a device, which defines the resolution level that a printer should produce. The more dots per inch, the higher the resolution.

DSLR (digital single-lens reflex) A camera that uses mirrors to show the potential image through the viewfinder. When the shutter opens, the mirror lifts away, and the same view strikes the sensor.

dynamic range The range between the darkest and lightest areas of an image.

E-F

exposure The amount of light that reaches the sensor. This can be manipulated to create a particular tone or mood in a photograph.

exposure compensation A control found on most cameras that allows users to overexpose (+ factors) or underexpose (– factors) from the metered value in an automatic mode.

extension tubes Hollow mechanical spacers that fit between a camera body and the lens, used to increase the lens focal length and magnify the subject for close-up work.

fast A term used to describe a lens with a very wide maximum aperture, allowing for faster shutter speeds to make a correct exposure.

file format The format used to save or record photographic data—JPEG or RAW, for most digital cameras.

fill-in flash (fill flash) Extra light added by electronic flash to soften hard shadows without becoming the primary light source. Generally used in sunny conditions, fill-in flash is less bright than sunlight, producing a subtle effect.

filter A piece of coated or colored glass or plastic placed in front of the camera lens that alters the light reaching the sensor. Filters can modify the color or quality of the light, change the relative rendition of various tones, reduce haze or glare, or create special effects.

fish-eye lens A type of lens that bends and distorts the world in the photograph.

flare Stray light that does not form the image but reduces contrast or forms patches of light. Caused by reflections inside the lens and between the many lens elements, it is particularly problematic in backlighting, and most severe with lenses containing high numbers of optical elements. Flare can be reduced by multiple coatings of all elements, or by using a lens hood to prevent light from striking the front element.

focal plane The layer of the scene that will be in focus in the photograph. Elements that are the same distance from the camera as the focal point are all in the same focal plane. The depth of focal plane is determined by depth of field.

f-stop A numerical value to denote the size of the lens aperture; the focal length of the lens divided by the diameter of the aperture. Wide apertures are denoted with small numbers such as f/2, small apertures with large numbers such as f/22. See also *diaphragm.*

G-H

gigabyte (GB) A unit measuring digital information equal to 1,024 megabytes (MB).

graininess Digital artifacts that appear in an image as a result of maximizing sensor sensitivity; otherwise known as *noise.*

high dynamic range (HDR) A multi-image solution where multiple frames of the same scene exposed for different tonal areas are combined into one image with a balanced exposure; the goal is a natural-looking image that appears the way the human eye registers a scene.

histogram A bar graph showing the relative number of pixels in different brightness ranges in a digital image.

hot shoe A mount on the camera intended for connecting a flash unit or a remote trigger for a flash unit. It contains electronic contacts that mate with the contacts on the "foot" of the accessory unit. These contacts are required for transmitting data between the camera and flash, and for automatically triggering the flash when the shutter is released.

I

image stabilization Techniques and technologies that reduce camera movement at slow shutter speeds.

ISO A standard for image sensor rating. ISO is an abbreviation for International Organization for Standardization, which sets the standards used to rate the light sensitivity of the sensor. Common ISO ratings range from 25 to 1600, but many digital cameras reach as high as 10,000 and more.

J-K

JPEG Named for Joint Photographic Experts Group, a file format for storing images in a compressed form to keep files small. It is also the standard format of photographs on the internet due to small file sizes and full-color palette. Variable degrees of compression can be used.

keyword A label added to data attached to a digital image to help with computer searches. Also called *tags*.

L

leading lines Elements in a composition that carry viewers' attention to a point of interest in the scene.

light meter A device that measures brightness of an object or scene; the camera's internal meter or a separate accessory light meter can be used.

long lens A lens with a long focal length used for taking photographs from a great distance.

M-N

macro The close-focusing ability of a lens, or a lens with such capability. Strictly defined, the term is employed when a subject is reproduced to at least life-size (or larger) on the sensor.

matrix or evaluative meter A type of metering for a Nikon (matrix) or Canon (evaluative) camera that divides the scene into several zones, each of which is analyzed for dark and light areas within.

megabyte (MB) A measurement of electronic data storage equal to approximately one million bytes.

megapixel (MP) One million pixels. The higher the number of pixels, the greater the resolution of a digital image.

memory card The small cartridge to which the camera sensor writes images for storing and eventually transferring to a computer; types of memory cards include CompactFlash (CF), Secure Digital (SD), and Micro Secure Digital (MicroSD).

metadata Mechanical information automatically attached to each image by a digital camera.

negative space An aspect of composition that refers to the empty space around the elements within a scene.

noise Specks of color that can populate an image when photographs are shot with a high ISO in low light. The size and resolution of the image sensor also affect noise levels.

O-P

optical aberration An optical flaw most common in wide-angle lenses at wide apertures appearing as reduced sharpness near the edges of the frame. It can be corrected by various optical methods, including the use of aspheric lens surfaces and by stopping down to smaller apertures.

panorama A picture offering an exceptionally wide field of view.

pixel Abbreviation for picture (pix-) element (-el). These are the smallest bits of information that combine to form a digital image. The more pixels—current cameras are measured in megapixels—the higher the resolution.

positive space The areas of the image occupied by subject matter.

prime lens A lens with a fixed focal length, as opposed to a zoom lens.

R

RAW file A type of image file that captures and preserves the maximum amount of data possible, allowing photographers to process images as they like and preserve the original files.

red-eye Light from a camera's flash reflected by the retinas in a person's eyes. This effect is easily corrected with editing software or, more commonly, by functions within the digital camera itself. Moving a flash unit away from the camera will reduce this effect in photographs.

Rembrandt lighting A natural look in a portrait created when the light illuminates the subject from the front and slightly to one side, forming a shadow on a portion of the face; named for its resemblance to the look captured by Rembrandt, the great master of portrait painting.

resolution A measurement of ability to resolve fine detail. In digital photography, a measure (in pixels) of the amount of information included in an image and its ability to resolve in fine detail; impacts the clarity and sharpness of a printed photograph.

rule of thirds A compositional technique where the subject is placed in one-third of the image; can create dynamic tension and interest.

S

saturation Referring to the intensity of color

as it exists in a scene, or an adjustment that modifies the intensity of color within an image in the postproduction process.

sensor An electronic chip containing light-sensitive pixels. The larger the sensor and the more pixels, the more information the sensor can gather.

shutter The mechanism built into a camera that opens for a designated period to regulate the length of time that light reaches the sensor through the lens aperture.

shutter priority A semiautomatic camera mode where a photographer sets the shutter speed and the camera adjusts to the f-stop required for a correct exposure, based on information from the in-camera light meter. Denoted on the mode dial as "S" or "Tv."

shutter speed The length of time that the shutter is open to allow light coming through the aperture to hit the sensor. This is expressed in seconds or fractions of a second, such as 1/60 or 1/250.

single-shot autofocus (AF) Technique where the focal point is held while a photographer holds the shutter halfway to set the focus on an object within the frame until the shutter is triggered.

smartphone camera A camera built into a smartphone that allows for capture and immediate editing and sharing when connected to the internet.

speedlight An external flash unit designed to sit atop the camera's hot shoe; can also be used off-camera and triggered wirelessly.

spot meter A metering system that reads the intensity of light reflected by only a single point within the scene; may be a function of the camera's built-in light meter or an accessory device.

stop-motion A technique used to capture multiple stills in rapid succession to create high-impact playback presentations of intense action.

strobe An electronic flash unit that produces an intense, short-duration burst of light.

sync speed The fastest shutter speed that can be used to ensure that the burst of flash is synchronized with the time that the shutter is open.

T

teleconverter A magnifying device mounted between camera and lens to increase the effective focal length of the lens. The most common are 2x (doubler) and 1.4x. Also called a *tele-extender, lens converter,* or *lens extender.*

telephoto A specific lens design in which the physical length of the lens is shorter than its focal length, although this term is often used for any long lens. Any focal length longer than 85mm is generally referred to as a telephoto.

TIFF A universal image file format (Tagged Image File Format) that can be read with imaging software on most computers. It is a popular exporting choice of photographers because the image does not degrade in its "lossless compression" mode. Some digital cameras can record images in uncompressed TIFF to eliminate the loss of information that occurs during JPEG compression.

tilt-shift lens A type of lens that corrects for perspective problems and allows architectural photographers to photograph tall buildings without converging verticals.

time-lapse A technique used to capture multiple stills of very slow events for playback in rapid succession for a presentation that shows a lot of action in a short amount of time.

TTL Abbreviation for "through the lens," generally indicating that the camera's internal light meter reads the amount of light reflected from the scene. Most often used to measure the output of speedlights that fire a quick pre-burst of flash, then adjust automatically to properly light a given scene.

tungsten light Light emitted by common incandescent bulbs that give a yellow-orange cast to a scene; can be used for effect or corrected with white balance.

U-V-W-Z

USB A standardized computer port (Universal Serial Bus) that accepts cables for attaching accessories such as a camera, memory card reader, or hard drive.

viewfinder An optical system that allows users to view the image area that will be included in the final picture. Types include optical (OVF), where a photographer sees a reflection of exactly what the camera sees, and electronic (EVF), where the sensor projects a digital preview of the image to the LCD screen.

visual hierarchy The arrangement of elements in a frame that suggest a ranking of importance, as well as the order in which viewers are guided to view them through use of other compositional elements.

white balance A control used to color-correct an image so that white appears truly white and to correct all other colors relative to that; often used to correct for light sources with an unnatural color cast.

wide-angle lens A lens with a short focal length and wide field of view. Any lens shorter than 35mm is referred to as a wide-angle.

zoom lens A lens with variable focal lengths, shifting between shorter and longer focal lengths with a rotating bezel.

FURTHER READING

BOOKS: HISTORY, CLASSICS & THEORY

Adams, Ansel, *Examples: The Making of 40 Photographs*

Adams, Robert, *Why People Photograph: Selected Essays and Reviews*

Ang, Tom, *Photography: The Definitive Visual History*

Berger, John, *Understanding a Photograph*

Berger, John, *Ways of Seeing*

Brandow, Todd, and William A. Ewing, *Edward Steichen: Lives in Photography*

Bredar, John, and Pete Souza, *The President's Photographer: Fifty Years Inside the Oval Office*

Cartier-Bresson, Henri, *The Decisive Moment*

Cunningham, Bill, *On the Street: Five Decades of Iconic Photography*

Essick, Peter, and Jamie Williams, *The Ansel Adams Wilderness*

Evans, Walker, *American Photographs*

Jenkins, Mark Collins, and Chris Johns, *National Geographic The Covers: Iconic Photographs, Unforgettable Stories*

Lubben, Kristen, *Magnum Contact Sheets*

100 Photographs That Changed the World (by editors of *Life*)

Sontag, Susan, *On Photography*

Steichen, Edward, *The Family of Man*

Stieglitz, Alfred, *Camera Work: The Complete Photographs*

Szarkowski, John, *Looking at Photographs: 100 Pictures from the Collection of The Museum of Modern Art*

Szarkowski, John, *The Photographer's Eye*

TIME 100 Photographs: The Most Influential Photos of All Time (Editors of *Time*)

BOOKS: TECHNIQUES

Ang, Tom, *How to Photograph Absolutely Everything: Successful Pictures From Your Digital Camera*

Carroll, Henry, *Read This If You Want to Take Great Photographs*

Davis, Harold, and Phyllis Davis, *The Photoshop Darkroom: Creative Digital Post-Processing*

Mark, Mary Ellen, *Mary Ellen Mark on the Portrait and the Moment*

Peterson, Bryan, and Susana Heide Schellenberg, *Understanding Color in Photography*

Peterson, Bryan, *Understanding Exposure* (4th ed.)

Sartore, Joel, *Photographing Your Family*

Sartore, Joel, and Heather Perry, *National Geographic Photo Basics: The Ultimate Beginner's Guide to Great Photography*

BOOKS: MONOGRAPHS & COLLECTIONS

Abell, Sam, *Life of a Photograph*

Allard, William Albert, *Five Decades: A Retrospective*

Allard, William Albert, *Portraits of America*

Beckwith, Carol, and Angela Fisher, *Faces of Africa: Thirty Years of Photography*

Cobb, Jodi, *Geisha: The Life, the Voices, the Art*

Davis, Wade, *Wade Davis Photographs*

Doubilet, David, *Great Barrier Reef*

Doubilet, David, *Water Light Time*

Grant, Benjamin, *Overview: A New Perspective of Earth*

Griffiths, Annie, *National Geographic Simply Beautiful Photographs*

Harvey, David Alan, *Cuba: Island at a Crossroad*

Johns, Chris, *Wild at Heart: Man and Beast in Southern Africa*

Lanting, Frans, *Into Africa*

Liittschwager, David, and Susan Middleton, *Archipelago: Portraits of Life in the World's Most Remote Island Sanctuary*

McCurry, Steve, *The Iconic Photographs*

McCurry, Steve, *Portraits*

Mitchell, John G., *National Geographic: The Wildlife Photographs*

National Geographic, *Getting Your Shot: Stunning Photos, How-to Tips, and Endless Inspiration from the Pros*

National Geographic, *In Focus: National Geographic Greatest Portraits*

National Geographic, *National Geographic Image Collection*

National Geographic, *Rarely Seen: Photographs of the Extraordinary*

National Geographic, *The Splendor of Birds: Art and Photographs from National Geographic*

National Geographic, *Through the Lens: National Geographic Greatest Photographs*

National Geographic, *Women: The National Geographic Image Collection*

Nichols, Michael, and Mike Fay, *The Last Place on Earth*

Nicklen, Paul, *Polar Obsession*

Sartore, Joel, *The Photo Ark: One Man's Quest to Document the World's Animals*

Sartore, Joel, *Rare: Portraits of America's Endangered Species*

Sartore, Joel, *Vanishing: The World's Most Vulnerable Animals*

Sartore, Joel, and Noah Strycker, *Birds of the Photo Ark*

Skerry, Brian, *Ocean Soul*

Virts, Terry, *View From Above: An Astronaut Photographs the World*

ONLINE RESOURCES

NATIONAL GEOGRAPHIC PHOTOGRAPHY WEBSITES

National Geographic Photography:

nationalgeographic.com/photography

National Geographic's website dedicated to spectacular photography. The site showcases amazing photos from around the world and provides invaluable photography tips.

National Geographic Picture Stories:

nationalgeographic.com/photography/photographers

Hear behind-the-scenes stories of some of the world's best photographs, straight from the National Geographic photographers who took them.

National Geographic Photo of the Day:

*nationalgeographic.com/photography/
photo-of-the-day*

Photo of the Day showcases inspiring photos from around the world and provides tips on how to achieve your own amazing photos. Be sure to submit your photos to Your Shot, for a chance to become featured in Photo of the Day.

OTHER ONLINE RESOURCES

Information, News, and Equipment Reviews

CAMERA LABS:

cameralabs.com

A nonprofit, noncommercial photography site with product reviews, tutorials, a conversation forum, and other interactive features.

CREATIVE PRO:

creativepro.com

A site with abundant resources in forums, articles, and blogs for all photography and design needs.

DAVID ALAN HARVEY ONLINE MENTORING PROGRAM:

davidalanharvey.com/mentoring

Renowned photographer David Alan Harvey provides online mentoring and critiques for intermediate to advanced students.

DAVID DUCHEMIN:

davidduchemin.com

Where world and humanitarian assignment photographer David DuChemin shares stories and offers tips, strategies, musing on the art, and even a free e-book.

DEADPXL ONLINE COMMUNITY:

dedpxl.com/learn

An online community of photographers led by photographer Zack Arias, with the ethos of being brave, sharing work, and inspiring one another to get out and make pictures.

DIGITAL PHOTO:

dpmag.com

Online edition of *Digital Photo* magazine with how-to and photo-sharing community features for all plus more for subscribers.

DIGITAL PHOTO PRO:

digitalphotopro.com

Online edition of *Digital Photo Pro* magazine, with techniques, equipment, photography styles, and examples from top professional photographers.

DIGITAL PHOTOGRAPHY REVIEW:

dpreview.com

A website dedicated to equipment reviews for the digital community with a buyer's guide and an active discussion forum.

DIGITAL PHOTOGRAPHY SCHOOL:

digital-photography-school.com

An independent website with useful tips for semi-experienced digital camera owners.

EPHOTOZINE:

ephotozine.com

A digital photography site with news, reviews, and help page.

EXIT:

exitmedia.net

The online edition of the Madrid-based bilingual magazine devoted to contemporary photography.

MEDIA DIVISION BLOG:

media-division.com/blog/

A site dedicated to all things design, with tutorials, reviews, and tips for Photoshop, Illustrator, and photography.

PHOTO.NET:

photo.net

An online photography community featuring forums, equipment reviews, and tips for every photography opportunity.

PICTURE CORRECT:

picturecorrect.com

This site provides valuable relevant information to photographers of all levels through tips, tutorials, and a shopping guide.

POPPHOTO.COM:

popphoto.com

The online home of photography magazines *Popular Photography* and *American Photo*. This site features news, reviews, and informative blogs.

SHUTTERBUG:

shutterbug.net

Online edition of *Shutterbug* magazine provides technique tips, reviews, and online galleries.

PLUGINSWORLD.COM:

pluginsworld.com

A frequently updated list of plug-ins for Photoshop and other software, such as InDesign and Illustrator.

ONLINE TUTORIALS

National Geographic/The Great Courses

Online courses, taught by National Geographic photographers, offer the skills and tools you'll need to elevate your photography practice.

Joel Sartore, "Fundamentals of Photography": *thegreatcoursesplus.com/fundamentals-of-photography*

Joel Sartore, "The Art of Travel Photography": *thegreatcoursesplus.com/the-art-of-travel-photography*

"Masters of Photography": *thegreatcoursesplus.com/national-geographic-masters-of-photography*

PHOTOGRAPHY INSTITUTE:

thephotographyinstitute.com

An online course in photography and the business side of the industry.

PHOTOSHOP TUTORIALS:

photoshoptutorials.ws

A valuable resource with a range of Photoshop and design tutorials from beginner to advanced.

PICTURE HOSTING AND SHARING

FLICKR:

flickr.com

An online photo management and picture-sharing website offering organizational features at low prices.

INSTAGRAM:

instagram.com

A free online photo- and video-sharing network with a streamlined feed and live story component.

PHOTOBUCKET:

photobucket.com

A site that provides photo, video, and album sharing and storage.

SHUTTERFLY:

shutterfly.com

A website dedicated to organizing and storing digital photography.

SMUGMUG:

smugmug.com

An independent website dedicated to sharing professional-quality images.

PHOTO-EDITING SOFTWARE

ADOBE CREATIVE CLOUD PHOTOGRAPHY PLAN

adobe.com/creativecloud

A collection of desktop and mobile apps for photo management, editing, and design, including Lightroom and Photoshop.

CAPTURE ONE

captureone.com/en

Powerful, easy-to-use photo-editing software.

LUMINAR 4

skylum.com/luminar

Developed by Skylum, this photo-editing software features creative filters and tools.

PHOTO-EDITING SMARTPHONE APPS

ADOBE LIGHTROOM

lightroom.adobe.com

Edit, organize, and share your photos on your smartphone or tablet. The mobile app can also sync with the desktop Lightroom app.

ENLIGHT

photofoxapp.com

Merge photos, adjust tone and contrast, add fonts and graphics, and more with this powerful mobile editing app.

POLARR

polarr.co

Great for beginners and more experienced photographers, this app offers filters, enhancements, layer support, curve tools, and local adjustments.

VSCO

vsco.co

With either a free version or a paid membership, a variety of photo-editing tools and filters help you share your work with a community of creators around the world.

SMARTPHONE PHOTO-PRINTING APPS

MIXTILES

mixtiles.com

Get your best photos out of your phone and onto your walls by quickly uploading them to be made into ready-to-hang prints.

PARABO PRESS

parabo.press

Quickly send your smartphone photos to be turned into posters, greeting cards, framed canvas prints, and more.

SOCIAL PRINT STUDIO

socialprintstudio.com

Never again does a great photo have to go unseen. Proudly display your work on a variety of products like daily calendars, wood prints, photo yearbooks, magnets, and more.

SHUTTERFLY

shutterfly.com

Download the app to move photos from your phone to Shutterfly, which offers free and unlimited storage. Also, order prints and photo products and easily share galleries with friends and family.

CONTRIBUTORS

HEATHER PERRY is a freelance photographer and writer whose first passion is photographing people in and around water. Her work has been published by National Geographic in magazines, books, and online, as well as in the *New York Times*, *Smithsonian*, and other publications. She has done commercial photography for National Geographic Channel, South African Tourism, and Sony. She's photographed stories on immigration issues, refugee populations, fishing communities, shipbuilders, and neighborhood kids in her home state of Maine, and has worked with swimmers in pools and oceans around the world. Perry participates as a photo expert on National Geographic–Lindblad Expeditions and enjoys sharing her photographic knowledge with travelers.

MARK THIESSEN has been a National Geographic staff photographer since 1990. He has published numerous feature stories and covers for *National Geographic* magazine and other National Geographic publications on subjects ranging from Peruvian mummies to the study of human performance. In 1996, Thiessen began a personal photography project on wildland firefighters that has taken him to the front lines of this phenomenon every summer. This work led to *National Geographic* magazine feature stories on Russian smokejumpers and, more recently, Alaska smokejumpers. Thiessen's photographs for the July 2008 *National Geographic* cover story "Under Fire: Why the West Is Burning" earned first-place recognition by Pictures of the Year International. He also documented film director James Cameron's dive to Challenger Deep, the ocean's deepest location at the bottom of the Mariana Trench. Thiessen directs the National Geographic photo studio at the Washington headquarters.

ILLUSTRATIONS CREDITS

INDEX

Boldface indicates illustrations.

Since 1888, the National Geographic Society has funded more than 13,000 research, exploration, and preservation projects around the world. National Geographic Partners distributes a portion of the funds it receives from your purchase to National Geographic Society to support programs including the conservation of animals and their habitats.

National Geographic Partners, LLC
1145 17th Street NW
Washington, DC 20036-4688 USA

Get closer to National Geographic explorers and photographers, and connect with our global community. Join us today at nationalgeographic.com/join

For rights or permissions inquiries, please contact National Geographic Books Subsidiary Rights: bookrights@natgeo.com

Library of Congress Cataloging-in-Publication Data

Names: Perry, Heather, author. I National Geographic Society (U.S.), publisher.
Title: National Geographic complete photo guide : how to take better pictures / Heather Perry.
Description: Washington, D.C. : National Geographic, 2020. I Includes bibliographical references and index. I Summary: "This is a collection of photographic knowledge designed to take you beyond the basics and make you a better photographer, no matter what your current abilities and talents. Here are tips and tricks of National Geographic photographers, expertly explained, with terms defined and examples provided"-- Provided by publisher.
Identifiers: LCCN 2020003173 I ISBN 9781426221439 (hardcover)
Subjects: LCSH: Photography. I Photography--Technique.
Classification: LCC TR145 .P425 2020 I DDC 771--dc23
LC record available at https://lccn.loc.gov/2020003173

Printed in China
21/RRDH/1

POWERFUL PHOTOS MAKE THE BEST STORIES.

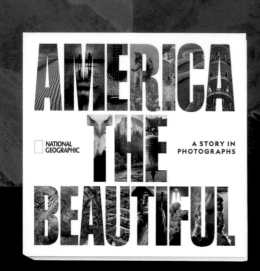

AMERICA THE BEAUTIFUL

NATIONAL GEOGRAPHIC

A STORY IN PHOTOGRAPHS

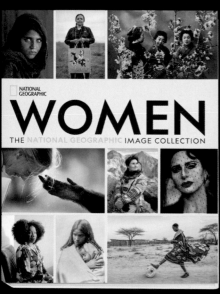

NATIONAL GEOGRAPHIC

WOMEN

THE NATIONAL GEOGRAPHIC IMAGE COLLECTION

NATIONAL GEOGRAPHIC

PHOTO BASICS

The Ultimate Beginner's Guide to Great Photography

JOEL SARTORE
Creator of the Photo Ark